THEORETICAL DEVELOPMENTS IN HISPANIC LINGUISTICS
Javier Gutiérrez-Rexach, Series Editor

Contemporary Advances in Theoretical and Applied Spanish Linguistic Variation

Edited by Juan J. Colomina-Almiñana

THE OHIO STATE UNIVERSITY PRESS · COLUMBUS

Copyright © 2017 by The Ohio State University.
All rights reserved.

Library of Congress Cataloging-in-Publication Data
Names: Colomina Almiñana, Juan José, editor.
Title: Contemporary advances in theoretical and applied Spanish linguistic variation / edited by Juan J. Colomina-Alminana.
Other titles: Theoretical developments in Hispanic linguistics.
Description: Columbus : The Ohio State University Press, [2017] | Series: Theoretical developments in Hispanic linguistics | Includes bibliographical references and index.
Identifiers: LCCN 2017003354 | ISBN 9780814213391 (cloth ; alk. paper) | ISBN 0814213391 (cloth ; alk. paper)
Subjects: LCSH: Spanish language—Variation. | Spanish language—Social aspects. | Sociolinguistics. | Languages in contact.
Classification: LCC PC4074.7 .C66 2017 | DDC 467—dc23
LC record available at https://lccn.loc.gov/2017003354

Cover design by Authorsupport.com
Text design by Juliet Williams
Type set in Minion and Formata

∞ The paper used in this publication meets the minimum requirements of the American National Standard for Information Sciences—Permanence of Paper for Printed Library Materials. ANSI Z39.48–1992.

9 8 7 6 5 4 3 2 1

To Javier Gutiérrez-Rexach, in memoriam

Contents

Acknowledgments — ix

Introduction — 1
    Juan J. Colomina-Almiñana

PART I
Historical Linguistics

Chapter 1 · Glimpses of Proto-Ibero-Romance in Neapolitan and
               Other Southern Italian Mainland Vernaculars — 17
    John M. Ryan

PART II
Phonetics and Morphosyntax

Chapter 2 · Rhotacism of /s/ in Elche Spanish: Social and Linguistic
               Factors Conditioning the Reduction — 43
    Whitney Chappell and Francisco Martínez Ibarra

Chapter 3 · Pragmatic and Semantic Factors for the Resumption
               Strategy in Spanish Relative Clauses — 63
    Irene Checa-García

Chapter 4 · The Role of Subjectivity in Discourse Marker Variation — 81
    Sarah Sinnott

PART III
Linguistic Attitudes and Discourse Analysis

Chapter 5 · Linguistic Attitudes in Argentine Spanish: *(De)queísmo,* DOM, and the Subjunctive   101
Mark Hoff and Rosa María Piqueres Gilabert

Chapter 6 · *Voseo* Vocatives and Interjections in Montevideo Spanish   124
María Irene Moyna

Chapter 7 · Genre and Register Variation: Academic Conference Presentations in Spanish in the United States   148
Carolina Viera

PART IV
Variation in the Minimalist Program

Chapter 8 · A Feature-Geometry Account for Subject-Verb Agreement Phenomena in Yungueño Spanish   165
Sandro Sessarego

Chapter 9 · Agreement and Valuation of Phi-Features in Judeo-Spanish: A Cross-Generational Account   183
Rey Romero

Chapter 10 · Psych Predicates, Light Verbs, and Phase Theory: On the Implications of Case Assignment to the Experiencer in Non-*Leísta* Experience Predicates   201
Ricard Viñas de Puig

Bibliography   225
List of Contributors   248
Index   254

Acknowledgments

Along the process of writing and composition, this volume has benefitted from the comments and wise advice of different persons. I want to express my most sincere gratitude to Eugene O'Connor and series editor Javier Gutiérrez-Rexach for their encouragement and help on the different steps of the production of this book and to two anonymous reviewers for their helpful suggestions to previous drafts. I am indebted to Irene Checa-García and James Cox, and especially to Nicole M. Guidotti-Hernández, who read parts of the collection and patiently listened to me when I gave them unsolicited lectures on some of the materials here contained. To all of them, many thanks.

A few days before the completion of the final manuscript, Professor Gutiérrez-Rexach passed away. Without his advice, constant help, and support this collection would have never been published. The authors want to express our most sincere condolences to his family, colleagues, and friends. We dedicate this volume to his memory.

Introduction

Juan J. Colomina-Almiñana

This volume is ambitious. Although there are, fortunately, a significant number of compilations on the general topic of Hispanic sociolinguistics, the present volume provides a different genealogy of Hispanic sociolinguistics with an alternate analysis of known and unknown Spanish varieties. *Contemporary Advances in Theoretical and Applied Spanish Linguistic Variation*, by analyzing different Spanish varieties using a plurality of methodologies and approaches and focusing on very diverse language variables, reframes the understanding of language variation and change as an intimate interplay between both linguistic features and social factors always occurring in unison in the same historical process.

The usual offerings focus on a general understanding of linguistic change as a byproduct of non-linguistic factors, normally centered on one specific level of speech (Serrano 1999a; Sessarego & Tejedo-Herrero 2016), a certain variant (Carvalho, Orozco & Shin 2015), or a concrete region (Rivera-Mills & Villa 2010). Thus, readers usually encounter books focused on one or two aspects of one concrete and well-known Spanish variety; centered on either phonetic, syntactic, or pragmatic issues in Hispanic linguistics; or interested in the Spanish spoken in one single geographical area. In contrast, this collection provides both a synchronic (Section II) and a diachronic (Section I) view of Hispanic sociolinguistics, focusing not only on the historical development of Spanish (as a Romance language) but also analyzing certain idiosyncratic elements of non-standard Spanish varieties across multiple regions, nations, and diasporas (Section IV). In addition, the volume offers an enchronic (Enfield 2009: 10) perspective of this phenomenon as well, analyzing how certain sustained cultural practices may drive concrete linguistic developments (Section III).

Before William Labov's seminal work on variationist linguistics in the 1960s, studies examining variable linguistic features considered linguistic variation as random and indefinite. In other words, any difference in the speech of two speakers of the same natural language should entirely depend on the speaker's preference for one variant or another. These pre-Labovian theories agreed that no constraint exists that allows the researcher to identify when one variant, that is, one of the options of a variable in language, will occur instead of another. Thus, the variation remained "unpredictable." Because no factors were believed to be responsible for variation beyond the speaker's will, only descriptive but not explanatory studies were possible. In practice, studies of variation only described language change primarily by casual geographical means.

With the study of nationality and folklore in Europe during the nineteenth century, and a little bit later in the Americas, many researchers started to approach linguistic variation based on geographical factors. They searched for links between linguistic variants and territory. These works not only showed an empirical link between geography and language variation that demystified certain essentialist approaches, but also built new methodologies for the systematic collection and treatment of linguistic data.

The use of variant codification systems and questionnaires for native speakers of these varieties quickly spread through Europe and the Americas, with the *Atlas Lingüístico de la Península Ibérica* (ALPI) being the first project to tackle Spanish variation. Its publication (Navarro Tomás 1962) was delayed due to the Spanish Civil war and very restrictive policies concerning "threats" to national unity (Viudas Camarasa 2003). Only two years after this thirty-year delayed publication, the *Proyecto de estudio coordinador de la norma lingüística culta de las principales ciudades de Iberoamérica* ("Norma culta" for short), directed by Lope Blanch, collected and tape-recorded interviews and conversations with a preselected set of educated individuals in the main cities of Latin America, the Caribbean, and Spain in order to describe the differences in "speech in informal and formal situations across the diverse dialects of Spanish" (Díaz-Campos 2011b: 2). Blanch's efforts constituted the first attempt to portray and study the full range of Spanish geographical variation and update data collection methodology by using sociolinguistic interviews rather than just questionnaires. Originally, the idea was to generate a more comprehensive and complete study of Spanish variation by comparing the speech of previously neglected Latin American Spanish varieties and by providing a richer and more naturalistic set of data. Following this path, the project focused on the phonetic differences of the Spanish found in La Havana, San Juan, Santo Domingo, and Ciudad de Panamá (primarily on the different pronunciations of /s/); a comparative study of some morphosyntactic features of the Spanish spoken in Ciudad de México, Madrid, Buenos Aires, and Caracas; and some descriptive analysis of lexical borrowing from Indigenous languages in contact with Spanish, such as Quechua and Nahuatl. Additionally, the first *Simposio sobre corrientes actuales en dialectología del Caribe hispánico* (1976) brought together scholars and researchers "studying socio-phonological variation and syntactic variation phenomena using the new sociolinguistic methodologies at the time" (Díaz-Campos 2011b: 2), demonstrating how Caribbean Spanish varieties have their own idiosyncrasies (i.e., De Granda 1968a; Otheguy 1973). Subsequent linguistic atlases focused on a single country (see Gimeno Menéndez 1990: 83–102), or have incorporated chapters about different Spanish speaking communities (Alvar 1996). Currently, most projects on Spanish variation have also incorporated some rural varieties as well as different social strata and other relevant variables in their descriptive analysis.

The field of Hispanic sociolinguistics has been expanding the interest in linguistic variation beyond geographical factors or mere descriptive analysis, incorporating myriad social factors (ALM 1990–1998; García Mouton & Moreno Fernández 1993). This increased interest in the influence of social factors on linguistic variation coincided with the expansion of the field of linguistics in general, particularly with respect to theories and methodologies, both in the formal and the functional traditions. The formalists' emphasis on describing language as a mental ability carried over into including processing complexity as a factor in variation research. Even research about social movements such as feminism and the civil rights struggles in the United States examined variations based on gender and social class stratification. Discourse analysis related research in particular focused on these kinds of concerns (see, for instance, Lakoff 1975).

Therefore, the expansion and enrichment of variation studies to include many different social variables has not only been due to a reaction against formalism and generativism. It has also been the consequence, particularly more recently, of incorporating some of the cognitive concerns of such formalist approaches. Another source of incorporation of cognitive processes as an independent variable is found within functional approaches (Gries 2013; Kristiansen & Geeraerts 2013). Although the inclusion of processing factors in variation studies are perhaps partly influenced by the Chomskian emphasis on language as a mental phenomenon, formal approaches to the explanation of language have been also a limiting force because of their reduction of the variation that was worth exploring. Silva-Corvalán (2001) and Almeida (2003) both mention the limitations encountered by taking into account only data coming from "ideal speakers" and how standards for speech worthy of explanation left much variation out of their studies. Chomsky's search for competence, or previously Saussure's classification of *parole* (vs. *langue*) as "external linguistics," resulted in variation being a phenomenon that was uninteresting and at most merely describable, but not explanatory.

Labov's variationist account, and more recently experimental or corpus correlational studies of language variation, have fortunately shown this approach to variation to be at best inaccurate. Variation can be studied and can provide key insights into the function of language. Moreover, formal linguistic theories are starting to explain variation in correlational terms, even if not always aiming to clarify it, such as the Minimalist Program. In addition, the initial reluctance to include morphosyntactic changes in variationist research because of the question of what constitutes "the same meaning" (Lavandera 1978; Silva-Corvalán 1989: 97–100) has been overcome by most researchers in Hispanic linguistics (Caravedo 2006; Carvalho, Orozco & Shin 2015). An important step in this direction was the incorporation of Díaz-Campos's (2011b: 2) factors influencing variant grammatical choice and discourse-communicative variables, such as those employed in corpus linguistics or in variationist studies on pronouns (Bentivoglio 2001; Ranson 1999; Lastra & Martín-Butragueño 2010). In the case of Hispanic linguistics, for instance, either optional subject pronouns (Otheguy & Zentella 2012) or resumptive pronouns (Silva-Corvalán 1996; Bentivoglio 2003; and Checa-García's chapter in this volume) have been analyzed.

The inclusion of morphosyntactic variation, with its own very distinctive methodological peculiarities (Schwenter 2011: 125; Silva-Corvalán 2001: 130–31), has revealed the need for more corpora with social information included in a digital format that makes it more searchable and for the incorporation of different basic tags, such as for parts of speech, interruptions of various kinds, silences, overlapping, interjections, and even different types of nonverbal communication data. This new information is of vital importance in efforts to pursue studies on pragmatic and discursive variation frequently behind morphosyntactic variation (Serrano 1999b). The data will also be useful for studies in the sociology of language and ethnolinguistics, such as on style or indexicality (Bucholtz 2009) or the application of interactional communication approaches (Serrano 2011: 193–96).

Partly responding to these needs, the PRESEEA, *Proyecto para el estudio sociolingüístico del español de España y América,* includes not only the "norma culta," but a pre-stratification by instruction level, gender, and age and a post-stratification that includes the following: profession, salary, and housing conditions. More importantly, each city develops their pre-stratification classification according to the specific social parameters that conform it. In addition, the project includes not only meticulous provisions on collection and transcription, but also proposals for studying the address system. Finally, each team can add their variables when collecting sociolinguistic information. For instance, the Málaga team has incorporated information on social networks to their corpus (Vida Castro & Villena Ponsoda 2007).

This has not been the only attempt to fill the gap in terms of readily available data that fits the recently enriched needs of the field. Among the new fields of sociolinguistic interests concerned with the Spanish language, it is probably the research about Spanish in contact with other languages, particularly Spanish with English in the United States, that has increased its scholarly production most significantly in the last twenty years. The study of variation in language contact situations has been so pervasive that we have seen a very stimulating debate around variation in L2 acquisition (Geeslin 2011), one very specific language contact situation whose connection to variation had remained mostly unexplored until a few years ago. The debate around the "permeability of grammar" (Otheguy & Zentella 2012: 11) has been enriched during the last two decades, and it has raised many interesting questions concerning Spanish variation. Where does it happen within grammatical structure? How much do variants spread within communities? Should we consider the extent of spread a consequence either of contact or a mere individual aspect of language acquisition? These and other central questions are what current research needs to address, and this is where the present collection makes its main contribution.

Parallel to the raising of all these questions, a—still probably low—number of corpora that deal with language contact data has started to appear that should be considered when talking of linguistic corpora oriented toward sociolinguistic research in Spanish. There are several corpora with sociolinguistic interviews: for instance, *Corpus del español de Raleigh-Durham (CERD), The New England Corpus of Heritage and Second Language Speakers,* and *Spanish in Texas Corpus*. Nonetheless, there are fewer corpora that do provide spontaneous informal conversation recorded by one of the speakers in different situations with other bilingual speakers (for example, in the *Miami Corpus* of bilingual Spanish-speakers in Florida and the *New Mexico Spanish-English Code-Switching Corpus* of conversations recorded in bilingual communities.) Unfortunately, even though these corpora provide spontaneous informal conversation that might help to the general goal of testing the convergence hypothesis, they are not available to the public (Torres-Cacoullos & Travis 2015). Also, longitudinal corpora of language acquisition by heritage speakers, ideally incorporating speakers of different social backgrounds and exposure to Spanish and English, are not very common, and currently the data is restricted to a few bilingual children in the Childes database. There are, nonetheless, some recent collections devoted to Spanish in contact with other languages (Molinero & Stewart 2006; Potowski & Cameron 2007; Klee & Lynch 2009), typically concerned with Spanish in the United States, or bilingual Hispanic communities, but not so much with the varieties in contact included in this volume (such as, for instance, Yungueño, Ladino, and Proto-Ibero Romance).

Given the tremendous growth in the last two or three decades of Hispanic sociolinguistics, both in terms of interests and methodologies, the field had a pressing need for a volume with an eclectic philosophy that would represent as much as possible these trends, methods, and interests. Built on a comprehensive view, this collection includes both qualitative and quantitative approaches, diachronic and synchronic studies, more theoretical and more applied studies, and more functional approaches as well as more formal accounts. This inclusive view reflects more accurately the current state of Hispanic linguistics, and the authors promote and encourage debate by employing new and diverse methodologies and views.

Although the present volume could be used in introductory courses as a complement to more broad introductions (such as Almeida 2003; Díaz-Campos 2013; García Marcos 1999; Lipski 1994a, 2008a; López Morales 1989; Moreno Fernández 1999; Escobar & Potowski 2015; Silva-Corvalán 2001, or even Zentella 1997), it will also provoke discussion in a more advanced Hispanic linguistics context. It answers the following questions: In what ways are studies of phonetic variation vs. morphosyntactic variation similar and dissimilar? How can qualitative studies complement quantitative ones? When is a qualitative or interactional approach to be used? How do diachronic studies help us to understand variation? What varieties of Spanish are currently understudied and how could we study them better? Is there a different approach for these varieties and their study? How do more classical studies of variation account for differences from the Minimalist Program? Are they complementary or at odds? Which one is to be preferred—if any— and why? Thus, the present collection serves students, academic specialists, practitioners, and professionals in the field of Hispanic linguistics.

Accordingly, the volume has been organized in four parts: historical linguistics, phonetics and morphosyntax, linguistic attitudes and discourse analysis, and variation in the Minimalist Program. Priority has been given to studies that better exemplify different methodologies, explore less studied data, or include cutting-edge methodologies. Part one focuses on diachronic variation. Part two is concerned with phonetic and morphosyntactic variation through more functional approaches employing corpus and interview data, perfectly balancing quantitative and qualitative analyses and incorporating pragmatics and discursive factors in morphosyntactic variation. Part three deals with the study of linguistic attitudes through well-established techniques in the field, such as the match-guised test, but also newer ones, like online usage of data and surveys. It also contains one chapter surveying conference papers using discourse analysis. Part four includes works employing minimalist methods. The volume also contains studies about less researched varieties of Spanish, and scholars concerned with monolingual as well as bilingual speakers in a situation of language contact will be satisfied with the contributions herein. Each of the ten chapters attends to, explains, and solves one or more current issues in Spanish linguistic variation and are written by a well-recognized expert on the matter or by a promising young scholar offering distinct perspectives of variation in Spanish.

Part I, "Historical Linguistics," includes John M. Ryan's "Glimpses of Proto-Ibero-Romance in Neapolitan and Other Southern Italian Mainland Vernaculars." This first chapter examines phonological, morphological, and syntactic structures shared by most southern Italian mainland vernacular dialects in the search for certain patterns that account for earlier stages of the Iberian Spanish variety. Grounded in historical linguistic methodologies, Ryan explores ancient Spanish texts such as *Cantar del Mio Cid, Jarchas,* and *Cartularios de Valpuesta* to demonstrate that certain structures are found in both the primeval Spanish-language incunabula and contemporary Italian mainland dialects. These structures show the use of the diminutive ending *-iello/-iella* as the preferred form, the presence of pre-inchoativized infinitive verbs ending in *-ir* and *-er* instead of *-ecer* (as in Latin), the post nominal placement of possessive adjectives, and the preference for the first-person singular future form ending in *-aggio*. The chapter concludes by arguing that these structures evidence the existence of a intermediate period where the Iberian Spanish variety showed post-tonic vocalic weakening to schwa instead of full syncope, the existence of a multi-syllabic palatalized first-person present tense form of *haber*, and an earlier binary subordinate conjunction system with /ke/ and /ka/, all clear proofs of the presence of a more primitive type of Romance language.

Part II, "Phonetics and Morphosyntax," contains three chapters. Chapter 2, Whitney Chappell and Francisco Martínez Ibarra's "Rhotacism of /s/ in Elche Spanish: Social and Linguistic Factors Conditioning the Reduction," fills a void in contemporary literature by providing the first quantitative analysis of the linguistic and social factors that constrain the rhotacization of /s/ in the variety of Peninsular Spanish spoken in Elche, Alicante. The analysis of the Spanish variety of this region shows how recent migratory waves of Spanish speakers in an area in contact with Catalan, which was the dominant language, impacts the rhotacization of /s/, among many other factors. Even though previous studies have analyzed /s/ variation in other Spanish varieties, no mention is made of the factors that condition the realization, or the particular characteristics affecting /s/ weakening in this region. To establish a pattern that predicts the variant's appearance, Chappell and Martínez Ibarra conducted thirty sociolinguistic interviews in Elche (Spain) to analyze the participants' /s/ realizations. The surveys were coded for the social factors of age, gender, education level, and language dominance (Catalan or Spanish) and the linguistic factors of word class (including the target and following word), preceding and following segment, preceding and following stress, the morphological status of the /s/, and speech rate. The results of their statistical analysis indicates that in social terms, rhotacization is significantly more likely among males, older speakers, and those who do not have a college degree. The reduction is also significantly more likely in casual speech involving faster speech rates. Additionally, the variant appears more often among bilinguals than monolinguals. Linguistically, rhotacization occurs almost exclusively at the word boundary, most likely with a following voiced segment, and takes place primarily before unstressed syllables. The chapter concludes that rhotacization of /s/ serves several purposes. As a nonstandard and stigmatized realization, rhotacization is most likely among speakers who are less influenced by the linguistic marketplace and who may attend more to covert than overt prestige. Linguistically, the flap represents a reduction of articulatory effort in weaker environments involving unstressed syllables and faster speech rates. Finally, the rhotacization of /s/ before vowels may also indicate an extension of the reduction process among speakers who rhotacize. To summarize, Chappell and Martínez Ibarra show how sociolinguistic data, when combined with theoretical methodologies, explains both linguistic and social constraints favoring the occurrence of certain variants.

Irene Checa-García in chapter 3, "Pragmatic and Semantic Factors for the Resumption Strategy in Spanish Relative Clauses," analyzes resumption (the use of a redundant element representing a previous occurrence in the discourse) as a strategy to build relative clauses in Spanish. After summarizing previous approaches linking the appearance of a resumptive pronoun to, on one hand, processing difficulties and, on the other hand, to pragmatic meaning, she examines ninety instances of relative clauses, including a resumptive pronoun collected in the oral corpus of spontaneous conversations in Peninsular Spanish (CORLEC). Checa-García combines quantitative and qualitative approaches to determine pragmatic and semantic values for the resumptive element strategy versus the gap strategy. Her results indicate that resumption in Spanish relative clauses has in some specific cases pragmatic and semantic marked values and makes us consider how the variant does not stand in free variation (for instance when used to express contrast). However, in many cases, where such conveyed meanings cannot be found, an appeal to processing and social factors are needed to explain the two optional variants. Hence, this study shows the need to consider more than one causation and to combine methodologies to differentiate which causation operates first and in what cases. Hence, what otherwise could look like a phenomenon with just one causation is a multifactorial phenomenon that requires us to operate in layers and distinguish at which layer different causations are operating.

Chapter 4, Sarah Sinnott's "The Role of Subjectivity in Discourse Marker Variation," employs a corpus collected from the newspaper *20 Minutos* (Spain). Sinnott shows that the variations between Iberian Spanish discourse markers *por tanto* and *por lo tanto* rely on the subjectivity of the relation found between antecedent and consequent in the argument. Sinnott demonstrates that a less subjective relationship tends to be linked to the occurrence of *por tanto* and that a more subjective relation favors the occurrence of *por lo tanto*. Sinnott concludes that *por lo tanto* then contributes to a greater argumentative strength than *por tanto*. Thus, the use of the former correlates with volitional consequents, whereas the use of the second correlates with non-volitional contexts. With quantitative analysis, Sinnott concludes that non-linguistic factors also constrain the use of one or another discourse marker in Peninsular Spanish.

Part III, "Linguistic Attitudes and Discourse Analysis," focuses on the way speakers perceive certain cases of variation in Argentine and Uruguayan

Spanish and an analysis of the genre and register characteristics in Hispanic studies. Chapter 5, "Linguistic Attitudes in Argentine Spanish: *(De)queísmo*, DOM, and the Subjunctive," written by Mark Hoff and Rosa María Piqueres Gilabert, provides new perspectives on native speaker attitudes toward Argentine Spanish variables such as *(de)queísmo*, differential object marking (DOM) of the inanimate, and the use of the present subjunctive in place of imperfect subjunctive. Hoff and Piqueres Gilabert measure the value judgment that Argentines make of speakers using the variants of these morphological variables. The combined methodology based on the match-guised technique shows that no significant difference occurs for *(de)queísmo*, whereas the non-standard variant of differential object marking of the inanimate is more positively ranked than the standard variant and the subjunctive variant. These are two separate variables each with a standard and a non-standard variable. Hoff and Piqueres Gilabert's study improves our conception of speech community consciousness in morphological variables by arguing against traditional notions of standard language and social evaluation.

In chapter 6, "*Voseo* Vocatives and Interjections in Montevideo Spanish," María Irene Moyna analyzes the Montevideo Spanish (Uruguay) vocative-interjective particles *che* and *bo/vo*. Employing data collected online and surveys of self-reported usage, Moyna shows that *bo/vo* is more likely to be used by young male speakers when the interlocutor is another young male, or when the interaction is impolite. Older female speakers reject the use of the *bo/vo* vocative as inappropriate, whereas younger speakers from both genders show neutral or positive attitudes. The *bo/vo* vocative then, Moyna concludes, retains certain pragmatic features (gender, politeness, among others) that *che* has lost. Her conclusions, then, also explain national differences between Argentine and Uruguayan Spanish varieties.

Chapter 7, Carolina Viera's "Genre and Register Variation: Academic Conference Presentations in Spanish in the United States," draws on manual and computer-assisted discourse analysis in a corpus of thirty-two Spanish conference presentations in Hispanic studies in the U.S. academic context (in both linguistics and literature studies). Viera identifies the obligatory stages—the genre structure—of a conference paper as well as the linguistic elements that speakers favor when creating their oral presentation, or register. Viera shows that all conference papers, even though they are organized differently depending on genre, share a structure that includes interpersonal stages. All use humor and other interactive features of language, and a certain degree of informality, to create a climate of confidence. Nonetheless, and even though all conference papers are written and given in Spanish, Viera's data show how in those on Hispanic linguistics the use of English is also common to establish solidarity with the audience and to project an academic identity that acknowledges bilingualism, a characteristic absent in the literary studies presentations.

Part IV, "Variation in the Minimalist Program," provides formal explanations to linguistic constraints in less studied Spanish varieties: Yungueño Spanish, Ladino, and non-*leísta* Spanish varieties. Based on the idea that linguists should look at what is in the words first, to the logical form, and then explain linguistic patterns, this final section answers some sociolinguistic questions in a more analytic and formal fashion. Its purpose is to show that, contrary to the general view, there is a certain homogeneity in a number of linguistic behaviors. So this study identifies general properties of our language and their communicational nature.

In chapter 8, "A Feature-Geometry Account for Subject-Verb Agreement Phenomena in Yungueño Spanish," Sandro Sessarego investigates subject-verb agreement in the Afro-Bolivian Hispanic variety Yungueño. Relying on a feature-geometry framework that integrates studies about the emergence of default values in SLA and the nature of feature variability (which generates necessary polemics about the formation of pidgin and creole languages), Sessarego proposes a model of contact-induced cross-generational language acquisition for approaching this and a number of other Afro-Hispanic varieties in the Americas.

Rey Romero in chapter 9, "Agreement and Valuation of Phi-Features in Judeo-Spanish: A Cross-Generational Account," analyzes the Judeo-Spanish varieties (Ladino) found in Istanbul, the Prince Islands, and New York City. Since the younger generation of speakers displays a speech pattern in which gender and number unvalued features are not satisfied, Romero examines the phi-feature valuation in determiners, pre-nominal adjectives, and post-nominal adjectives to center the features that represent the array of inflection processes. Employing the Minimalist Program to approach these phi-features in his fieldwork, Romero shows how the lack of gender agreement is the result of elements that are not specified in the lexicon. His approach demonstrates the existence of a cross-generational pattern with post-nominal adjectives, which are specified and accepted the most, followed by pre-nominal adjectives and determiners, which are agreed on the least. Romero concludes that variation in phi-features agreement is a common characteristic of endangered languages and languages in shift, which means that these patterns may be based on universal language acquisition processes.

In chapter 10, "Psych Predicates, Light Verbs, and Phase Theory: On the Implications of Case Assignment to the Experiencer in Non-*Leísta* Experience

Predicates," Ricard Viñas de Puig looks at non-*leísta* varieties of Spanish to assess the syntactic behavior of psych verbs resulting from light verb constructions. Viñas de Puig proposes a cross-linguistic common structure for experience predicates based on where the Experience is merged with a V-head. His approach helps to reveal a predication structure with the Theme, while the Experiencer is projected by a higher functional projection, v_{EXP}. Considering the lack of variation in the Case assigned to the Experiencer argument in these constructions, Viñas de Puig concludes that the functional projection heading of these predicates is responsible for Case assignment and the introduction of an external argument. Thus, arguing against several norms in the literature, this projection must be considered a non-unaccusative phase head (v^*).

Contemporary Advances in Theoretical and Applied Spanish Linguistic Variation has a unique place within studies of Hispanic linguistics. It distinguishes itself from more general books, such as Hualde, Olarrea, Escobar, and Travis (2010) or Azevedo (2009), by not restricting sociolinguistics to one or a few chapters. It is necessarily the sole focus of the collection as a whole. Moreover, instead of chapters on different areas of sociolinguistics with some summarized examples and exercises for the reader, this volume offers original research where one can approach critically emergent problems in the field, such as the role of language contact in variation, gender and variation, how age affects speech, the influence of general language acquisition features, and even the influence of migration and immigration in language molding and usage. Another main feature that separates this volume from others is that it is written in English in order to be used not only in Spanish language courses, or by Hispanic linguistics scholars, but also by any scholar interested in linguistic variation in general.

It focuses on linguistic variation, while showing across the different studies that language variation is a constant process of change over time and not only a static phenomenon representative of a social class or concrete demographic. Hence, it also demonstrates the need to approach language variation in many different ways. It is in this sense that this collection offers an alternate history of language variation.

The volume includes more novel approaches to variation and contains at least three main contributions to the rich spectrum of sociolinguistics books focused on the Hispanic world. First, it covers variation in less commonly studied varieties such as Proto-Ibero Romance, Yungueño Spanish, and Ladino, which are new areas of interest in a broader world where certain minorities and their languages are crucial. Second, it also includes very recent and innovative approaches to variation coming from formal theories, such as feature geometry and the Minimalist Program, in order to spark a debate about methodology that is more comprehensive of the very diverse approaches to variation currently practiced in the field. Third, the volume includes chapters that combine quantitative and qualitative analysis of different linguistic variables. Besides providing an approach to the linguistic, contextual, and situational elements that statistically favor the occurrence of the forms in question, some of the chapters also attend to the intentional features influencing the speaker's deployment of speech. By incorporating such novel approaches that focus on some more classical linguistic variation, even if incorporating more novel data, causation, causation treatment/conceptualization, or methodologies, this volume contributes to the field of Hispanic sociolinguistics in reflecting the diversity of methodologies and approaches that have enriched the field in the last decades, but that in some ways are in logical progression from earlier studies to the most recent ones.

PART I
Historical Linguistics

Glimpses of Proto-Ibero-Romance in Neapolitan and Other Southern Italian Mainland Vernaculars

John M. Ryan

1. Introduction

Projects to reconstruct proto-languages are far from new. For years linguists and philologists have been using both the comparative and other methods to reconstruct ancient languages such as Proto-Indo-European (Jones 1786), as well as more recent ones like Proto-Romance. Although printed and written texts arguably provide by far the most direct attestation of change over time, these go back only so far (Castellani 1976: 5–7). Occasionally, we are surprised by some new record that predates those previously discovered, as the recently found Spanish *Cartularies of Valpuesta*, some of which date back to the early 9th century (Ruiz Asencio 2010).

1.1. HISTORICAL WRITTEN TEXTS FROM THE IBERIAN PENINSULA

Thanks to both the ongoing discovery and preservation efforts of philologists and linguists as recent as the current century, historical written texts originating in the Iberian Peninsula have been found to be the most representative and earliest of any texts produced in Romance, spanning from a highly prescribed variety of Classical Latin to the Modern Spanish of today. Existing written texts in a Latin of the classic variety have been attested as early as the first century with the philosophical treatises of Seneca and poetry by both Martial and Quintilian. Only a few centuries later, a Galician monk by the name of Etheria or Egeria (indicated in the leftmost gray box in figure 1.1) would demonstrate the changes that were taking place in the Latin of a particular Iberian type in a narrative of her pilgrimage to the Holy Land (Harrington 1972: 1–4). Figure 1.1 illustrates the evolution of Romance from these earliest Latin texts. The problem with documenting the next stage of writing in the Iberian Peninsula is the lack of written texts for a period of approximately 420 years, and prior to the twentieth century this gap was believed to be even greater. For example, before the discovery in the previous century of such Ibero Romance texts as the *Cartularios*, *Jarchas*, or *Glosas Emilianenses*, it was believed that the earliest writing in Romance of the peninsula was *El Cantar del Mío Çid* dating from 1140 CE. As it currently stands, the earliest medieval texts for any Romance language are the *Cartularios de Valpuesta* (indicated in the rightmost gray box in figure 1.1), currently dated at 804 CE, almost 240 years earlier than the *Cantar del Mío Çid*.

1.2. USING PRESENT-DAY LANGUAGES AS EVIDENCE FOR EARLIER LANGUAGE FORMS

As indicated in the preceding section, although substantial advances have been made during the twentieth century in demonstrating progressively earlier variations of Ibero Romance in actual written texts originating in the peninsula, there continues to be a gap of over four hundred years. Although it is possible, it is highly unlikely that other, earlier texts will be found that predate the *Cartularios*. Aside from the analysis of existing texts, another line of inquiry is the variationist perspective with regard to the analysis of languages that are still spoken but have been sufficiently isolated geographically, politically, and, until relatively recently, technologically. These modern languages have been suggested to contain certain older forms not found elsewhere, such as the Classical Latin velar obstruent /k/ before /i/ and /e/ in Sardinian, retention of such earlier noun cases as the dative and genitive in Romanian, or certain phonological or morphological archaisms found in Modern Portuguese or Sephardic Spanish. This has led some linguists to go so far as to suggest one particular variety of the Italo-Romance as being closest to Latin or as being the "oldest Romance language," such as Sardinian (Pei 1968: 23) or Sicilian (Privitera 2004: 15); however, one such variety that has not been suggested as a contender is the southern Italian mainland vernacular, most notably represented by Neapolitan.

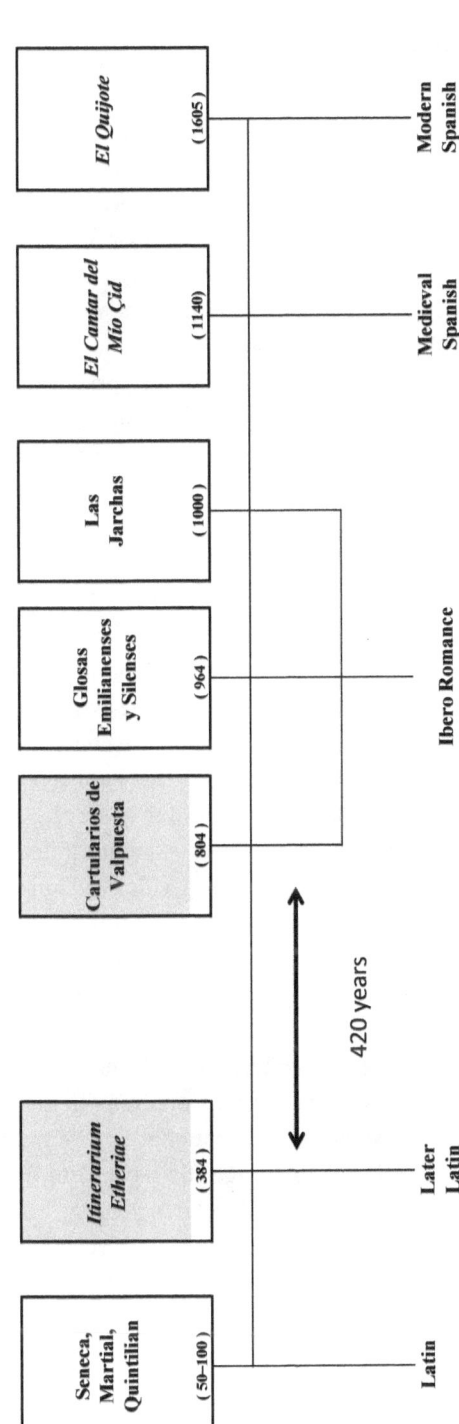

Figure 1.1
Evolution of peninsular texts from Latin to Modern Spanish.

2. Purpose and Objectives

This chapter revisits the variationist approach to diachronic linguistics, which seeks among particular isolated (hence, conservative) varieties of modern spoken languages linguistic evidence for older forms and structures. As such, this chapter explores a variety of phonological, morphological, and syntactic structures that are shared by most southern Italian mainland vernaculars, as represented by Neapolitan, and furthermore, which can be either 1) documented in earlier written versions of Romance, particularly of the Iberian variety, or 2) suggestive of forms that existed prior to existing written records. As additional evidence, a final section illustrates the archaic nature of Modern Neapolitan lexical items as compared to modern Italian reflexes.

3. Methodology

Although technically used to describe characteristics pertaining to the customs or language spoken in or around Naples, the term Neapolitan has become a catch-all, macrodialectal term[1] used to describe most Italian dialects in the south, particularly in the Campania region (Ledgeway 2009). The southern vernacular, a more general term that has been applied to this variety, has been shown to exhibit a variety of linguistic characteristics that are quite different from those of northern or standard Italian, also known as Tuscan (Clivio et al. 2011: 10), and, more specifically, Florentine (Maiden 1995: 3–5) and has experienced an evolution from Latin that is entirely separate from the north (Ledgeway 2009: 5–13). In fact, Neapolitan is considered a separate language from Italian and is spoken by 5.7 million people (*Ethnologue* 2002).[2]

Some of the principal linguistic differences between Neapolitan and Tuscan are the extent and preservation of archaic structures in the former, which can be explained by both its history and economy. Southern Italy has had a long history of political, cultural, and linguistic separatism from the north, one which included incessant natural disasters, rampant poverty, disease, and limited education and illiteracy (Bartalesi-Graf 2011: 1–31). Even after the unification of Italy in 1861, the North and South remained essentially

---

1. Neapolitan is not unlike the term "castellano" in the Spanish-speaking world, which technically refers to the variety of Spanish that originated and is still spoken in Castile, but is applied more liberally by speakers of most other regional varieties of Spanish.
2. Estimated from 2002 data.

un-united linguistically until the mid-1900s. Not until the 1950s did mass education and technology help spread the use of northern Italian as the official language. Before this time, it was not uncommon for the uneducated to speak ONLY the southern vernacular. Still today, the North and South remain two very different places both culturally and linguistically.

Southern Italy is historically an agricultural economy, although there have been several unsuccessful attempts to bring more industry into the region. This continued agricultural economy has contributed historically to successive massive emigrations of unskilled workers from the South to places like the United States and Latin America. This is also responsible for the very little cultural or linguistic change within the region throughout its history, with more people leaving the region than newcomers settling there.

3.1. RESEARCH QUESTIONS

This study will try to answer the following research questions:

1. What structures in Modern Neapolitan are different from those employed by modern standard Italian or modern standard Spanish but resemble attested existing older primitive Romance structures?
2. In what ways do these structures compare with structures that can be attested in Classical Latin, Vulgar Latin, or early Ibero Romance?
3. In the case of structures that cannot be attested in older forms, how might they serve as clues to proto forms that predate those that are attested?

4. Data[3] and Discussion

4.1. PHONOLOGY

This section focuses on two verbal phonological characteristics of Modern Neapolitan that suggest earlier forms. The first is the retention of Latin short

---

3. For clarity of illustration this study adopts the convention of using upper case Roman (no-italics) to represent Classical Latin forms, italicized upper case Roman for both attested and hypothetical Vulgar Latin and Ibero Romance forms, and lower case italics for Modern Italian, Spanish, or Neapolitan forms. If only a portion of a particular word or structure is the focus

Ĭ as /i/, where this has changed to /e/ in other languages. The other is a much more involved example of the reduction of post-tonic vowels that may suggest a pre-attested form in Ibero Romance.

4.1.1. Retention of Latin Short Ĭ as /i/

One phonological feature of Modern Neapolitan that gives us the glimpse of a variety of Romance that is closer to its Latin ancestor is the retention of Latin tonic short Ĭ in words that in other modern Romance varieties have converted to /e/. For example, (1) (a) through (d) show preservation of the short high vowels in Modern Neapolitan that all have otherwise converted in Modern Italian:

	LATIN	Neapolitan	Modern Italian	Gloss
(1)	(a) PISCE	pisə	pesce	'fish'
	(b) DICTU	dittə	detto	'said'
	(c) BIVO	bivə	bevo	'I drink'
	(d) MITTERE	mittərə	mettere	'to send'

4.1.2. Weakening versus Full Syncope of Post-Tonic Latin Vowels

One of the earliest phonological changes that began to take hold between Latin and early Romance was the weakening of post-tonic vowels, particularly in the environment of a liquid. The tendency for loss of post-tonic vowels was present in Latin speech in the earliest days of the Empire, as illustrated in (2) (a) through (d), by Marcus Valerius Probus, a grammarian of the third to fourth century and author of *Appendix Probi*:

	LATIN	Gloss
(2)	(a) SPECULUM, NON SPECLUM	'mirror'
	(b) VIRIDIS, NON VIRDIS	'green'
	(c) VETVLVS NON VETLVS	'old'
	(d) ARTICVLVS NON ARTICLVS	'article'

Of all the Romance languages, Spanish continued this early trend and extended it beyond the realm of liquids as in (3) (a) and (b):

---

of discussion within a particular example, only that portion of the word or structure has been underlined.

	LATIN	Intermediate Ibero Romance	Gloss
(3)	(a) FE<u>MI</u>NAS >	FE<u>M</u>NAS	'women'
	(b) HO<u>MI</u>NES >	HO<u>M</u>NES	'men'

It is generally agreed that this change in particular is what gives Modern Spanish its unique phonetic shape[4] as compared to the other Romance languages (Dworkin 2012: 175). This is because, in most cases, loss of post-tonic vowels would in turn set in motion a number of other phonological changes that are responsible for the modern sounds we hear today, as in (4) and (5).

	LATIN	Intermediate Ibero Romance		Modern Spanish
(4)	(a) FE<u>MI</u>NAS >	(b) FE<u>M</u>NAS >	(c) FE<u>MR</u>AS >	(d) he<u>mb</u>ras
(5)	(b) HO<u>MI</u>NES >	(b) HO<u>M</u>NES >	(c) HO<u>MR</u>ES >	(d) ho<u>mb</u>res

According to both (4) and (5), the traditional explanation for these changes is (a) the post-tonic I in the second syllable -MIN- was lost completely; resulting in (b) an unlikely phonological combination of two different nasals, i.e., -MN-, for speakers of that time; followed by (c) denasalization and, more specifically, rhotacization of the second nasal, which produced a new combination of -MR- obtained in Early Medieval Spanish; and (d) further adjustment of -MR- via epenthesis to -*mbr*- has led to the words we use today (Lloyd 1987: 204).

At the other end of the spectrum lies Modern Italian or Tuscan, which, unlike Spanish, has retained post-tonic vowels as illustrated in (6) (a) and (b):

	LATIN	Modern Italian	Gloss	Pronunciation
(6)	(a) FE<u>MI</u>NAS	*femmine*	'women'	[fe'-mːi-ne]
	(b) HO<u>MI</u>NES	*uomini*	'men'	[wo'-mi-ni]

In both cases, each word has retained the full articulation of the original post-tonic Latin vowels. When we compare the same word reflexes above in Modern Neapolitan, however, as seen in (7) (a) and (b), we observe a different pattern for the pronunciation of post-tonic vowels:

---

4. The exact timing of this change in Spanish is uncertain. However, the thirteenth-century Spanish poet Gonzalo de Berceo alternates between *femna* and *fembra* in his various writings, suggesting that the change might have been one in transition at the time (Corominas & Pascual 1980–1991, vol. 3: 340).

	LATIN	Modern Neapolitan	Gloss	Pronunciation
(7) (a)	FE<u>MINA</u>S	*femm<u>e</u>ne*	'women'	[fɛ'-mːə-nə]
(b)	HO<u>MINE</u>S	*uomm<u>e</u>ne*	'men'	[wo'-mːə-nə]

Modern Neapolitan and other southern Italian dialects have not gone as far as either Spanish in losing post-tonic Latin vowels or as Italian in retaining them, but instead have reached an intermediate stage and reduced these to schwa. Unlike Modern Italian or Spanish, in which every vowel of a word, whether tonic or atonic, receives full articulation, Modern Neapolitan employs a system in which only tonic vowels receive their full articulation, and all remaining atonic vowels are reduced to schwa (Clivio et al. 2011: 82). As also seen in (11) and (12), a secondary effect of this reduction is the reduplication of the consonant preceding the reduced vowel. Given that both Italian and Neapolitan orthography is highly representative of their pronunciation, this doubling effect is represented graphically with double consonants.

To summarize, table 1.1 compares the putative effects on post-tonic vowels in Spanish and northern (Tuscan) and southern (Neapolitan) Italian as evolved from the Latin FEMINAS and HOMINES. It is no coincidence that FE<u>MINA</u>S and HO<u>MINE</u>S are the two words chosen to demonstrate the phonological effects on post-tonic vowels among the three languages specified, since, as we will see below, those dealing with the evolution of the original Latin sequence -MIN- have particular relevance to this chapter. Having compared the evolution of these words among the three languages specified, we are now ready to address a discrepancy that appears in the evolution of the sequence -MN- to Modern Spanish. As seen above, it was the general tendency in early Ibero Romance for words like FE<u>MINA</u>S and HO<u>MINE</u>S to lose the post-tonic vowel/syllable, which in turn resulted in the new sequence -MN- to contend with phonologically. As also seen above, through the combined processes of denasalization and rhotacization, the second nasal, or -N-, was converted to -R-, which subsequently, in an effort to ease articulation, led to the epenthesis of [b], ultimately forming the Modern Spanish combination *-mbr-*.

On its face this explanation seems adequate; however, a problem arises when one considers that the sequence -MN- already existed in Latin and this combination did not in fact ultimately yield the *-mbr-* sequence in Spanish, but rather followed a different path involving progressive assimilation of the first nasal M to the second N, yielding -NN-, which ultimately became [ɲ], represented orthographically by -ñ-. Although there are only a few of these

Table 1.1
Comparative summary of putative effects on post-tonic vowels. The discrepancy in phonological rules regarding the sequence -MN- in Spanish and a new proposal for the origin of epenthetic [b] in [-mbr-].

LATIN	Northern Italian	Southern Italian	Spanish
FE<u>MI</u>NAS	fe<u>mm</u>ine (preservation of post-tonic vowel)	fe<u>mm</u>ənə (reduction of post-tonic vowel to schwa)	fe<u>mn</u>as > fe<u>mr</u>as > fe<u>mbr</u>as > e<u>mbr</u>as (syncope of post-tonic vowel, rhotacization, and epenthesis)
HO<u>MI</u>NES	uo<u>m</u>ini (preservation of post-tonic vowel)	uo<u>mm</u>ənə (reduction of post-tonic vowel to schwa)	ho<u>mn</u>es > ho<u>mr</u>es > ho<u>mbr</u>es > o<u>mbr</u>es (syncope of post-tonic vowel, rhotacization, and epenthesis)

words, they nonetheless exist and, as illustrated by (8) (a) and (b), follow a path that is quite different from the -MN- sequence in words like FE<u>MI</u>NAS and HO<u>MI</u>NES.

	LATIN	Intermediate Ibero Romance	Modern Spanish
(8)	(a) AUTU<u>MN</u>US >	AUTU<u>NN</u>U(S) >	otoño
	(b) SO<u>MN</u>IUM >	SO<u>NN</u>IU(M) >	sueño

At this juncture, it is appropriate to ask why words like FEMNA or HOMNE would not then have led to such Spanish reflexes as the hypothetical outcomes *feña in (9) (a) or *hoñe in (9) (b).

	LATIN	Hypothetical Ibero Romance	Modern Spanish
(9)	(a) FE<u>MN</u>AS >	*FE<u>NN</u>AS >	*feñas
	(b) HO<u>MN</u>ES >	*HO<u>NN</u>ES >	*hoñes

Based on the information presented thus far, one possible answer to this question might be that words that entered the Iberian Peninsula already as -MN- were able to follow this path immediately, while, on the other hand, those words that entered as -MIN- had to pass through an additional phase of post-tonic vowel reduction, taking longer and resulting therefore in a different combination, i.e., -mbr-. However, as (10) (a) will attest, there are some words like DO<u>MI</u>NU(S) that took the latter path and did not result in *-mbr,* as would have been expected and which would have derived the ill-formed (10) (b):

	LATIN		Transition in Ibero Romance		Modern Spanish
(10) (a)	DO<u>MIN</u>US	>	*DO<u>MN</u>U(S)* > *DO<u>NN</u>U(S)*	>	*dueño*
(b)	DO<u>MIN</u>US	>	*DO<u>MN</u>U(S)* > **DOMRU(S)*	>	**dombro*

As (10) (a) suggests, there were in fact, not one, but two potential paths for words that originally entered the peninsula as -MIN-, namely, 1) a more common one that would ultimately yield *mbr-*, and 2) a less common one that would ultimately yield *-ñ-*. So the next logical question to this analysis is what could have been the trigger that determined which of the two directions a word could take?

One hypothesis for the different paths taken by such words as DO<u>MIN</u>US and FE<u>MIN</u>A, despite the similarity in form, is that perhaps words like FE<u>MIN</u>A and HO<u>MIN</u>E might not have actually sounded quite like what we think, that is, being fully reduced to *FEMNA* or *HOMNE* with full post-tonic vocalic loss, but rather perhaps they sounded more like the intermediate Neapolitan version of *femmena* [fe'-mːə-nə] 'woman' or *uommene* [uo'-mːə-nə] 'men' with not a fully elided post-tonic vowel, but instead a weakened version, such as schwa. If this were the case, the resultant sequence of consonants would not have been -MN- but rather -Mᵊ N- as indicated by the revised analysis of (4) and (5) in (11) and (12).

	LATIN		Intermediate Ibero Romance				Modern Spanish
(11) (a)	FE<u>MIN</u>AS	>	(b) *FEMəNAS*	>	(c) *FEMəRAS*	>	(d) *he<u>mbr</u>as*
(12) (a)	HO<u>MIN</u>E	>	(b) *HOMəNES*	>	(c) *HOMəRES*	>	(d) *ho<u>mbr</u>es*

In this new analysis, the intermediate stage between (a) and (b), which was previously proposed as a full post-tonic vocalic loss, can now instead be simply thought of as a reduction to interconsonantal *ə*, which might have been sufficient to prohibit the normal path to palatalization (-MN- > *ñ*) by breaking the sequence -MN- so that progressive assimilation would not take place as it did in (8) and (10). This would explain why a word like DO<u>MIN</u>U(S) could have suffered palatalization (-MN- > *ñ*) while FE<u>MIN</u>A took a different path (-MəN- > *-mbr*).

John M. Ryan · 27

To summarize this section involving Neapolitan phonology, in addition to the preservation of the Latin tonic short Ĭ, it has also been suggested that postvocalic reduction in Modern Neapolitan may be an archaic feature that was also present in early Ibero Romance and therefore helps to explain why the sequence -MIN- in Ibero Romance might have gone in two possible directions. The next section of the chapter focuses on morphology of the verb system and suggests how structures in Modern Neapolitan may also provide clues to unattested forms in pre-written Ibero Romance.

4.2. MORPHOLOGY

This section focuses on four morphological characteristics of Modern Neapolitan, two of which have been directly attested among the earliest Ibero Romance documents, and two others, though not directly attested, can be corroborated by other, circumstantial evidence, suggesting pre-attested forms.

4.2.1. Diminutive Suffix -(i)ello/-(i)ella

A distinctive morphological trait that is preserved today by Neapolitan, and for which there is evidence for similar behavior in both later Latin and early Romance texts, is the predominant use of the diminutive suffix *-(i)ello/-(i)ella* instead of the many other suffixes that came into later use by Modern Italian (such as *-ino/-ina* or *-etto/-etta*) or Modern Spanish *(-ito/-ita, -ete/-eta,* or *-ín/-ina)* as in (13) (a) and (b):

	Neapolitan	Italian	Spanish	Gloss
(13) (a)	*vasiello*	*bacino*	*besito*	'little kiss'
(b)	*vucchella*	*bocchina*	*boquita*	'little mouth'

For Spanish, just as *-ito/-ita* might be considered the diminutive suffix of choice today, *-(i)ello/-(i)ella* was the predominate form before the fifteenth century (González Ollé 1962: 178) and simply continued the usage of the post-Classical Latin diminutive suffix -ELLUM (e.g., CASTELLUM > *castiello*). As the Spanish diminutive suffixes *-ito/-ita, -ete/-eta* were late arrivals in Ibero Romance, diminutives before this time were exclusively represented by the suffix *-(i)ello/(i)ella,* as illustrated by (14) and (15):

(14) "Non habeant labore de **castiello** neque in fossato"
'May they not toil in castle nor in grave'
Cartulario de Covarrubias (c. 972) (Seco 2003: 129)

(15) "Garid vos, ay **yermaniellas**"
'Say ye, oh little sisters'
Jarchas (c. 1075–c. 1140) (Gámez Elizondo 2013)

Modern Neapolitan, through both its coexistence with and the influence of standard Italian, is beginning to use today the other diminutive endings as well, although -*iello/-illa* are still used more widely (Fierro 1989: 65).

4.2.2. Infinitives in Pre-Inchoative Form That in Spanish Have Since Been Inchoativized

Like the diminutive example in the preceding section, another productive morphological phenomenon that began in Latin and would continue into the early history of Ibero Romance was the addition of an inchoative suffix -*ecer* to verbal infinitives (Dworkin 1985). At first this was done to enhance the meaning of the original verb (usually, but not always, to indicate the "beginning" of a particular action) and both verbs would coexist. In most cases, however, the period of coexistence did not endure, and over time only one of the verbs would prevail.[5] An overview of the Romance languages shows two possible ways this could happen. One would be the simple preference for the inchoativized form over the original pre-inchoativized form, as exhibited by Modern Spanish (e.g., *florecer* versus an older form *florir*). The other, more complicated, alternative was an absorption by the pre-inchoativized paradigm of just eight inchoativized forms into the present tense indicative and subjunctive, as exhibited by Italian and Neapolitan, and so in these languages, unlike Spanish, the inchoative suffix never permeated the entire verbal paradigm, including the infinitive (e.g., *fiorire* [Italian] and *fiorì* [Neapolitan]).

What this implies is another indication of the close relationship between the morphology of Neapolitan and older forms in Ibero Romance, in that, with the exception of the post-inchoativized forms of the present indicative tense, all other older forms (including the infinitive) have been maintained in Modern Neapolitan, as illustrated in (16) (a), (b), and (c):

---

5. In a few cases both pre-inchoative and inchoativized verbs have survived in Modern Spanish, such as *aburrir* and *aborrecer*, or *dormir* and *adormecer*. In this case, one verb did not oust the other because they carry differing meanings.

	LATIN	Neapolitan	Spanish	Gloss
(16)	(a) AD DORMIRE	addormì	adorme<u>cer</u>	'to fall asleep'
	(b) FLORERE	fiorì	flore<u>cer</u>	'to flower'
	(c) PARERE	parè	pare<u>cer</u>	'to seem'

In terms of Ibero Romance texts, use of the original verb *adormir* in (16) (a) has been attested in Mozarabic documents of the 11th and 12th centuries (Al-And. XVII: 111, from Corominas & Pascual 1980–1991, vol. 2: 518) before which it would eventually become *adormecer* in Modern Spanish. The verb *florir*, in (16) (b), must have existed as an earlier verb form before it would eventually become *florecer* in Modern Spanish and also from which the old participle *florida* (hence the name of the American state) would have arisen. Other verbs like that in (16) (c), which eventually gave rise to verbs like *parecer* in Modern Spanish, are still common in Modern Neapolitan and suggest what Ibero Romance might have been like before fusion of the inchoative ending on the original infinitival stem.

4.2.3. Multi-Syllabic First-Person Present Tense Indicative Form

Another instance where one might catch a glimpse in Modern Neapolitan of what would have been earlier, hence unattested, Ibero Romance forms is the retention of multisyllabic, first-person singular present tense indicative forms of the verbs HABERE 'have' in (17) (a) and SAPERE 'know' in (17) (b):

	LATIN	Neapolitan	Italian/Spanish	Gloss
(17)	(a) SAPIO	sacciə	so/sé	'I know'
	(b) HABEO	aggiə	ho/he	'I have'

In Modern Spanish and Italian, these forms have evolved into simplified monosyllabic variants such as *sé* or *so* for *saber* or *sapere*, respectively, and *he* or *ho* for *haber* and *avere*, respectively. What is also interesting is that for Modern Neapolitan these fuller forms have since palatalized and diphthongized yielding *saccia* from SAPIO and *aggia* from HABEO. We see the same palatalization and diphthongization in the present subjunctive form in Modern Spanish in the form of *haya*.

These present tense, first-person singular forms of *haber* and *saber* are not directly attested for in the earliest existing Ibero Romance documents. However, taken together, the following evidence suggests their existence and, most likely, at least for *haber* in palatalized form.

The first clue to a multisyllabic form for the first-person singular of *haber* is the direct attestation of a third-person singular multisyllabic form of *haber* in Ibero Romance, as in (18):

(18) "Et *abe* ipsas kalumnias contra se"
'And he has those calumnies against him.' (León, 11th Century from Seco 2003: 75)

As (18) will attest, *haber*, which coincidentally still had lexical meaning of possession in the 11th century, retained its full third-person singular form at the time so there is no reason why a fuller form in the first person could not have existed as well.

The second clue for the existence of a multisyllabic first-person present indicative form of both *saber* and *haber* is the multisyllabic first-person subjunctive forms in Modern Spanish and Italian, as illustrated in (19) (a) and (b):

	LATIN	Italian/Spanish	Gloss
(19) (a)	SAPIA(M)	sappia/sepa	'I may know'
(b)	HABEA(M)	abbia/haya	'I may have'

Both northern Italian and Spanish have retained the full, multisyllabic, first-person present tense subjunctive forms from Latin SAPIA(M), (19) (a), and HABEA(M), (19) (b), with palatalization occurring only in the Spanish form and diphthongization occurring in both Spanish and Italian forms. Though unattested, through analogy with these subjunctive forms, we could reconstruct the earlier forms *sepo* and *hayo* from SAPIO and HABEO as possible first-person singular indicative forms existing at one time (Lloyd 1987: 298). This would suggest that SAPIO did not palatalize in Spanish but HABEO did, as it did for Neapolitan.[6]

Finally, the third clue to the potential existence of a fuller, multisyllabic first-person form in Ibero Romance as is found in Modern Neapolitan is the analytic first-person singular future form, which is based on the fuller, multisyllabic form of *haber*. Although the multisyllabic first-person singular present tense form of *haber* itself has not been directly attested in existing Ibero

---

6. Additional analogical evidence for a first-person singular indicative form of *sepo* from SAPIO is the corresponding form *quepo* for the Modern Spanish verb *caber* derived directly from the Latin CAPIO (from CAPERE, which was conjugated identically to SAPERE in many tenses, including the present [Lloyd 1987: 298]).

Romance documents, what have been attested are multisyllabic first-person future tense forms, which are formed by the combination of an infinitive + the present tense of *haber*. Syllabically, the Modern Neapolitan form (based on the multisyllabic first-person singular present tense of *haber*) is much closer to the original Vulgar Latin formation of AMARE HABEO than are the Modern Italian or Spanish forms, as seen in (20):

	Vulgar Latin	Italian/Spanish	Neapolitan	Gloss
(20)	AMARE <u>HABEO</u>	amer<u>ó</u>/amar<u>é</u>	amar<u>raggio</u>	'I will love'

Thanks to evidence provided by the *Jarchas*, this longer form of the first-person singular future is attested in Ibero Romance of the 11th century:

(21) "Tan t'amaray tan t'amaray"
 "Gar que fareyu . . . por el morireyu"
 Jarchas (c. 1075–c. 1140) (Gámez Elizondo 2013)

As illustrated by (21), in addition to evidence for the analytic future tense form based on an early multisyllabic first-person present indicative form of *haber*, there is also evidence that this early form was palatalized precisely like the Modern Neapolitan counterpart.

4.2.4. Regularization or Weakening of Previous Latin Strong Verbs of the -ĔRE (Third) Conjugation

One final example that lends credence to the viability of morphological coincidence between Modern Neapolitan and the historical path taken by Ibero Romance in the case of the weakening of what used to be strong verbs in Latin is (22) (a) through (d):

	LATIN	Neapolitan	Italian	Gloss
(22) (a)	MISIT	mettette	mise	's/he put'
(b)	DIXIT	dicette	disse	's/he said'
(c)	COGNOVIT	canuscette	connobbe	's/he knew'
(d)	SAPUIT	sapette	seppe	's/he knew'

This regularization is also found in Modern Spanish as compared to Latin for verbs like *meter—metió, conocer—conoció*.

Yet another instance of the regularization of verb forms between Latin and Romance was that of past participles, which corresponded to the four verb conjugations, -ARE, -ĒRE, -ĔRE, and -IRE. For -ĒRE and -ĔRE verbs the participle ended in *-uto* and still does for Modern Neapolitan. In the case of medieval Spanish we find the past participial form of *-uto* in the *Cantar del Mío Çid* for the verbs *vencer* and *meter*. Both of these verbs originated in the Latin third conjugation forms VINCĔRE and MITTĔRE. It is interesting to note here that although these verbs formed strong past participles in Latin, namely, VICTUS and MISSUS, they are formed as regular verbs in medieval Spanish (i.e., *vençudo* and *metudo*), as in (23) (a) and (b).

(23) (a) "*vençudo so*"
　　　'I am conquered.'
　　(b) "... *e metudo en carta*"
　　　'And put in a letter'
　　　　El Cantar del Mío Çid (c. 1140)
　　　　(http://www.vicentellop.com/TEXTOS/miocid/miocid.htm)

Of course, today the participles for these forms are formed like all regular participles in *-er*, namely, by adding *-ido* to the verb stem, resulting in *vencido* and *metido*. Participles in *-uto* suggested that at this time there still existed at least some physical remnants, if not the four original and entirely separate Latin conjugations.

4.3. SYNTAX

This section discusses two instances of syntactic phenomena found in Modern Neapolitan that are suggestive of earlier forms in Ibero Romance. The first of these has to do with post-nominal placement of possessive adjectives, a phenomenon that has been directly attested for in existing Ibero Romance documents. The second case is the preservation of two distinct forms in Modern Neapolitan, one of which is "che," descended from the form QUOD (and its differing gender and case forms), and the other "ca," originating in the forms QUAM and QUIA. As explained further below, although two forms have been attested in Ibero Romance, their usage suggest even among the earliest documents a final period in which "ca" has almost completely been replaced by "que."

4.3.1. Post-Nominal Placement of Possessive Adjectives

In Modern Romance, although post-nominal placement of possessive adjectives is possible for stylistic considerations, there is a preference for prenominal placement, especially in everyday conversation, as illustrated by (24) for Spanish and (25) for Italian:

(24) Spanish: todos <u>tus</u> hijos 'all your children'

(25) Northern Italian: la <u>mia</u> casa 'my house'

In Classical Latin and Ibero Romance, however, although possessive adjectives may appear occasionally before a noun, as in (26), there seems to be a more general preference for placement after the noun as in (27) and (28):

(26) Classical Latin: MEA CULPA 'my fault'

(27) Classical Latin: (a) A DEXTRIS <u>MEIS</u> 'on my right side'
　　　　　　　　　　　(b) NOMEN <u>TUUM</u> 'your name'

(28) Ibero Romance: NOMINE <u>MEO</u> 'my name'
　　(Sahagún [c. 933] from Seco 2003: 388)

Modern Neapolitan, like Latin and Ibero Romance, also has a preference for post-nominal possessive adjectives, as in (29) (a) and (b).

(29) (a) tutt'e criature <u>tue</u> 'all your babies'
　　 (b) casa <u>mia</u> 'my house'

4.3.2. Preservation of the Distinction between /ke/ and /ka/

Examples abound in diachronic linguistics, both within and outside the Romance family, whereby phonological changes, such as the loss of word final consonants or neutralization of earlier vocalic differences, effect the need for revision of a previous system, particularly in the areas of morphology and syntax. Perhaps there is no better example of this phenomenon on as grand a scale as that exhibited by historical changes in the Latin nominal case system, ultimately affecting both the morphology and syntax of nouns in the daughter languages and necessitating an overall gravitation from a more morphologically active (synthetic) system to a more syntactically active (analytic) system.

Another, lesser known instance of a phonological process affecting the morphology and syntax of the daughter languages is the gradual loss and merging of what were originally in the classical language a variety of WH-forms. These forms would ultimately merge into one single lexeme in most varieties of modern Romance. Appearing among these early forms were the following:

1. Relative and interrogative pronouns QUIS/QUAE/QUOD 'who' or 'that' (and their differing inflected case forms);
2. The subordinating conjunction QUOD 'which' or 'that,' which in later Latin replaced the classical conjunction UT and NE in purpose and resultative clauses (Sidwell 1995: 370–71);
3. A subordinating suffix -QUAM 'which' or 'ever' that was fairly productive in Latin as evidenced in such forms as QUISQUAM 'whoever,' UMQUAM 'ever,' or NUMQUAM 'never,' POSTQUAM 'after which,' and PRIUSQUAM or ANTEQUAM 'before which';[7]
4. The comparative conjunction QUAM 'than,' as it is still used in the Spanish name for the past perfect tense, or *pluscuamperfecto* = PLUS QUAM PERFECTO, literally, 'more than perfect'; and
5. The coordinating (or enunciative) conjunction QUIA 'for' or 'well.'

All five forms have since merged into a single lexeme in most varieties of modern Romance (e.g., *que* in Spanish and *che* in Italian). However, as illustrated in other parts of this chapter, once again an interesting exception to this historical process reveals itself in Modern Neapolitan, whereby a complete merger hasn't taken place; but rather two different forms have emerged from these five forms, namely, /ke/ descending from the forms in QUOD and /ka/ descending from the forms in QUAM and QUIA. These are represented orthographically in Neapolitan by "*che*" and "*ca*," respectively.[8]

---

7. Interestingly, the only trace of this subordinating suffix -QUAM, which has subsequently survived in Modern Spanish, is the frozen adverbial form *nunca* 'never,' which arose from the classical form NUMQUAM but for which the suffix has been bleached semantically and no longer retains its separate conjunctive function. Rather, *nunca* is interpreted as a single morpheme.

8. For an extensive treatment on both historical and modern usages of *che* versus *ca* in Neapolitan, see Ledgeway 2009: 863–81.

Coincidentally, Iberian documents from the medieval period also show two forms to have existed alongside each other, namely, "*que*" (occasionally also spelled "*ke*") and "*ca*"; however, by this time, the *ca* that was being used had been found to be employed solely in its coordinative or enunciative sense, that is, the reflex of QUIA, as in (30) (a) and (b).⁹

(30) (a) "el se está en Valencia—guardando e vigilando,
ca bien sabe que Álvar Fáñez—tiene de todo cuidado."
'He is in Valencia—looking and keeping watch,
For he knows full well that Álvar Fáñez—has everything cared for.'
Cantar del Mío Cid (c. 1140)
(http://www.vicentellop.com/TEXTOS/miocid/miocid.htm)

(b) "En España deseo de luego empezar;
en Toledo la magna, un afamado lugar
ca non sé de cual cabo empiece a contar,
ca más son que arenas a orilla de la mar."
'In Spain I wish of course to begin;
In Toledo the great, a famed place
For I do not know from which end I should begin to tell,
For more are the sands on the beach.'
Berceo, G. *Milagros de Nuestra Señora* (c. 1245–55) (Marín 1968: 36)

In other words, the *ca* in early existing Iberian documents are never found to represent either a subordinative use (as in the form of a subordinating suffix) or a comparative conjunction. This suggests that by the period of the earliest documents, QUAM had already merged with QUOD and only appeared as *que* for both of these uses. Eventually, Spanish medieval usage of *ca* would too be replaced by another conjunction, a fact that by the early sixteenth century, according to Juan de Valdés, was underscored by his commentary that

---

9. In addition to the case of *nunca* in Modern Spanish, which was suggested in footnote 7, one other instance of *ca* in the sense of -QUAM has been found to occur only once in medieval documents, namely, the *Glosas Silenses*, in the compound form *depuisca*, in the sense of *después (de) que*. However, it is maintained here, as was for *nunca*, that by this time the subordinating suffix had bleached semantically, as suggested by the following gloss of *depuisca* (appearing between brackets), which does not precede a clause and is translated by Seco as the adverb "*después*." "DE MUNQUE [*depuisca*] POST PURIFICATIONEM" *Glosas Silenses*, 22 (c. 950–1000) (Seco 2003: 190)

ca sounded archaic and would be the more common *"porque"* (de Valdés 1984: 154–55).

To summarize the discussion here, figure 1.2 compares the trajectories of all five Classical Latin forms into Neapolitan and Modern Spanish, with the binary /ke/-/ka/ system of Neapolitan being more representative of a pre-medieval Iberian usage. It has been shown that the earliest Ibero Romance documents provide evidence of a limited binary system in which the conjunction *ca* was only being used as late as the medieval Spanish period as a coordinative conjunction. As figure 1.2 illustrates, continued Neapolitan usage of two conjunctions, including *ca* in the subordinating function, suggests a pre-existing system that prevailed in Ibero Romance as well. Remnants of *ca* in both modern Spanish, as with *nunca*, or in late Ibero Romance, as in *depuisca*, hint at an earlier, richer subordinative system as well.

4.4. LEXICON

Before concluding this chapter, one last foray into Neapolitan as a potential exemplar of early Romance lies in the area of the lexicon. Unlike previous sections, this section does not make comparisons between Neapolitan and early Ibero Romance; rather, its purpose is to show evidence of Modern Neapolitan forms, as are illustrated in the first column of (31) (a) through (g), when compared to reflexes in Modern Italian of the third column, which are much closer to the original Latin equivalents in the middle column:

	Neapolitan	LATIN	Modern Italian	Gloss
(31) (a)	*sora*	SORORE	*sorella*	'sister'
(b)	*frate*	FRATRE	*fratello*	'brother'
(c)	*facere*	FACERE	*fare*	'do'
(d)	*dicere*	DICERE	*dire*	'say'
(e)	*ascetà*	EXCITARE	*svegliare*	'wake up'
(f)	*iamma*	EAMUS	*andiamo*	'let's go'
(g)	*'nnante*	IN ANTE	*davanti*	'before'

The examples in (31) illustrate that Neapolitan forms resemble those in Latin across all grammatical categories. In terms of nouns, or examples (a) and (b), both *sora* 'sister' and *frate* 'brother' are Neapolitan forms that, unlike their northern Italian counterparts of *sorella* or *fratello*, have not suffered diminutivization, a later lexical process in the history of these two words.

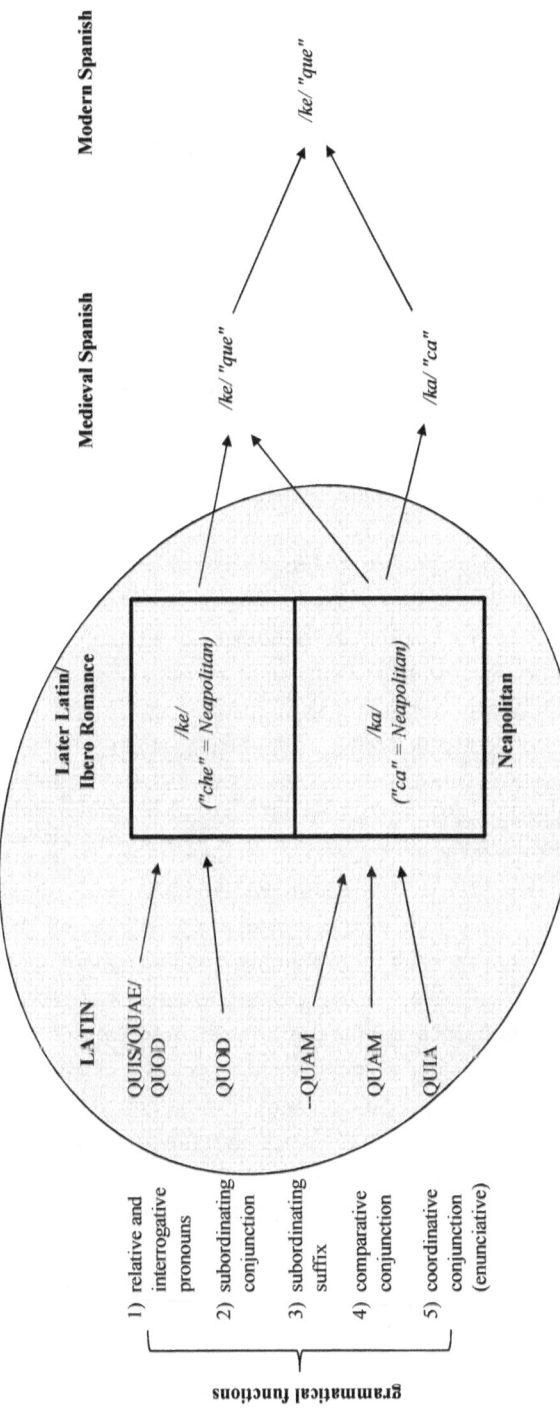

Figure 1.2
Comparison of Historical Trajectories of Neapolitan /ka/-/ke/ with Spanish /ke/.

Likewise, the Neapolitan infinitival forms of the verbs *facere* 'do' and *dicere* 'say,' as in (c) and (d), are identical to their Latin counterparts, unlike the northern forms that over time have been truncated into *fare* and *dire*, respectively. Some Neapolitan verbs, like (e) *ascetà* from EXCITARE, preserve the meaning these had in later Latin, in this case, 'wake up.' Some verb forms, such as (f) *iamma* 'let's go,' are direct reflexes of Latin verb forms, all but lost in other Romance varieties, in this case the first-person plural present subjunctive form EAMOS from IRE 'go.' Finally, also existent in Neapolitan are prepositions that have been constructed from the combination of earlier sequences that have been replaced in the north by other forms, as in the case of (g) *'nnante* 'before,' a reflex of IN ANTE, which has been lost to *davanti*.

5. Final Remarks and Conclusions

The purpose of this chapter was to demonstrate that certain basic phonological, morphological, syntactic, and lexical structures in Modern Neapolitan are reminiscent of forms found in early Romance, as documented here for the development of Spanish from Latin. In some cases I have offered documentation of the direct retention of Latin features and in others suggested the preservation of forms that can be documented in early Romance texts, or provide strong clues for forms that may have existed prior to forms that can be documented.

These structures in Modern Neapolitan, such as the exclusive use of diminutives in *-iello/-iella*, pre-inchoative infinitives in *-ir* or *-er* instead of *-ecer*, and post-nominal placement of possessive adjectives, etc., are reminiscent of forms found in early Ibero Romance, as documented here for the development for Spanish from Latin. Other processes or structures found in Modern Neapolitan, such as post-tonic vocalic weakening to schwa, the multi-syllabic palatalized first-person present tense forms of *haber/saber*, and a dual subordinating conjunction system of /ke/ and /ka/, although they are not directly attested in early Ibero Romance, may provide clues to forms that we suggest here predate written evidence.

To conclude, the assertions made in this chapter are quite plausible considering what we know about the history of Italy's south, as discussed earlier in this chapter. When compared to its more economically successful and industrialized counterpart to the north, Italy's south represents a historical paradox, on the one hand having served as the early seat of the Roman Empire and, on the other, the embodiment of continuous corruption, neglect, poverty, as well as a region of repeated natural disasters. The historical lack of attention to these matters, compounded by little capital investment, as well as political, cultural, and linguistic separation from the north well beyond Italy's overall unification in the nineteenth century, allowed the south to proceed along the same simple agricultural path that characterized it since the days before the empire.

Another interesting historical fact that further supports a possible link between Neapolitan and Ibero Romance is the relative proximity in timing between the Roman invasion and occupation (in 326 BCE) of the then Greek city of Neapolis, historically coveted by competing nations for its obviously advantageous commercial location, and the arrival of imperial troops on Iberian shores (in 218 BCE). The closeness in timing of settlement in both these areas would suggest that both Neapolitan and Ibero Romance stem from a variety of Latin of the same period. This, compounded with historical isolation in their own right, could very well be important contributing factors to giving Neapolitan, as compared to other modern varieties of Romance, the historical edge in capturing the essence of an early Ibero Romance.

Observations made here have both pedagogical potential as well as implications for reopening the additional investigation into areas of diachronic Ibero Romance linguistics that may have previously been thought to be fully studied, such as the long held position of full syncope of Classical -MIN- that has been challenged in this chapter. With regards to the teaching of Ibero Romance linguistics, it has been shown here that in the absence of available texts, certain phonological, morphological, and syntactic structures in Neapolitan might be used to demonstrate the earliest of transitional stages both between Latin and Ibero Romance and between Ibero Romance and Spanish.

Finally, and in closing, this study provides additional evidence for the way in which the variationist approach can inform the field of diachronic linguistics by providing a more holistic (and realistic) perspective, one that incorporates language variation into the larger picture of language change. Any serious study seeking to understand how language either changes or does not change over time must consider what happens on the ground, with particular historical and sociopolitical factors contributing to the continued use of the vernacular, which consequently, as suggested here for the case of southern Italy, plays a large part in the maintenance of older forms. In a land where so little has changed in over two millennia, and most speakers are now bilingual in both Neapolitan and Italian, it should not be surprising that one middle-aged woman, the owner of a corner bar in a remotely located southern Italian hill town, when asked to describe under what circumstances she might use Italian, and under what others she might use Neapolitan, indicated without a moment's hesitation that she uses Italian with people she doesn't know and Neapolitan "with just about everyone else."[10]

Acknowledgments

This project was supported by a University of Northern Colorado Spring 2015 Faculty Reassignment Award, 2015 Provost Travel Award, and the 2013–2014 College of Humanities and Social Sciences Professional Development Fund.

---

10. 1999 Interview with unnamed respondent in San Clemente di Galluccio, Province of Caserta.

PART II
Phonetics and Morphosyntax

Rhotacism of /s/ in Elche Spanish
Social and Linguistic Factors Conditioning the Reduction

Whitney Chappell and Francisco Martínez Ibarra

1. Introduction

Not only is /s/ the most commonly occurring consonant phoneme in Spanish (Navarro Tomás 1968), it is also the most widely studied in Hispanic linguistics (Brown & Torres Cacoullos 2002) given its extensive dialectal and sociolectal variation. Aspiration, deletion, gemination, voicing, hypercorrection, and myriad other processes affecting /s/ have been documented in the Spanish-speaking world (see Lipski 1994a). In spite of the large body of work /s/ processes have generated, studies investigating the rhotacism of /s/ in Spanish, e.g., *los dos* 'both' produced as [loɾ.ðos] rather than the standard [loz.ðos], are scarce.

The few mentions of rhotacism of /s/ in Spanish note that both Castilian and Andalusian dialects may variably produce a rhotic before [ð] at the word boundary, and Andalusian dialects may also rhoticize before [β, ɣ, m, n, l] (Solé 1992: 261). In each of the aforementioned environments, regressive voicing assimilation tends to take place, resulting in /s/ realized as [z], which may then in turn be weakened to [ɾ]. This [z] to [ɾ] phenomenon is not specific to Spanish, as dialects of Catalan also rhoticize [z] before [β, ð, ɣ, m, n]. In fact, the rhotacism of voiced /s/ has been attested in several language families, including Italic, Germanic, and Sanskrit, among others (Painter 2011; Roberts 2012; Solé 1992).

While rhotacism of /s/ has been mentioned in several dialects of Spanish, a quantitative analysis of the linguistic and social factors conditioning its realization has yet to take place. The present study seeks to fill the void in the literature by examining rhotacism in Elche Spanish, a coastal city of approximately 230,000 people in southeastern Spain, where Spanish and Catalan have coexisted for centuries. In Elche Spanish, rhotacism may be observed word-internally or word-finally before a voiced consonant, e.g., *musgo* 'moss' can become [muɾyo] and *los motes* 'the nicknames' becomes [loɾ motes], or word-finally before a vowel, e.g., [loɾ ekos] for *los ecos* 'the echos.' The inclusion of this previously overlooked prevocalic rhotacism will also shed light on the linguistic contexts in which /s/ rhotacism is most likely, providing a contemporary account of a variable reduction that has received little attention in both theoretical and applied work on Spanish linguistic variation.

2. Literature Review

2.1. DEMOGRAPHICS AND LANGUAGE USE IN ELCHE

Elche is located in the southeast of Spain on the Mediterranean coast, and the city is the capital of the administrative division of the Low Vinalopo, within the province of Alicante in the Autonomous Community of Valencia (ACV). Elche is the third most populated city in the ACV, with a total population of 230,224 according to the 2013 census. The majority of the population lives within the city limits and only about 12% live in a more rural environment.

In 1960, only 73,320 people resided in Elche, but two large waves of immigration have propelled the population to its current state. The first wave took place in the 1960s and 1970s; in this period the city grew to 162,873 residents, largely due to economic development and employment opportunities related to the shoe industry. The majority of the newly arrived immigrants came from neighboring regions such as Murcia, Albacete, and Andalusia and spoke Spanish as their first and only language. A second significant wave of immigration occurred from the 1990s to the beginning of the twenty-first century, predominantly comprised of foreign immigrants. The majority of this group came from South America, Eastern Europe, and North Africa and were driven by employment opportunities in the construction industry.

The boom of monolingual Spanish speakers and foreign immigrants to Elche reinforced a process of language shift that has existed in Valencia for centuries: since the sixteenth century, Spanish has been gradually supplanting Catalan use (Gimeno Menéndez & Gómez Molina 2007: 99–101). As Spain transitioned to democracy following Franco's death, numerous national and regional laws were created to govern linguistic responsibilities, safeguard cultural identities, and regulate the teaching of both Spanish and Catalan, but Elche is characterized as an area with a predominance of Spanish in both economic and family domains (Gimeno Menéndez & Gómez Molina 2007: 99–101). Data from public surveys and academic research support such a linguistic description of Elche: according to Martinez Ibarra (2013), the majority of the population (97%) reports speaking Spanish on a daily basis quite frequently. However, only 21% claim the same for Catalan, and individual percentages of daily Catalan use rarely rise above 25%. Domains of use differ as well: while Spanish is used in all contexts of interaction, private or public, Catalan is primarily found in private contexts of interaction such as the home or local stores in certain neighborhoods.

The Spanish of Elche includes several distinct dialectal features that may be due to contact with Catalan and/or language-internal developments. Some of these features include *seseo*, lexical borrowings from Catalan, the use of the expletive particle *qué* in direct questions, and prepositional use that differs from Standard Spanish. Spatial limitations prevent a thorough discussion of these features, and we refer the reader to Gimeno Menéndez and Gómez Molina (2007) for more information. The following sections will focus specifically on the rhotacism of /s/ in Elche Spanish, the dialectal feature of particular interest in this study.

2.2. /s/ VOICING IN SPANISH AND CATALAN

Because rhotacism variably occurs where [z] is produced, section 2.2 provides a brief introduction to both standard and non-standard /s/ voicing in Spanish. In addition to the environments that condition /s/ voicing in Spanish, the potential influence of /s/-voicing rules in Catalan phonology must be explored as well. Given the bilingual nature of the community under investigation, the possible transfer of voicing rules from Catalan to Spanish may help explain cases of Elche rhotacism. For this reason, the present section details Spanish /s/ voicing and Catalan /s/ voicing in both standard and nonstandard contexts.

The voicing assimilation of /s/ before a voiced consonant is a cross-dialectal and well-documented phenomenon in Spanish. In traditional phonological accounts, /s/ becomes [z] before a voiced consonant but not before a vowel or voiceless consonant (Morgan 2010). This process takes place both word-internally and word-finally, as illustrated below in (1).

(1) | asbesto | [azβesto] | 'asbestos' |
aspa	[aspa]	'blade'
asa	[asa]	'handle'
las botas	[laz#βotas]	'the boots'
las posas	[las#posas]	'you place them'
las odas	[las#oðas]	'the odes'

While traditional phonological accounts have treated this voicing assimilation as categorical, variation in degree of voicing is widely observed, with /s/ voicing decreasing in more formal registers and slower speech (A. García 2013; Navarro Tomás 1977; Torreblanca 1978). Additionally, the following consonant's manner of articulation and type of prosodic boundary following the /s/ play a key role (Campos-Astorkiza 2014), with more /s/ voicing before open approximants than before closed, more plosive-like approximants and less /s/ voicing across an intonational phrase boundary. This variability suggests that rather than a generative phonological rule, a gestural blending account (Browman & Goldstein 1989) more successfully captures the /s/-voicing variation. Under such an account, /s/ voicing is the product of increased overlap of the conflicting laryngeal gestures for /s/ and a following voiced consonant, allowing for gradient and variable realizations of /s/ voicing.

Like modern standard Spanish, /s/ voicing takes place in Catalan before a voiced consonant word-internally and word-finally but not before a voiceless consonant. Unlike Spanish, which has a single apical-alveolar fricative phoneme, /s/, Catalan has both the voiceless apical-alveolar /s/ and a voiced apical-alveolar /z/ (Davidson 2014). In word-initial and in word-medial position these phonemes are contrastive, e.g., *casa* 'house' and *caça* 'he/she/it hunts,' but the phonemic contrast is neutralized word-finally, and the production of [s] or [z] is determined by the following segment: with a following pause, a voiceless fricative occurs, e.g., *gos* 'dog' with [s], but a phonological, post-lexical voicing rule is applied in the presence of a following vowel, e.g., *gos estrany* 'strange dog' with [z]. This rule applies to all word-final fricatives followed by a vowel (see Bonet & Lloret 1998: 118–19; Pieras 1999: 212; Prieto 2004: 208, 216). These patterns are illustrated in (2).

(2) *és veritat*   [ez#βəɾitat]   'it's true'
    escoles   [əskoləs]   'schools'
    parles català   [paɾləs#kətəla]   'you speak Catalan'
    és horrible   [ez#uribblə]   'it is horrible'
    (Examples from Wheeler 1979)

Several studies have found complete voicing assimilation in most obstruent sequences, but some cases of incomplete neutralization can be observed as well (Carbonell 1992; Cuartero Torres 1998). Cuartero Torres (2001) found the fricative in /s#d/ sequences categorically realized with full voicing, suggesting that the phonological process of word-final, prevocalic /s/ voicing in Catalan may impact bilinguals' /s/ productions in the same environment in Spanish. Given the bilingual nature of the region, contact with Catalan is certainly a possible explanation for prevocalic /s/ voicing in Elche.

Lending credence to the argument that Spanish /s/ voicing is a contact phenomenon in Catalan-speaking regions, Davidson (2014) found that [z] is the preferred /s/ variant word-finally in his analysis of Barcelona Spanish. Further bolstering this claim is the fact that his participants' level of exposure to Catalan also significantly impacted Spanish /s/ voicing, and Catalan-dominant individuals observed more /s/ voicing constraints than other groups. In the same region, McKinnon (2012) found that intervocalic voicing is most likely in word-final position and in spontaneous speech, which suggests that both language contact and gestural overlap may play a role in Barcelonian /s/ voicing.

While the contact situation with Catalan helps to explain word-final, intervocalic /s/ voicing in parts of Spain, it should be noted that this type of voicing occurs in non-contact dialects of Spanish as well. Torreira and Ernestus (2012) recently found that Madrileño Spanish speakers produce uninterrupted /s/ voicing in approximately one third of intervocalic contexts, with /s/ voicing most likely in rapid speech and, to a lesser extent, in word-final position and unstressed syllables. In addition to non-contact regions of Spain, intervocalic /s/ voicing has been documented in Ecuador (Aguirre 2000; Calle 2010; Chappell 2011; C. García 2011; Lipski 1989; Robinson 1979; Strycharczuk 2012), Mexico City (Schmidt & Willis 2011), Costa Rica (Chappell & García in press), Buenos Aires (Bárkánya 2013), and it has also been mentioned in Panama, El Salvador, and Colombia (Torreblanca 1978: 501).[1]

---

1. The presence of similar constraints governing /s/ voicing in many non-contact varieties suggests that word-final voicing is preferred regardless of language contact, likely due to higher

The preceding section has demonstrated that /s/ voicing occurs in Standard Spanish and Catalan before a voiced consonant both word internally and word finally. In Catalan, both /s/ and /z/ occur word-internally and /s/ voicing takes place categorically word finally before a vowel. While exposure to and dominance in Catalan has been shown to influence prevocalic /s/ voicing in Barcelonian Spanish, intervocalic /s/ voicing also occurs in similar environments in nonstandard dialects of Spanish that are not in contact with other languages, making the influence of Catalan uncertain. Regardless of Catalan's influence, the existence of /s/ voicing both preconsonantally and prevocalically in Catalonian Spanish provides for numerous possible contexts for rhotacism, which are detailed below in section 2.3.

2.3. RHOTACISM

Cases of rhotacism are abundant in Romance languages, with the rhotic often serving as a reduction of another segment diachronically or synchronically. For example, in Romanian, /n/ has been reduced to [ɾ] between vowels, e.g., *buni* > *buri* and *bine* > *bire* (Lázaro Carreter 1962: 357, as cited in Rufo Sánchez 2006: 6), and coda /l/ is realized as [ɾ] in Sevillian Spanish, such that *alto* 'tall' and *maldad* 'wickedness' become [aɾto] and [maɾðað], respectively (Amado & Lida 1945; García de Diego 1978; Jiménez Fernández 1999; Morgan 2010; Narbona, Cano, & Morillo 1998). There exists a consensus in the literature that intervocalic /s/ in Latin was produced with voicing (Allen 1978: 35; Leumann 1977: 180; Meiser 1998: 95), and the intervocalic voiced [z] was then reduced to a rhotic, e.g., *Valesius* > *Valezius* > *Valerius* (Lázaro Carreter 1962: 357, as cited in Rufo Sánchez 2006: 5). Rhotacism in Latin can be identified in two ways: first, in cases of comparative evidence, e.g., **swesor* became *soror* 'sister' in Latin, and second, in paradigms that show word-final *s* alternating with word-medial intervocalic *r*, e.g., *flos* and *floris* 'flower' (Roberts 2012: 80).

In addition to yielding diachronic changes, rhotacism of /s/ variably appears synchronically in several varieties of peninsular Spanish before a voiced consonant, including Castilian and Andalusian Spanish in addition to Balearic Catalan, illustrated below in (3).

---

rates of temporal reduction word-finally (File-Muriel 2007; Johnson 2004) and the position's decreased importance in terms of lexical accessibility (MacEachern 1995). This reduction leads to a reduced sibilant duration, and a reduced duration is correlated with an increase in voicing (Torreira & Ernestus 2012).

(3) (a) Castilian and Andalusian dialects of Spanish [z] > [ɾ] / ____ $ [ð]
  los demás   [loɾ ðemas]   'the others'
  buenos días [bwenoɾ ðias] 'good morning'
  desde   [deɾðe]   'from, since'
 (b) Andalusian dialects of Spanish [z] > [ɾ] / ____ $ [β, ð, ɣ, m, n, l]
  los van a coger [loɾ βan a kɔxɛ] 'they'll catch them'
  me has mojado [m(e)aɾ moxao]   'you splashed me'
  los lirios   [loɾ liɾjɔh]   'the lilies'
 (c) Balearic dialects of Catalan [z] > [ɾ] / ____$ [β, ð, ɣ, m, n]
  es dit   [əɾ ðit]   'the finger'
  fantasma   [fəntaɾmə] 'ghost'
  es nins   [əɾ nins]   'the children'
  From Solé (1992: 261).

In Catalan, rhotacism has been described as a feature associated with younger speakers in informal speaking styles (Recasens i Vives 1993; Segura i Llopis 1996, 1998). Little has been said about rhotacism in Valencian Spanish, but the phenomenon is observable there as well. In fact, the rhotacism of [z] occurs in more environments than those mentioned above in (3): in addition to rhotacism before a voiced consonant, rhotacism can take place variably before a vowel as well, as shown in (4).

(4) Elche Spanish [z] > [ɾ] or [ɹ] / ____ $ [+cons, +voice]
          desde   [deɾðe]   'from, since'
          [z] > [ɾ] or [ɹ] / ____ # [+cons, +voice]
                 [+vowel]
          los goles [loɾ ɣoles] 'the goals'
          los otros [loɾ otɾos] 'the others'

In addition to Italic languages, rhotacism has also been documented in Germanic and Sanskrit languages (Painter 2011; Roberts 2012; Solé 1992), showing that the phenomenon is not an isolated occurrence nor is the process limited to a single language family. The appearance of rhotacism in typologically diverse languages suggests that the reduction of [z] to [ɾ] (or sometimes [ɹ]) is phonetically motivated. Acoustically, [z] and [ɾ] are both similar in terms of duration, intensity, and formant transitions (Painter 2011), and perceptual studies have demonstrated listener confusion between the two phones (Solé 1992; Painter 2011). When Romero and Martín (2003) manipulated the duration of [z] in American English, they found that adult listeners tend to identify [z] as a flap when the fricative's duration is reduced, e.g., *lizard* [lızɚd] is perceived as *littered* [lıɾɚd].

The confusion makes sense in articulatory terms, as both [z] and [ɾ] are voiced alveolar realizations differing only in manner of articulation. Should articulatory undershoot occur (Lindblom 1963), involving a decrease in the fricative's duration and insufficient buildup of pressure to produce a fricative, a listener may perceive a change in constriction degree, identifying the leftover vocalic transitions as a flap (Romero & Martín 2003). Further support for the similarities between [z] and [ɾ] comes from children's speech: English-speaking children often substitute a rhotic for [z] at different stages of development (Smith 1973: 79, 262).

This section has shown that [z] and [ɾ] are articulatorily and acoustically similar, with perceptual confusion occurring between the two phones in typologically distinct languages. While it is clear that rhotacism of /s/ does occur in several varieties of Spanish, it remains to be seen where the lenition occurs in Elche Spanish and why. Given this lacuna in the literature on rhotacism, we seek to answer the following questions:

1. In which linguistic contexts is rhotacism most likely in Elche Spanish?
2. Which social groups are most likely to produce rhotacism in Elche?
3. Why is the variant more likely in those linguistic contexts or social groups?

3. Methodology

3.1. PARTICIPANTS AND TASKS

In order to examine the rhotacism of /s/ in Elche Spanish, the second author, who is a native of Elche and can speak both Spanish and Catalan, approached potential candidates as a member of the local community and conducted thirty sociolinguistic interviews in Spanish in August 2014. Interviewees were recruited by means of the snowball technique (Goodman 1961) or "friend-of-a-friend" method (Milroy 1980), and we controlled for gender, age, and education level. Of the thirty participants, sixteen were male and fourteen were female, with ages ranging from twenty-five to sixty years old. In order to qualify for the study, the participants needed to be adults over the age of eighteen who had been living in Elche for more than ten years. Although some subjects had not spent their entire lives in Elche, all participants had lived in the city for at least twenty years at the time of the interviews. The speakers recorded come from a range of neighborhoods within the city limits, including Altabix, Carrús, El Pla, the city center, and Pont Nou. In terms of linguistic backgrounds, all thirty interviewees spoke Spanish fluently and eleven could speak Catalan as well; among those who spoke Catalan, three reported it to be their first language. With respect to the participants' education levels, nine held a college degree, nine had a high school diploma, and eleven had not attained a high school diploma. (See the appendix for more information about each participant.)

After providing their IRB-approved written permission to participate in the study, all thirty participants were recorded using an Olympus WS-400S standard digital recorder. Each participant completed two tasks: i) a casual conversation between the interviewer and interviewee that lasted approximately thirty minutes and ii) a reading task involving seventy-nine target sentences intended to elicit rhotacism. The interviews were conducted in quiet environments that were convenient to the interviewee, including the participants' homes, places of employment, or quiet parks in their neighborhoods.

In the casual conversation, topics included daily routines, likes/dislikes, or recent trips; sensitive subjects such as politics and religion were avoided. In the second task, participants were asked to read sentences that had been manipulated to control for the significant predictors of nonstandard /s/ in previous studies (see section 2.2), including preceding and following syllable stress, preceding and following phonological context, word-internal and word-final /s/, morphological status of the /s/, and target and following word class, among others.

3.2. DATA ANALYSIS

For the task of coding the data, interviewees were first organized into two main groups: (i) participants who produced at least one case of rhotacized /s/ and (ii) those who did not produce any rhotics for /s/. For the former group, we coded all coda /s/ realizations throughout the interview and all coda /s/ realizations in the reading task. In the case of interviewees who did not produce any rhotacized /s/, thirty tokens from the casual conversation were coded beginning at the ten-minute mark, including ten word-internal and twenty word-final tokens of /s/. All /s/ tokens from the reading task were included.

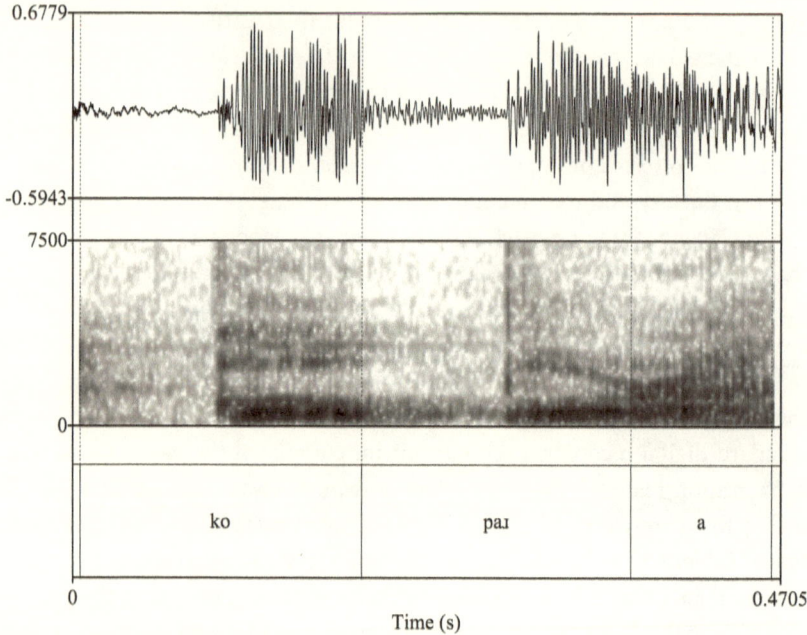

Figure 2.1
Participant V's production of rhotacized /s/ in *copas a* 'drinks to.'

In terms of our variants, we coded for [s], [z], [ɾ], and "other," which included the elision of /s/ and gemination of a following consonant. The phones [s] and [z] were identified by their high-frequency noise in the spectrogram and frication in the waveform, differing only in the spectrogram's voicing bar and the continued glottal pulses for [z]. We found the acoustic analysis of rhotics to be a difficult task, as the perception of a rhotic may be triggered simply by a shortened [z] without any other acoustic differences (Romero & Martín 2003). We attempted to keep the coding as acoustically motivated as possible, and we used a lowered third formant to identify cases of rhotacism along with a lack of noise in the spectrogram and no aperiodic energy in the waveform. Cases that were ambiguous were excluded from analysis, but instances that were perceptually deemed clear rhotics in the absence of other acoustic cues were included in the rhotic category. Elided /s/ and geminates were determined based on the absence of any acoustic correlate of the /s/ in the spectrogram and waveform, sometimes accompanied by a durational increase of the following consonant. These realizations were conflated in the present analysis, as they are not our primary object of

Table 2.1
Independent variables coded in our analysis of the data.

Category	Levels
Gender	Female, Male
Task	Reading, Sociolinguistic Interview
Age	18–29, 30–49, 50+
Education	Did not finish high school, High school diploma, College degree
Language Dominance	Spanish dominant, "Balanced" bilingual, Catalan dominant
Type of /s/	Verbal marker, Plural marker, Lexical /s/
Target Word Class	Adjective, Adverb, Determiner, Discourse marker, Noun, Preposition, Pronoun, Verb
Following Word Class	Adjective, Adverb, Conjunction, Determiner, Discourse marker, Noun, Preposition, Pronoun, Verb
Preceding Vowel	/a/, /e/, /i/, /o/, /u/
Following Segment*	Voiceless consonant, Voiced consonant, Vowel
Preceding Syllable Stress	Unstressed, Stressed
Following Syllable Stress	Unstressed, Stressed
Preceding Word Length (Syllables)	1, 2, 3, 4+
Speech rate	Continuous
Target word frequency†	Continuous
Following word frequency	Continuous
String frequency	Continuous

*Following segment was initially coded for all distinct phones, e.g., /d/, /m/, /e/, /k/, etc., but voiced consonants, voiceless consonants, and vowels were grouped together based on their similar behavior.
†Target word frequency and following word frequency were measured using the *Real Academia Española's Lista total de frecuencias* "Total list of frequencies." String frequency was measured with number of appearances of *word 1* + *word 2* in the spontaneous speech of the corpus.

interest. An example of rhotacized /s/, noticeable by third formant lowering in the spectrogram and a corresponding decrease in amplitude in the waveform, is presented in figure 2.1. Upon determining the variant produced, the /s/ realizations were coded for the social factors of age, gender, education level, and language dominance (Catalan or Spanish), in addition to the linguistic factors found to be predictive of nonstandard /s/ realizations in previous research. The factors that were coded are presented in table 2.1. In order to determine the factors that condition rhotacism in Elche Spanish, a mixed effects binomial logistic regression model was fitted to rhotacism as compared to the other possible variants, including speaker, target word, and following word as random effects. While age, gender, and education were controlled in the present study, we were not able to control the speakers' linguistic background due to the availability of the participants and paucity of Catalan-dominant speakers in Elche. Unfortunately, an interaction in the data between linguistic background and education level problematizes potential conclusions about Catalan's influence on Spanish rhotacism, on the one hand, or the effect of education on rhotacism, on the other. For this reason, linguistic background and education level are not included in the analysis below, as it is difficult to tell with our current sample whether any effect is due to the linguistic background of the speakers or their education level. These factors should be investigated more thoroughly in future studies when the sample allows for linguistic background to be controlled.

4. Results and Discussion

Early in our observations, it became apparent that while cases of word-internal rhotacism can occur, e.g., *musgo* 'moss' as [muɾɣo], they are very uncommon compared with word-final rhotacism, e.g., *los marcianos* 'the aliens' as [loɾ maɾsjanos]. In fact, only nine cases of rhotacism occurred word medially in the present corpus, which is likely due to several factors. First, rhotacized /s/ occurs in two phonological contexts word-finally: both following vowels and voiced consonants may trigger rhotacism in the word-final environment, but only following voiced consonants may trigger rhotacism word internally. That is, because the word-final /s/ in *es algo* 'it is something' is in coda position, that /s/ may be rhotacized to [eɾ algo], but the word-medial /s/ in *esa* 'this', being in onset position, would not become [eɾa].[2] Second, the relatively infrequent /s/ + voiced consonant sequence word internally, e.g., *asma* 'asthma,' *Oslo,* and *rasgo* 'feature,' may contribute to the relative scarcity of rhotacism word internally.

As only nine tokens of word-medial rhotacism occurred in the present corpus, the analysis that follows will only explore the social and linguistic factors conditioning word-final rhotacism, where the predictive power is stronger. The raw frequency breakdown of the variants in this word-final

---

2. While no cases of word-medial, prevocalic /s/ rhotacism were observed in this particular corpus, the second author has observed rhotacism in one specific environment: word-medial morpheme boundaries in which the /s/ may be conceived of as morpheme-final (and consequently syllable-final) allow for rhotacism, e.g., *des#alar* 'to remove wings' may become [deɾalaɾ]. Word-medial, morpheme-final /s/ is also analyzed as a syllable-final case of /s/ in the phonologically triggered /s/ voicing in Cuenca, Ecuador (see Robinson 1979).

Table 2.2
Raw frequency breakdown of the word-final variants given following phonological environment.

	Voiceless consonant	Vowel	Voiced consonant	Total
[s]	83.8% N = 176	72.1% N = 452	24.3% N = 90	N = 718
[z]	3.8% N = 8	16.5% N = 104	48.1% N = 178	N = 290
[ɾ]	0% N = 0	10% N = 62	10.6% N = 39	N = 101
Other (Gem. or elision)	12.4% N = 26	1.4% N = 9	17% N = 63	N = 98
Total	100% N = 210	100% N = 627	100% N = 370	

environment based on following phonological context is illustrated in table 2.2. As shown in table 2.2, not a single rhotic occurs before a voiceless consonant; rather, the rhotic occurs exclusively before a following voiced consonant and before a following vowel. In fact, the rhotic is more common before a vowel than before a voiced consonant, which is somewhat surprising considering that the prevocalic environment had not been mentioned as a factor conditioning rhotacism in previous studies.

Let us now turn our attention to the overall significance of each factor retained in the mixed effects binomial logistic regression model, as illustrated in the random forest in figure 2.2. First, figure 2.2 illustrates the importance of the random effect of speaker, which indicates a very high rate of inter-speaker variability in terms of rhotic production. While some speakers rhotacize /s/ frequently, others never produce rhotics. Beyond the individual speaker, the most important fixed effects are following segment, gender, task, and speech rate.

While following segment and gender both appear as important predictors of rhotacism in the random forest provided in figure 2.2, a mixed effects binomial logistic regression model fitted to the data shows that the two effects are not independent; actually, the two factors interact. This is shown in table 2.3. In terms of social factors, Recasens i Vives (1991) and Segura i Llopis (1996, 1998) claimed the use of rhoticized /s/ in Catalan is most frequent in colloquial speech by young adults. Our results partially support this finding in Elche Spanish, as rhotacism is much more likely in spontaneous speech than it is in a reading task. However, age was not selected

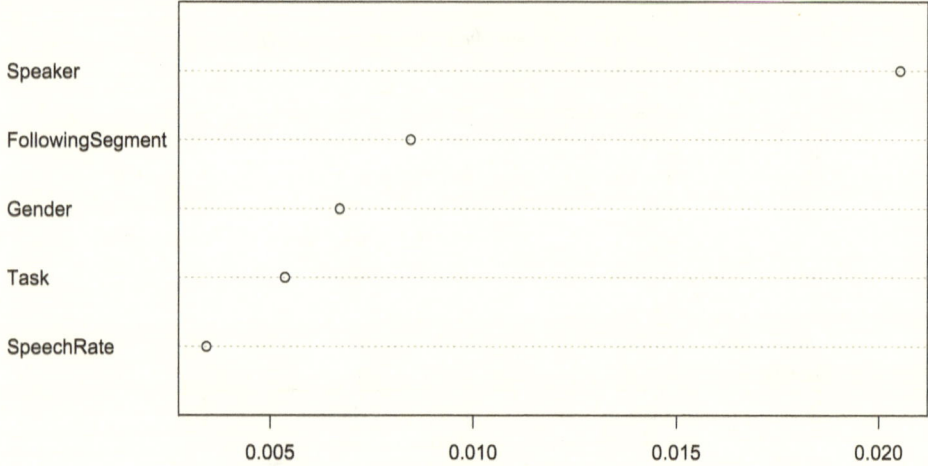

Figure 2.2
Random forest of all significant factors illustrating the most important predictors of rhotacism (top) to the least important (bottom).

as a significant predictor of rhotacism, suggesting that the variant is less age-graded in Elche Spanish. The most notable social distinction in our data occurs for the gender variable. While both men and women rhotacize, men rhotacize differently than women, as shown in figure 2.3. While neither men nor women rhotacize before a voiceless consonant, women clearly produce a higher percentage of rhotics before a voiced consonant, while men produce more rhotics before a vowel. Interestingly, this gender difference prevocalically parallels [z] production prevocalically: although both men and women infrequently produce [z] before a voiceless consonant and both voice /s/ the most before a voiced consonant, men produce higher rates of [z] before a vowel. Earlier studies' conclusion that only voiced /s/ becomes rhotacized paired with this study's finding that both men and women tend to produce the highest rates of [ɾ] where they also produce more [z] suggests that the extension of rhotacism hinges on the extension of /s/ voicing in Elche Spanish. In other words, environments with the highest rates of /s/ voicing will also show higher rates of rhotacism.

However, the conclusion that rhotacism is a direct result of higher rates of /s/ voicing does not entirely capture the patterning of the phenomenon. While men do produce [z] more than women in the prevocalic position, men voice /s/ more before a voiced consonant than before a vowel. If rhotacism were to follow this pattern, men would produce more rhotics than women

Table 2.3
Significant factors contributing to the rhotacism of /s/ in word-final contexts.

	Estimate	Std. Error	z-value	p-value
(Intercept)	−6.537	1.098	−5.955	<.01
Gender : Following Segment Interaction* (reference level is female, voiced consonant)†				
Male : Following vowel	2.2	0.775	2.839	<.01
Task (reference level is reading)				
Spontaneous	1.865	0.539	3.46	<.01
Speech Rate				
Faster speech rate	0.192	0.073	2.609	<.01
	AIC 518.7	BIC 562.8	Log likelihood −250.3	

*While gender alone and following segment alone are kept in the model, their values are not presented here to avoid confusion, given the ambiguity in interpreting linear effects (the original factors) when an interaction exists between them. Additionally, following voiceless consonants are excluded from the model, as no variation was observed given a following voiceless consonant.

†As no variation took place before a voiceless consonant, only followed voiced consonants and vowels are included in the model.

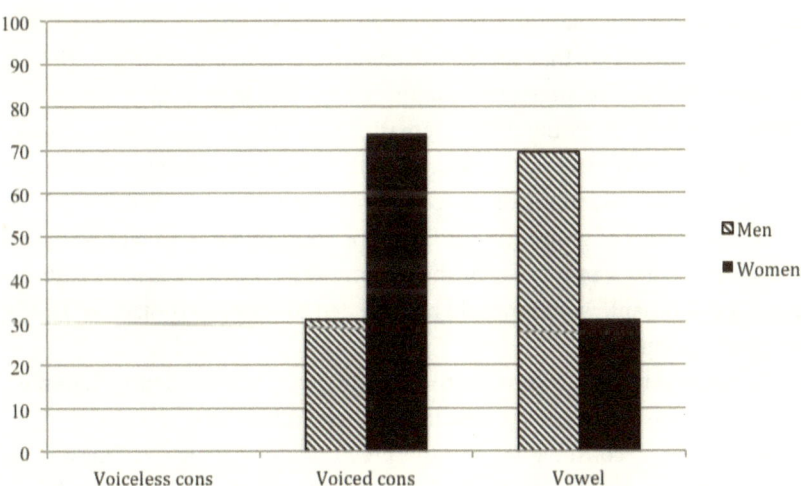

Figure 2.3
Percent of rhotacism by men and women based on following phonological context.

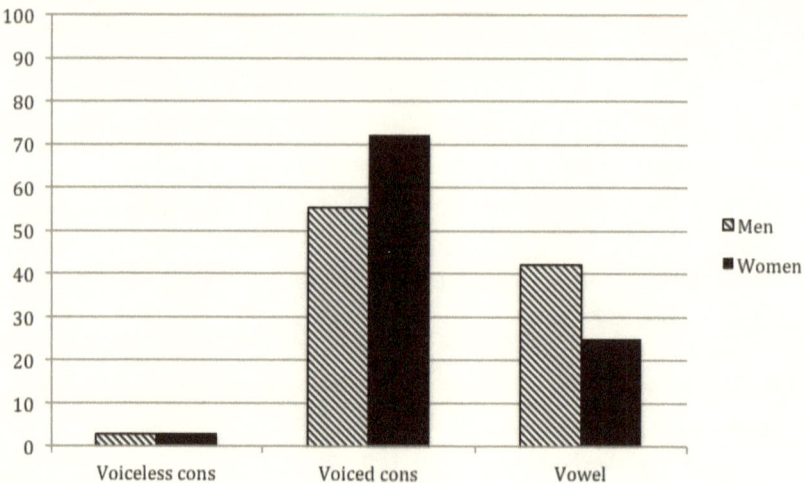

Figure 2.4
Distribution of [z] production by gender given following phonological environment.

prevocalically but would continue to rhotacize most before a consonant, which is not how the variant behaves in figure 2.3. In order to explain this difference, our explanation turns to salience and stigma.

It is well known that given a change from above or stable variation, women tend to use prestige variants more than men (Labov 2001: 274; Holmquist 2011), avoiding more stigmatized realizations. Although attitudes toward rhotacism were not measured in this study, anecdotal evidence and comments from members of the community indicate that rhotacism of /s/ is above the level of awareness for Elche speakers, and it is, in fact, a stigmatized, vernacular variant. Given the community's overtly negative attitudes toward the variant, women would be expected to produce rhotacized /s/ less frequently than men.

While it is true that women produce the rhotic less frequently than men, such a conclusion oversimplifies the genders' differential treatment of the rhotic in the preconsonantal and the prevocalic environment. The women in this study rhotacize /s/ most in cue-impoverished environments (Steriade 1997), where transitional cues are blocked by a following consonant. Men, on the other hand, rhotacize /s/ most in cue-rich environments, where internal cues accompany transitional cues from the preceding and following vowels. In other words, men are increasing their use of the vernacular forms in the most salient environments, perhaps advertising their in-group status

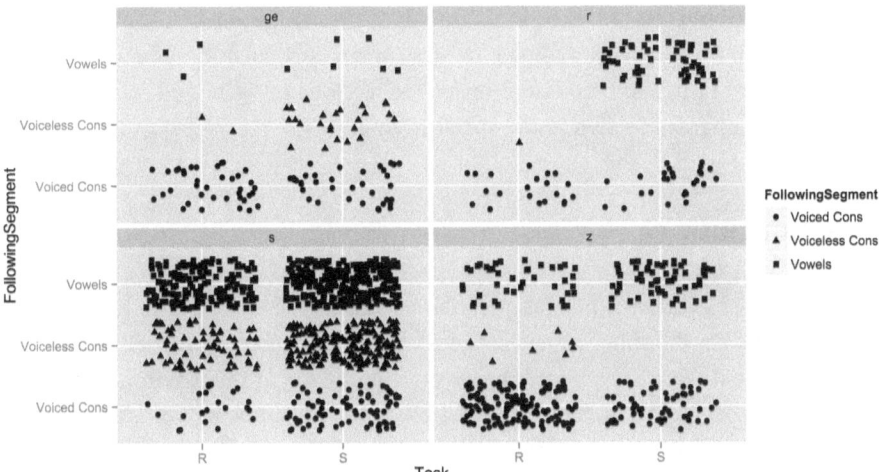

Figure 2.5
Dot plot of [s], [z], [ɾ], and gemination/elision (ge) given following segment in the sociolinguistic interview (S) and the reading task (R).

where the socially meaningful marker of local identity can be most successfully heard by a listener (Chappell 2016a).

As noted above, following segment and gender are the best predictors of /s/ rhotacism, but task and speech rate also contribute to rhotic realizations. Although there is no interaction between task and speech rate, speech rate itself is a significant predictor of rhotacism, suggesting that coarticulation leads to more rhotacism in faster speech. Previous perceptual studies have found that decreasing the duration of [z] leads to [ɾ] perceptions (Romero & Martín 2003), and faster speech rates may not allow for a sufficient pressure build-up to produce frication. In short, it seems that faster speech rates increase coarticulation and lead to more articulatory reduction.

The lack of interaction between speech rate and task in the model indicates that rhotics do not simply occur more in the sociolinguistic interview due to faster rates of speech. As figure 2.5 illustrates, while most variants occur in both the reading and conversation tasks, [ɾ] occurs most in the casual sociolinguistic interview, particularly in the prevocalic environment. In fact, figure 2.5 shows that speakers eschewed rhotics entirely before vowels in the reading task but did produce rhotics pre-consonantally, which again suggests that prevocalic [ɾ] is more salient and more stigmatized than preconsonantal [ɾ]. Rather than explaining rhotacism of /s/ purely in terms of gestural overlap (Browman & Goldstein 1989), social evaluations of the variants should also be taken into account to determine where a stigmatized realization is likely to be avoided. In other words, articulatory reductions do not occur in linguistic isolation; social conceptions mitigate said reductions based on linguistic salience and social stigma.

5. Conclusions

This study has offered the first quantitative analysis of the social and linguistic factors conditioning rhotacism in Elche Spanish, finding that rhotacism occurs most word finally and the greatest predictor in this environment is following segment: rhotacism is most likely with a following voiced consonant and a following vowel, and it is least likely before a voiceless consonant. Gender interacts with following segment in an interesting way: while both men and women produce rhotics before a voiced consonant, men produce rhotics significantly more before a vowel, which we propose is due to a combination of [z] extension, salience, and stigma. Having extended /s/ voicing to prevocalic environments more than women, men have more opportunities to reduce [z] to a rhotic. In addition to different gender-based opportunities for rhotacism of [z], we contend that social motivations may play a role as well. That is, women tend to avoid the stigmatized reduction in a cue-rich, prevocalic environment where it is most clearly perceived, while men may use the opportunity to saliently advertise their local identity, particularly in informal, faster speech, which can lead to greater gestural overlap.

This study expands on the contemporary body of knowledge in variationism, targeting a process that has been historically overlooked in Hispanic linguistics: /s/ rhotacism. However, as the first exploration of this phenomenon in Elche Spanish, a great deal more research is needed to fully capture the complexity of the phenomenon. Future studies would benefit from a larger sample size to allow for more participants and tokens of /s/ rhotacism. In terms of social factors, a controlled sample and thorough analysis of language dominance should be conducted: an even distribution of Catalan-dominant speakers, Spanish-dominant speakers, and more balanced bilinguals would allow for a better understanding of the role of Catalan in the process of rhotacism. The participant's family origin should be controlled as well, as individuals exposed to Andalusian Spanish at home may differ in the /s/ rhotacism constraints to which they attend.

In spite of these shortcomings, the present work builds on linguistic knowledge in several fields. First, our findings contribute to dialectology by shedding light on a local phenomenon that had not been addressed in previous literature. Beyond a simple dialectal survey of the phenomenon, we have also found a connection between a social group's extension of one phenomenon (/s/ voicing) and a subsequent increase in rhotacism, which supports historical accounts of voiced /s/ becoming /r/ and phonetic/perceptual studies on the similarities between [z] and rhotics. Finally, the study contributes to sociolinguistics, finding that rhotacism in Elche Spanish is not simply the product of linguistic or social constraints. Rather, this phonological process reveals a delicate interplay between gender and following segment, which highlights different social groups' treatment of the nexus between stigma (or prestige) and salience.

Appendix: Participants

	Gender	Age	City Area	Languages	Education
A	M	28	Altabix	Spanish	College
B	M	29	Pont Nou	Spanish	College
C	F	29	El Pla	Spanish	College
D	M	27	El Pla	Spanish/Catalan	High School
E	F	27	Altabix	Spanish	High School
F	F	28	Carrús	Spanish/Catalan	High School
G	M	25	Carrús	Spanish	No High School
H	M	24	Centro	Spanish	No High School
I	F	24	El Pla	Spanish	No High School
J	M	36	El Pla	Spanish	College
K	F	32	Altabix	Spanish	College
L	F	31	Altabix	Spanish	College
M	M	35	Pont Nou	Spanish/Catalan	High School
N	M	33	Pont Nou	Spanish	High School
O	M	43	El Pla	Spanish	High School
P	F	37	Carrús	Spanish	High School
Q	M	33	Carrús	Spanish	No High School
R	M	34	Carrús	Spanish/Catalan	No High School
S	F	37	Pont Nou	Spanish/Catalan	No High School
T	F	41	Carrús	Spanish	No High School
U	M	60	Pont Nou	Spanish/Catalan	College

	Gender	Age	City Area	Languages	Education
V	M	51	El Pla	Catalan/Spanish	College
W	F	54	El Pla	Catalan/Spanish	College
X	M	52	Centro	Spanish/Catalan	High School
Y	F	50	Centro	Spanish	High School
Z	M	59	Centro	Spanish	No High School
AA	M	60	Carrús	Spanish/Catalan	No High School
AB	F	55	Pont Nou	Spanish/Catalan	No High School
AC	F	57	Pont Nou	Spanish	No High School

3

Pragmatic and Semantic Factors for the Resumption Strategy in Spanish Relative Clauses

Irene Checa-García

As stated in the introduction to this volume, variation is a pervasive phenomenon in language that needs to be explained if we are to fully understand how languages work. The approaches to this phenomenon have been very diverse but also increasingly more systematic. In this chapter, I attempt to present a mix of a quantitative and a qualitative approach that I have applied to the study of resumptive pronouns in relative clauses. The variation at hand has been studied before using corpus linguistics and quantitative analysis. This approach has been very fruitful, but restricted to basic semantic and syntactic factors. Yet, several pragmatic factors have been proposed to account for this variation as well. After establishing some basic hypotheses that arise from systematizing the previous literature, I gathered corpus oral data and tested the hypotheses by looking at the proportion of each variant but also their role in context. This mix of quantitative and qualitative analysis is necessary given the pragmatic nature of the factors affecting the phenomenon, so only a careful look into the context case by case allows for an accurate classification of the variants according to such pragmatic factors. Furthermore, as will be seen in the conclusions discussing the results of the study, the same phenomenon can stand in both free variation in some cases, while carrying semantic and/or pragmatic meaning in others. Differentiating all these cases is of crucial importance to accurately explain variation phenomena, and this chapter aims to show such importance and how to proceed methodologically in such cases.

1. Resumptive Pronouns in Spanish Relative Clauses

The presence of a resumptive element (RE) in Spanish relative clauses has been attested in a number of studies and for a number of varieties in Spanish (Bentivoglio 2003, 2006; Borzi & Morano 2009; Cerrón-Palomino 2006; Fernández Soriano 1995; González García 2001; Lope Blanch 2001; Samper Padilla, Hernández Cabrera & Pérez Gil 2005; Silva-Corvalán 1996; Suárez Fernández 2010; Suñer 2001, among others), as well as in other languages (Prince 1990; Polinsky et al. 2013; Heestand, Xiang & Polinsky 2011; Ariel 1999, among many others). Resumption consists of the use of an element to refer back to a previous one already used within the same syntactic unit, typically a clause. It can occur in simple clauses, questions, or relative clauses (henceforth RCs), for instance. Its presence has been detected in numerous languages, though its grammaticality status varies from language to language, being ungrammatical in Spanish except when coreferring to the indirect object. Sentence (1) offers an example of a RE in an ungrammatical function (genitive), the RE is in bold case:

(1) (ACON006D, H2)[1]

Hay	un	tí-o	de-l	trabajo		
There is	*a*.M	*guy*-M.SG	*from-the*.M.SG	*work*		

que...	eh...	**su**	cuñad-o		es
that...	*uh...*	POSS.ADJ.SG.3rd	*brother-in-law*-M.SG		*is*

el	que	me	lo	ha	vendido
the:M.SG	*that*	*me*:DAT	*it*:M:ACC	*has*	*sold*

*There is <u>a guy from work</u> that, uh, **his** brother-in-law is the one that sold it to me.*

Sentence (2) offers an example of an RC with an RE in the indirect object function and hence accepted as grammatical in Spanish:

---

[1]. Original conversation file name and speaker number in that conversation in CORLEC (see section 3 on methods). Glosses follow the Leipzig glossing rules (Comrie, Haspelmath & Bicker 2008).

(2) (CCON028A, H1)

Yo	conozc-o	gente	que	**le**
1st:SG:NOM	know-1st:SG:NOM	people	that	PRN **DAT.SG**

h-a	toc-ado	l-a	quiniela
have.AUX-PRS.3rd.SG	touch-PTCP.PST	the-F.SG	soccer betting system

I know <u>people</u> that have won the soccer lottery (literally: *that* **to them** *the lottery touched*).

Likewise, different factors have been claimed to favor its presence. In the case of Spanish, these factors can be grouped as follows: language contact, processing/memory demands, mere performance error, and marking of a pragmatic meaning.

Checa-García (2012) reviewed the claims for these factors. As Checa-García pointed out, resumptive elements appear in different environments (and not just island environments), but even if they were to be considered "performance errors," they are a window into processing difficulty and worth the effort of finding common characteristics of such more difficult environments as well as the sources of difficulty. The possibility of medieval Arabic resumptive constructions having an influence on Spanish resumptive ones, proposed by Gehman (1982) and Galmés de Fuentes (1996), is questioned by Lope Blanch (1986) and Suárez Fernández (2010). On one hand, Lope Blanch argued that the social bilingualism present in Spain at the time was too weak for Arabic to have such an influence (Lope Blanch 1986). Regardless of the strength of medieval social bilingualism, the examples offered by Gehman of Spanish resumptive elements are from translations of Arabic texts, so it could rather be the effect of a too literal translation. Furthermore, other Romance languages not in contact with Arabic present this phenomenon, also detected in Vulgar Latin.

After rejecting the two first accounts, we are left with processing and memory demands (semantic or syntactic) and pragmatic information being encoded by the use of this construction. In this chapter I will explore this later possibility. In the next section, I will present different accounts of resumptive elements that propose a pragmatic meaning behind its presence. I will test these hypotheses with oral data in section 4, after describing the data used and tagging and segmentation processes in section 3 on methods. Finally, I will offer a preliminary account of the role of pragmatics for resumptive elements in Spanish RCs in the last section.

2. Pragmatic Factors Affecting the Presence of a Resumptive Pronoun in Spanish Relative Clauses

Pragmatic and information factors have been also pointed to as factors for the presence of an RE, used to convey a different meaning, not at the truth condition level, but at a pragmatic level. What this meaning is and how it influences choosing to use an RE vary depending on the author. González García (2001), for instance, proposed that the use of REs in Spanish relative clauses is the result of what he calls a "thematization" and it seems to correspond to a kind of topicalization of the antecedent, the same kind that operates in left dislocation with pronoun retrieval, as shown in (3), with no topicalization and no resumptive pronoun (3a), vs. (3b) with topicalization and a resumptive pronoun.

(3a)
Yo   quiero   el   pastel
I   want-1st:SG:PRS:IND   the-M:SG   cake
I want the cake.

(3b)
El   pastel   **lo**   quiero   yo
the:M:SG *cake*   *it:ACC:MASC*   *want-1st:SG:PRS:IND*   *I*
I am the one who wants the cake (topicalization).

Although a very suggestive claim, González García's study does not present empirical evidence for it. This claim needs to be operationalized and then tested. In order to be operationalized, a more precise definition of what is meant by *thematization* needs to be offered. However, he is not alone in noticing a parallelism between the use of resumptive pronouns in simple clauses and relative clauses and some "emphatic" value to the use of a resumptive pronoun. With respect to the former, Brucart (1999) pointed out the use of resumptive pronouns for duplicated indirect objects in simple clauses, and the use of "intensive pronominal forms" such as those in his example (17), reproduced here as (4a), relative clause, and (4b), simple clause.

(4a) (Brucart 1999: 405 slightly modified)
Conozc-o   a   profesores   que
know-1st:SG:NOM   *ACC*   *teacher-s*   *that*

provoc-an   ell-os   mism-os
provoke-3rd:PL:NOM:PRS:IND   *they-PL:M:NOM*   *self-PL:M*

l-a   animadversión   de   su-s   estudiant-es
the-SG:F   dislike   of   Poss-3rd:PL   student-PL
I know teachers that provoke themselves their students' dislike.

(4b) (Brucart 1999: 405)
Algun-os   profesores   provoc-an
Some-M:PL   teacher-PL   provoke-3rd:PL:NOM:PRS:IND

ellos   mismos
they-PL:M:NOM   self-PL:M

l-a   animadversion   de   sus   estudiantes
the-SG:F   dislike   of   Poss-3rd:PL   student-PL
Some teachers provoke themselves their students' dislike.

In (4a), the RE is duplicating the Head NP or antecedent (henceforth HNP) for the same reasons it does in the equivalent simple clause, to add that intensive NP. However, that is not exactly the case for (4b). While in simple clauses the duplication of indirect objects depends on their semantic role (Fernández Soriano 1999), we will see in section 4 whether this is the case in RCs or, like Fernández Soriano proposed, whether the motivations are different and more in the line with processing difficulties, like the level of embedding.

Trujillo (1990) argued that REs, and in particular resumptive pronouns, have an emphatic value, a similar value to an intensifier for the content of the RC as it applies to the HNP, but only in restrictive RCs. It is worth noting that Trujillo's examples are of restrictive RCs with the RE acting as the subject and postposed to the verb of the RC, a position that seems to contribute significantly to the emphatic value. Along those lines, Cerrón-Palomino (2006)[2] noted that there is a significant number of REs in the subject function even though this is the highest function in the Keenan and Comrie (1977) accessibility hierarchy and, therefore, structurally at the easiest end for relativization, and hence processing, from the point of view of production. While resumption could be a strategy to ease the processing of syntactic functions whose relativization is harder, such as the genitive, its

---

2. One interesting thing to note about Cerrón-Palomino's data is that he prompted RCs through an interview with the speaker. However, he noticed how his speakers produced very few or no REs during the recorded interview and started to produce them only after chatting more informally with the researcher. In those cases, Cerrón-Palomino wrote down most of the instances of RCs with a RE that were produced, but was not able to write down all the RCs. This means that the proportion of RCs with REs is inflated in his data, as he himself comments.

use for direct objects and even more so for subjects cannot be accounted for by recurring to such production complexity. Thus, after looking at his examples he proposes that all of them are subjects standing in contrast. In his examples (Cerrón-Palomino 2006: 246) there are very clear cases, such as his (17) reproduced here as (5), and other less clearly expressing a contrast,[3] like his (18) reproduced here as (6). HNP is <u>underlined</u> while RE is in **bold** case.

(5)
Ten-go   otr-as   receta-s   ahí   que,
have-1st:Sg:Prs:Ind:Nom   other-F:Sg   recipe-Pl   there   that,

es-as   sí   son   recetas   argentin-a-s
those-F   yes   are:3rd   recipe-Pl   Argentine-F-Pl
I have other recipes over there that . . . those are in fact Argentine.

(6)
Ten-ía   un-a   amig-a   que   **ella** . . .
have-1st/3rd Sg:Pst:Impf:Ind   a-F:Sg   friend-F:Sg that   she . . .

en   l-a   universidad   leía   carta-s
In   the-F:Sg   university   read-1st/3rdSg:Pst:Impf:Ind   letter-Pl
I had a friend that . . . at the university used to read letters.

Therefore, a contrastive meaning could be part of the explanation, but perhaps not for all cases, as we will see in section 4.

Another RC construction with REs that has an emphatic value in Spanish is non-restrictive RCs with a consecutive value (Brucart 1999), of the type "un X que ____" (*an X such that . . .*), where the relativizer is typically a direct object. In these consecutive constructions the RE is needed for the non-restrictive RC to convey a consecutive meaning, however, it is controverted whether these are really RCs, or a consecutive construction that uses the form of an RC. In any case, they seem to have parts of their structure fixed in order to serve a particular meaning, and hence a different construction, although a particular construction can bear less specific ones inside (Goldberg 2006).

---

3. I will discuss how these two examples are different when I explain in more depth the notion of contrast that I will be using for the present study.

Borzi and Morano (2009)[4] proposed that by using an RE the speaker is trying to establish a contrast or to introduce new information (in fact, for them a contrast is defined by being unknown information). Unlike González García, Borzi and Morano did translate their proposal of this special information status into terms susceptible of being quantified (their frequencies determined). In particular, they claimed that the following variables are signs of more new information status: negation in the RC, more or less distance from the antecedent (that is, the distance between an HNP and a relativizer),[5] the presence of two elements contrasting in the main clause and relative clause (not necessarily the one designated by the HNP and the relativizer), determination of the HNP, syntactic function of the HNP, and the presence of "possessive tener" vs. other verbs or meanings of "tener." When one of these characteristics is present, the RC conveys new information, so it is necessary to place an element representing the old information in front of the RC, the RE, to maintain the usual information distribution: old information first and new information after. In this way, as González García (2001) proposed, RCs with REs mirror the structure of pragmatically marked sentences of the type exemplified in (3b) above.

Their account, however, presents several problems. First, although all contrastive information is new, not all new information is constrastive (Lambrecht 1994), so it is best to separate the two concepts as potentially different factors. Another problem is that, according to them, the RE introduces a topic about which the speaker is not sure what to say next, such as (6) above. Although this seems very clear in some of their examples, it is not a systematic difference, that is, in some cases where there is an RE, it is clear that the speaker does not know how to continue, like in (5) above, and in some cases where the speaker hesitates after producing the HNP or the relativizer, an RE was used or there was an implied contrast or new information. See, for example, (7), where there is a hesitation right after using the relativizer, the speaker is still processing what new information to say about the prepositional complement of the RC, acting as a circumstantial complement for place, "en el fascículo seminal este," but no other place complement, such as "allí" (*there*) or "en él" (*in it*), is produced after the relativizer (or anywhere else in the sentence).

---

4. Very intriguingly, the proportions of RCs with an RE are much higher than they are in any other study on Spanish: seventy-two RCs with REs and 205 without, that is 35.12%, vs. 7.8% in Silva-Corvalán's data, for instance, even though they are only considering direct object resumptive pronouns instead of all functions in Silva-Corvalán. Perhaps this is due to the speakers participating in the portion used of that corpus, if this is so, it would be worth exploring.

5. The distance is measured in words, as well as pauses and hesitation expressions, and the results are grouped into two categories—more distance and less distance—although the number of intervening material divided into these two categories is not mentioned.

(7) (ACON006B, H1)

Pues	en	"El Mundo"	de	hoy,	en	el	fascículo
Well	in	"The World"	of	today,	in	the	supplement.M.SG

semanal	este,
weekly	this.M,

que...	vien-e...		eh...	ah...	un-a
that...	come-3rd. SG.PRS.IND		eh...	uh...	a-F.SG

página	enter-a	con	l-a	foto
page.F.SG	full-F.SG	with	the-F.SG	picture.F.SG

en	grande	de-l	tí-o	y	to...	un-a
in	big	of-the.M.SG	guy-M.SG	and	all...	a-F.SG

entrevista	y	tal
interview.F.SG	and	such

Well, in todays's El Mundo, in the weekly supplement that comes (in it) ... eh ... uh ... a full page with the picture, big format, of the guy and a ... an interview and all that.

More importantly, the way they operationalized the notion of new information is problematic. On one hand, it is unclear whether it is the combination of their presence that makes some referent be new information, or rather any of the items is sufficient to identify new information referents. On the other hand, most of their newness factors are better understood as increasing processing difficulty, rather than representing a particular information status, and they have been treated that way in much of the previous literature on the topic in Spanish and other languages. For example, negated clauses are considered harder to process, the distance between coreferential NPs also makes it harder to track such coreferences (Brucart 1999), and some syntactic functions are more difficult to code in a relativizer than others, as shown in the relativizing hierarchy by Keenan and Comrie (1977). The determination of the HNP is interpreted in processing terms as well by the file card theory of Prince (1990). In addition, determined NPs can be both new or old information, but are perhaps more typically presupposed by the speaker to be old information in the hearer's mind. In sum, if we are going to consider newness of information status a factor, we need to define it unequivocally and in terms independent from processing complexities.

Additionally, their account could only explain REs that are placed at the beginning of the sentence, which is typically the location of the direct object and the indirect object as well as the case of the subject. In regard to objects, this is because clitic, non-tonic, pronouns are always placed in the pre-verbal position, immediately preceding the verb. This, however, is a syntactic fact that is not caused by information status. In the case of possible differing subject positions, the canonical position—where old information is presented first—is in front of the verb. More crucially, it is possible for REs to be in other positions, not always in front of the verb and at the beginning of the sentence, as we will see later.

To conclude this review of previous literature on pragmatic meanings of the resumptive relative clause construction, it seems that an emphatic/intensifying value can be associated with the presence of an RE, but only in quite fixed constructions that then receive a more specific meaning, consecutive. For other cases, differing information structure factors have been invoked: a parallelism between simple clause structure and RCs and the positioning of an element representing old information to start the clause, both for the direct and indirect objects, as well as a contrastive meaning, for subjects. In order to determine if such hypotheses are true, it is imperative to contrast them with data, which requires, as said above, good and operational definitions of such information structure concepts. I will attempt to do so with the two informational terms invoked to explain REs, newness and contrast, in the second part of the methods section. I will subsume the "thematization" explanation by González García under information status new/old, since it seems to be the reverse of new information (Gutiérrez Ordóñez 1997).

3. Methods of the Present Study

3.1. DATA

For the purposes of this study, I used the Universidad Autónoma de Madrid Corpus of Peninsular Spanish, specifically the CORLEC,[6] which comprises conversations in informal Spanish. The corpus was tagged for RCs, their antecedents, resumptive elements, and the syntactic function of all elements, as well as other characteristics of the NPs involved and the relations between

---

6. The CORLEC is the Corpus de Referencia de la Lengua Española Contemporánea, which consists of oral production in conversation, mostly from conversations between family and friends (25%) and in media (over 40%).

them. Not all RCs in the corpus were included in the study. Nominalized RCs, as in (6), were eliminated, since no antecedent was necessary in those cases. Those RCs with a very generic NP functioning as the antecedent or an HNP forming a fixed expression were eliminated as well, such as "las veces que," "el año que viene," "en el momento que," etc. Since there is no possibility of a resumptive element or variation in the characteristics of the HNP (definite vs. indefinite, human or not human, etc.), it was impossible for their fixed elements to maintain a special pragmatic meaning and have it marked with a resumptive element. We did include RCs whose relativizer functions as an indirect object (unlike Silva-Corvalán 1996). Although it is true that its use is grammatical, the RC construction containing an RE does alternate with an RC without an RE, or a gap construction, as I will show in section 4.

The total number of RCs selected was 1,237. Only ninety contained an RE. Thus, approximately 0.73 % of the clauses contained an RE, a proportion similar to that found in other studies (Silva-Corvalán 1996).

3.2. VARIABLES DEFINITIONS

3.2.1. Information Newness

Information being new or old is a classic concept in information structure theory and pragmatics, so much so that it has been defined in different ways, and it is not my goal here to discuss these definitions exhaustively or in great depth. Most authors, Prince (1981) for instance, understand new and old information to be a property of particular referents, and their familiarity is a result of them having been mentioned or evoked before, being inferable, or none of these. As can be easily seen, the definition of new or old information requires taking into account the extralinguistic context of the conversation (as much as we can know about it) as well as the linguistic context, particularly the previous one. The definition cannot be reduced to the set of factors that Borzi and Morano coded. Lambrecht (1994), in contrast, rejects the idea that the newness of information is a property of referents, but rather belongs to whole propositions. Given this, the presupposed or asserted nature of referents must be further examined. Gutiérrez Ordóñez (1997) equates new information with the notion of rheme/contribution and old information to that of theme/support. Interestingly, both Lambrecht and Gutiérrez Ordóñez offer versions of the same test to detect new information within a sentence, whether we think it is propositional in nature or relies on referents, which attempts to negate what we think is old information and what is new.[7] Only new information can be negated, it is not possible to negate old information because it has been already presupposed. We reproduce here as (8) Lambrecht's example 2.11 (Lambrecht 1994: 51) to show what is expressed as old, presupposed information, and what is new information.

(8) *I finally met the woman who moved in downstairs.*

Here the new information is the pragmatic assertion: I finally met a person. But the speaker assumes the hearer knows that this person is a woman and that she moved in downstairs through a pragmatic presupposition. This presupposition is the old information, and it cannot be negated because it is being presupposed. Therefore, if someone hearing (8) were to say, *That is not true*, it would refer to the fact that the speaker met this person, not to the fact that there is a woman who moved downstairs, which negates that part, and s/he would have to be more explicit. This is what Lambrecht calls a "lie-test." I will adopt Gutiérrez Ordóñez's test, which is a version of Lambrecht's, because it allows for questioning all kinds of segments in a sentence, and consists of the application of the structure "Not A, but B" to the segment being evaluated as new information. Only new information can have this structure applied to it, as old information is already presupposed.

3.2.2. Contrastiveness

As in the case of new and old information, the term "contrast," or "constrastiveness," has been defined in a number of ways. The common core to this notion in such definitions coincides more or less with Halliday (1967: 206), that it is "contrary to some predicted or stated alternative." Variations on the notion stem from the question, how many alternatives are there and how are those "predicted" (if they are not simply stated)? Bolinger (1961) preferred to see the phenomenon as gradient, where those cases whose alternatives are more restricted and more clearly selected as being the clearest instances of contrast. Along those lines, Lambrecht (1994) proposed that the notion of contrast is not an informative, grammaticalized one, but a pragmatic effect

---

7. Gutiérrez Ordóñez does not seem to claim either. He points to either sentences or phrases as conveying new information, depending on what is the answer to a frequently unspoken, underlying question (following Ducrot 1972), which is for Lambrecht what is being asserted rather than presupposed.

derived from conversational implicatures. For the purposes of our study we will use a more restricted notion, where the set of alternatives is available from the preceding textual context. If we say something like (9):

(9) *I don't watch soccer.*

"soccer" can contrast potentially with any other sport or even any other "watchable" activity. The meaning is contrastive only if the other choices are presented or their range limited in the previous discourse, as Silva-Corvalán puts it (1984: 8):

"La noción de alternativas en oposición, y no simplemente una lista de alternativas, en cuanto a que solo una de ellas es la correcta con respecto a la situación contrastiva, es crucial en la definición de contraste."

'The notion of opposing alternatives, and not just a list of alternatives, in the sense that only one of them is the correct one with respect to the contrastive situation, is crucial when defining contrast.'

To clarify this, let's look at examples (5) and (6) again:

(5)
Ten-go   otr-as   receta-s   ahí   que,
have-1st:SG:PRS:IND:NOM   *other-F:SG*   *recipe-PL* *there*   *that,*

es-as   sí   son   recetas   argentin-a-s
those-F   *yes*   *are:3rd*   *recipe-PL*   *Argentine-F-PL*
I have other recipes over there that . . . those are in fact Argentine.

(6)
Ten-ía   un-a   amig-a   que   **ella** . . .
have-1st/3rd SG:PST:IMPF:IND *a-F:SG*   *friend-F:SG*   *that*   *she* . . .

en   l-a   universidad   leía   carta-s
in *the-F:SG*   *university*   *read-1st/3rdSG:PST:IMPF:IND*   *letter-PL*
I had a friend that she . . . at the university used to read letters.

In (5) the presence of "sí" makes the fact that the recipes are Argentine contrast with others that are not. In addition, the use of "other" implies that there is another set of recipes of a different nature, such difference and contrast is made explicit with the RC. Cerrón-Palomino (2006) argued that in (6) there is a contrast between that friend and other people that like parapsychology, presumably because the conversation was about people liking parapsychology. However, here the set of "anyone in the world liking parapsychology" is certainly very open, and it would be similar to claim a contrast between this one friend and all of my other friends, which is the very nature of any restrictive RC. Therefore, I will not consider examples of the type presented in (6) as conveying a contrastive meaning, unless something in the prior discourse is directly contrasting it, such as in (10):

(10) -A mis amigos no les gusta la parapsicología.
'*My friends do not like parapsychology.*'
-Pues yo tengo una amiga que ella . . . leía cartas.
'*Well, I have a friend who she . . . reads cards.*'

Here, the second speaker is contrasting these particular friends of the previous speaker to one of her/his friends.

3.2.3. Indirect Objects and Semantic Roles in Simple Clauses

Fernández Soriano (1999) pointed out how the semantic roles of indirect objects is what makes the reduplication of the pronoun mandatory. Less canonical indirect objects' semantic roles, such as experiencer or unalienable possessor, as in verbs like "gustar" (to like) or "doler" (to hurt), make the use of a clitic pronoun mandatory, whether there is a noun phrase expressing the indirect object or not. As for why it would be duplicated when it is not mandatory is an ongoing question. However, she made a point of distinguishing this duplication in simple clauses from that in relative clauses. In this instance, she discussed the distance between the HNP and relativizer, and in particular the level of subordination, so clitics appear more if they are the complement of a subordinate clause embedded within an RC. So do relativized indirect objects behave like their reduplication counterparts in simple clauses? That is, are they always present if their semantic roles are non-canonical, namely non-recipients, and are they sometimes present and sometimes not when their semantic roles are less canonical, such as possessors or experiencers?

In sum, this study will take into account newness of the HNP within the RC coupled with RE position, the parallelism with reduplicating pronouns in simple clauses for indirect objects, and the presence of an opposing specific contrast between the RE and some other element or elements in the case of subjects.

3.3. HYPOTHESES

I will propose the following hypotheses:

- H1: There is a pragmatic meaning consisting of the expression of old information through an RE at the front of the RC whenever an RE appears in such clauses in Spanish.
- H2: There is a pragmatic meaning consisting of the expression of a contrast through an RE in an RC whenever such RE appears in the subject function.
- H3: The presence of an RE in an RC when acting as an indirect object is due to the same semantic reasons that explain the presence of indirect object reduplication in simple clauses.

I will contrast these hypotheses with my data, analyzing the information status of REs when present, in ninety clauses, for newness and contrastiveness, particularly in the case of subjects; I will also look at the semantic roles of indirect objects and other characteristics of the RCs that relativize this function, with and without RE.

4. Results of the Present Study

4.1. OLD INFORMATION AND RESUMPTIVE ELEMENTS

According to the first hypothesis, H1, there is a pragmatic meaning consisting of the expression of old information through an RE at the front of the RC whenever an RE appears in such clauses in Spanish. The RC makes use of an RE to keep the usual information order: old information first, to support the introduction of new information. If this is so, the RE should appear in first position. Those cases where there was a clarification inserted between the relativizer, such as (11),[8] were considered first position, as were the cases where there was a negation between the relativizer and the verb, since

---

8. The inserted portion is in italics in the original Spanish.

negation always has to precede the verb and any clitics that accompany it in Spanish, such as (12), where there is no choice but place "no," a non-argumental complement, as the first element. Finally, indirect object pronouns always precede direct object pronouns, so in these cases there is no possibility of placing a direct object resumptive pronoun in the first position.

(11) (CCON018b, H1)
Se	h-a	carg-ado	a	un	chic-o	que
3rd PR.REFL	h-as	fail-ed	to	a.M.SG	child-M.SG	that

no	sé		por qué	se	
Neg	know.1st Sg.Prs.Ind		why	3rd PR.REFL	

le	h-a	carg-ado
3rd Sg.Pr.Dat/Acc[9]	h-as	fail-ed

S/he failed a boy that I don't know why he failed him.

(12) (CCON037b, H2)
Lo	que	pas-a		que	se	
It.Acc	that	happen-3rd SG.PRS.IND		that	3rd SG.RFL	

hab-ían		com-ido	un	plato ...	
have-3rd PL.PST.IMP.IND		eat-en	a.M.SG	dish.M ...	

que	no	lo	encontr-ábamos
that	NEG	3rd.M.SG.ACC	find-1st PL.PST.IMP.IND

What happens (is) that they had eaten a dish that we could not find it.

Hence, also in those cases direct object resumptive pronouns were considered to be in first position, although as mentioned above, to be placed before the verb is not optional but mandatory for direct object clitics. Table 3.1 shows the distribution of an RE within the RC. Despite all these inclusions of what constitutes first position, REs do not always occur in such a position. There is a majority of objects, direct and indirect, occurring in first position, which could be due to the mandatory pre-verbal position. Interestingly, the lowest frequency of an RE in first position is direct objects, even below non-objects, while the highest is for indirect objects.

---

9. The speaker is a "leísta," he speaks a variety of Spanish where pronominal agreement for direct and indirect objects is not based on their syntactic function, but on gender, with "le" being used for masculine objects and "la" for feminine ones, irrespective of their syntactic function.

Table 3.1
Distribution of REs within their RC with relative frequencies for first versus other positions.

	First position		Second position	
RE function	Absolute Frequency	Relative Frequency	Absolute Frequency	Relative Frequency
D. O.	27	58.70	19	41.30
I. O.	9	100.00	0	0.00
D. O + I. O	36	65.45	19	34.55
Not an object	22	62.86	13	37.14
Total	58	64.44	32	35.56

Among those REs in first position, the vast majority of them, fifty-one, are old information, as they do not pass the negation test. There are seven cases where the RE could maybe be negated, and those are cases where the RC that allocates the RE is more distantly located from its HNP. Distance between the HNP and both the relativizer and the potential position of its function in the RC have been pointed out as factors for the presence of an RE: the larger the distance, typically measured in the number of words, the more likely an RE will appear (Cerrón-Palomino 2006; Checa-García 2012).

In conclusion, it does not seem that the presence of an RE implies that there is a thematization of its referent and that the RE represents old information about which new information is said.

4.2. CONTRASTIVENESS AND RESUMPTIVE ELEMENTS

To explain the use of an RE when its function is an easier one to process, Cerrón-Palomino (2006) has proposed that there is a pragmatic meaning consisting of the expression of a contrast through an RE. Data from the UAM corpus of spontaneous conversation contained only ten cases of subjects being relativized and presenting an RE. Of these, and according to the more restrictive sense of "contrast" presented above, and without being able to take into account stress as a marker because of the lack of sound files for the corpus, only three of those cases were contrastive contexts. Given this proportion, we have to conclude that RE are subjects not necessarily due to a contrasting use. Other possible causes such as distance between relativizer and HNP or level of embedding need to be taken into account to explain this case. That said, in at least two of the three constrastive cases the use of an RE does seem to be due to the expression of a contrast.

4.3. INDIRECT OBJECTS AS RESUMPTIVE ELEMENTS

In my data I have found that there were a total of seventeen cases where the relativized function is an indirect object, and only two of those cases were without an RE. In both of those cases the semantic role of the RC indirect object is recipient. In this sense, it seems that the resumptive pronoun is only absent when in a semantic role that allows it in simple clauses, and the behavior here is similar. However, it is also worth noting that in one of the two cases without a resumptive indirect object pronoun the preposition "a" is missing from the relativizer. In the other case, there is another RC attached to the same HNP preceding the RC containing the indirect object. The absence of problems in the marking of the relativizer's function has been found to be a factor for not using an RE (Checa-García 2012). In the other case, since the function of the referent of the HNP in the first RC was a subject, this could have carried over to the next clause, although this hypothesis would need further exploration, as syntactic priming is a controverted notion. Finally, with only two instances and diverse possible factors influencing the choice of a gap strategy vs. a resumption one, I can only tentatively conclude that in this case RCs seem to follow similar rules as simple clauses regarding the use of resumptive pronouns as indirect objects. More evidence is needed in order to substantiate this claim.

5. Conclusions: The Weight of Pragmatics and Simple Clause Parallelism for Resumptive Elements' Presence in Spanish Relative Clauses

The pragmatic meanings proposed to explain the use of an RE in an RC are present in some cases, but those are actually a minority. In the majority of RCs with an RE other factors seem to be responsible for the RE rather than the expression of a pragmatic meaning. This is both the case for contrastive meaning marking, only present in three of ten cases, and the old information status marking, presented in only fifty-one out of ninety cases. Furthermore, while the expression of contrastive meaning relies, at least in part, on the use of the RE, there are several reasons to question that the role of the RE is to indicate this status. The majority of the first position REs are either direct or indirect objects, all of them represented by a non-tonic pronoun, which is mandatory to place pre-verbally, and therefore typically, though not always, in first position. In addition, as Lambrecht (1994) pointed out, new information is about presupposed propositions, rather than referents (even if the proposition is there exists an X). Moreover, as it was patent from example (8), restrictive RCs typically introduce old information, as a whole.

In contrast, and although the sample is too small to be able to be certain, if indirect objects of the RC have the semantic role "recipient" they can lose their resumptive pronoun, but that seems to be impossible in the case of other roles. What makes recipients be represented by a resumptive pronoun or not remains to be determined.

In light of this evidence, it seems that pragmatic, and in one case semantic, meanings are expressed through an RE in Spanish relative clauses. When this is the case, the resumption strategy does not stand in free variation with the gap strategy (no RE). There are still, however, many cases where the two strategies are in free variation, competing with each other, and recent research points to processing factors to explain such variation.

With this investigation, I hope to have shown the utility of looking at oral data while using both quantitative and qualitative analysis. This chapter also shows how behind the same phenomenon there can be several factors of different nature, such as the processing difficulty investigated in earlier literature and pragmatic and semantic factors as well. The latter are particularly relevant in this volume for two reasons: they force us to use qualitative analysis, less common among variationist studies perhaps, and they show how the same variants can stand in free variation in some cases but not in others, when certain pragmatic meanings conditions them. In such cases, they can be said to convey a different meaning and therefore cannot be said to be a variant of the same construction.

4

The Role of Subjectivity in Discourse Marker Variation

Sarah Sinnott

1. Introduction

This chapter contributes to the volume's overall goal of highlighting new perspectives on linguistic variation by examining the variation of a pair of Spanish discourse markers that has previously gone unstudied: *por tanto* and *por lo tanto*. This variation is explored from a pragmatic perspective, from which we can see how the two markers differ in terms of their use in context. Specifically, we will see how discourse marker choice correlates with particular types of antecedent-consequent relationships and how it therefore can be utilized by speakers to demonstrate their perspective of the strength of these relationships.

In this chapter I set out to answer the following questions that underlie the variation of *por tanto* and *por lo tanto*: What are the contextual features that correlate with the variation of these two markers? What does this correlation reveal about why a speaker might choose one variant over another? Throughout this chapter I will demonstrate that the use of *por tanto* and *por lo tanto* correlates with the level of subjectivity of the relationship between the antecedent and the consequent connected by the marker. By appealing to the notion of subjectivity, specifically as described by, for example, Pander Maat and Sanders (2000) and Pander Maat and Degand (2002), we gain further understanding of the distribution of the two markers in

Peninsular Spanish. I will demonstrate that relationships that are less subjective tend to be linked by the discourse marker *por tanto* and that more subjective relationships tend to be linked by *por lo tanto*. This hypothesis aligns with the theory explored in Sinnott (in press) that *por lo tanto* contributes greater argumentative strength than *por tanto*. In other words, and regarding the second question posed above, a speaker may choose to use *por lo tanto* to express a stronger relationship between the antecedent and the consequent and *por tanto* when no such additional strength is required or desired. Regarding the relationship between subjectivity and argumentative strength, I hypothesize that if *por lo tanto* is indeed utilized to achieve greater argumentative strength as proposed by Sinnott, then it is likely to appear frequently in subjective contexts. The specific realm of subjective context that I will explore is the volitionality of the consequent. I aim to show that the use of *por lo tanto* correlates with volitional consequents and that use of *por tanto* correlates with nonvolitional contexts.

The chapter is structured as follows. In section 2 I will present a review of previous research and insights into the discourse markers in question, including a review of the theory of their argumentative strength proposed by Sinnott (in press). In section 3 I will discuss the notion of subjectivity, and in section 4 I will explain the methodology employed in this chapter. In section 5 I will exposit and discuss the results found in the data. This will be followed by final conclusions and suggestions for future research in section 6.

2. Previous Research of *Por tanto* and *Por lo tanto*

While there has been a recent surge of investigation of discourse markers (see, for example, Blakemore 2004; Travis 2005; Fraser 2009), there is a dearth of information regarding *por tanto* (henceforth PT) and *por lo tanto* (henceforth PLT) specifically. The majority of descriptions come to us through grammars of Spanish or style guides for writing. Within these sources, the markers are generally either treated as if they were one and the same, or one is left out altogether. Martín Zorraquino and Portolés Lázaro, for example, stated that PT "cuenta con la variante *por lo tanto*" (1999: 4001) 'exists alongside the variant *por lo tanto*.' Montolío stated that "*por (lo) tanto* . . . puede aparecer con o sin el elemento anafórico *lo*" (2008: 101) 'can occur with or without the anaphoric *lo*.' Her usage of parentheses is demonstrative of her treatment of the markers as one and the same. Butt and Benjamin only mentioned PLT in their examination of discuss markers in their grammar of Spanish, saying that it is used to "show that what follows is the result of what preceded" (2000: 459). While these descriptions do not distinguish the two variants, they do provide a basic idea of their function, which is to link a *p* and a *q*, where *q* is a consequent reasoned from the basis of *p*. This is demonstrated in (1), taken from the corpus described in the methodology in section 4. (Note that all examples are reproduced exactly as in the original blog posting and therefore may contain typographical errors.)

(1) *además conocen a la familia de Samu,* **por lo tanto***, es mas que un "yerno"*
'what's more, they know Samu's family, **por lo tanto**, he is more than a son-in-law'

While there has not been much research specifically into the variation of PT and PLT, variation between other discourse markers has been explored from a variety of perspectives.

I will begin with the influential work of Sweetser (1990). She claimed that discourse markers function in one or more of the three cognitive domains: content, epistemic, and speech act. As such, the discourse markers might be used to connect two real world actions (content), a segment with a conclusion arrived at through mental reasoning (epistemic), or a segment and a particular speech act (speech act). *Because*, for example, can function in all three of these domains, as shown in (2–4) (examples from Sweetser 1990: 77).

(2) John came back because he loved her.

(3) John loves her, because he came back.

(4) What are you doing tonight, because there is a good movie on.

Here we see that in (2) *because* connects two real-world events, i.e., the causality occurs in the content domain. In (3) we see a conclusion based on reasoning, i.e., the causality occurs in the epistemic domain. And in (4) we see the speech act domain in which *because* is being used to introduce the speech act of suggesting a movie.

Sweetser also used these domains to explain the variation in use between some discourse markers. For example, she stated that *since* cannot be used in the content domain. Other researchers have made similar claims about other discourse markers. For example, Keller (1995) utilized these domains to account for a change in the use of *weil* in German. *Weil* previously had only been used in dependent clause order in German, however it is now being used in spoken German in main clause order. According to Keller, *weil* used in dependent clause order links segments of content causality. Keller refers to this as *factual weil*. When *weil* appears in main clause order, it expresses epistemic causality. Keller refers to this as epistemic *weil* and claims that it is taking over the territory of *denn*, a discourse marker historically used to express epistemic causality in German.

Pander Maat and Sanders (2000) attempted to account for the Dutch causal connectives *daarom, daardoor,* and *dus* utilizing Sweetser's domain theory, but found that it was not sufficient. One issue was that both *daarom* and *daardoor* were used in the content domain. In addition, both *dus* and *daarom* can be utilized in the content and in the epistemic domains. In order to account for this, the authors proposed a more fine-tuned breakdown of the domains in which they considered their relative subjectivity. This will be discussed in greater detail in section 3 since it is of great importance to the current study.

Regarding PT and PLT specifically, Sinnott (in press) is, to my knowledge, the only work treating the variation between the two. Sinnott explored the variation between PT and PLT from the perspective of Sweetser's cognitive domains (described above) as well as argumentation. Working from the hypothesis that PLT contributed more argumentative strength (in the sense of Anscombre & Ducrot 1976) than PT, Sinnott compared their use in the domains of epistemic causation and content causation. She hypothesized that if PLT contributed more argumentative strength, then it would be used more frequently in cases of epistemic causality because the consequents presented in this domain are more easily refuted than those in the content domain. This is due to the mental reasoning nature of epistemic consequents versus the more factual nature of content consequents. Sinnott also compared their use within arguments vs. otherwise assuming that PLT would be used more often within arguments than PT. Therefore she investigated the distribution of the connectives when the speaker was arguing versus when they were not. Her conclusions were based on data from a corpus of online blog language.

Sinnott found that PLT was used more frequently than PT to introduce epistemic consequents, although not to a statistically significant level. When it came to arguments, however, PLT was used significantly more frequently than PT when the speaker was arguing a point made by another participant in the blog. The combination of these findings led Sinnott to the conclusion that PLT was utilized when a speaker was most invested in convincing the hearer that *q* was a valid consequent of *p*. She claimed then that PLT adds greater argumentative force to the discourse than PT. In other words, speakers use PLT when they want to add argumentative strength to their conclusions.

As noted in two of the studies mentioned above—Pander Maat and Sanders (2000) and Sinnott (in press)—the domain theory was not found to be sufficient in accounting for discourse marker variation. Pander Maat and Sanders continued their work in Dutch by adding the notion of subjectivity to their findings in domain theory. This will be discussed further in Section 3.

The current study provides a continuation of Sinnott's (in press) work with PT and PLT. Upon finding that the domains of epistemicity and content were not sufficient for accounting for the distributional behavior of the markers, she suggested that the next step would be to take a closer look at the level of subjectivity expressed in utterances in which they appear. This study represents that next step. In the following section I will discuss the concept of subjectivity, paying special attention to its relation with causality.

3. Subjectivity

According to Athanasiadou et al. (2006), the notion of subjectivity is relatively new in the field of linguistics despite its prominence in the social sciences. Despite its recency, it has received a great deal of attention from a variety of perspectives. The two most prevalent, according to Narrog (2012), have been the pragmatic perspective, spearheaded by Traugott, and the conceptualist perspective, proposed by Langacker. Traugott (2010: 30) explored the use of certain linguistic cues in context and how these cues come to index subjectivity, or, "speaker attitude or viewpoint." These linguistic cues include, for example, mental verbs, epistemic modals, and discourse markers. For Traugott, utterances that convey the speaker's viewpoint are subjective.

Langacker (2006), on the other hand, saw subjectivity as reflecting the *vantage point* of the speaker. According to his theory, no utterance is objective or subjective, but rather elements within that utterance are. Any element that remains implicit, or *offstage*, is maximally subjective. This includes, at least, the speaker. Any element made explicit, or *onstage*, is objective, which includes, at least, the referent of the utterance.

For the purposes of this chapter, I will look to a model of subjectivity that is more closely aligned with Traugott in that the expressions used and their context are key in determining the subjectivity of an utterance. The model that I employ is that utilized by Pander Maat and Sanders (2000) and Pander Maat and Degand (2002), who studied the use of Dutch and French causal connectives in terms of their relative subjectivity. Because this chapter also deals with the subjectivity of causal connectives, I will discuss their notion of subjectivity in some detail and I will generally follow their model in this investigation.

According to Sanders (2005) causality and subjectivity are two of the most basic cognitive principles that are reflected in language. He and others have found that variation in causal connectives can be accounted for in terms of their relative subjectivity, although, as noted in Sanders, there is a great need for more empirical evidence to support the hypothesis that subjectivity and causal connectives are interrelated. As of that 2005 paper, there had only been studies completed on some of the causal connectives in Dutch, German, French, and English.

By combining subjectivity with the domains approach, Pander Maat and Sanders (2000) were able to divide the domains further into epistemic, content volitional, content nonvolitional, and speech act. They define subjectivity in the realm of causality as "the distance between the speaker and the Subject of Consciousness (SOC) that is responsible for the causal relation" (57). The SOC is described as the person whose perspective is represented, or "the actor of the action in the second segment" (66), when that action is a volitional consequence to the antecedent. The SOC is explored further in Sanders, Sanders, and Sweetser (2009), where the SOC is described similarly as the person "involved in the construction of the causal relation" (22). They explain that the SOC in epistemic relations is typically the same as the speaker, therefore the distance between the SOC and the speaker is small or nonexistent. In volitional content causality relations the SOC is often not the speaker, and therefore the distance between the SOC and the speaker is greater. In cases of nonvolitional content causality there is not an SOC because there is no person, including the speaker, involved in construing the causal relationship.

According to Pander Maat and Sanders (2000), there is a continuum of subjectivity ranging from the least subjective relations, or those that occur unintentionally in the inanimate world, and the most subjective relations, or those that occur in the mind of the speaker when he is also the SOC. Pander Maat and Degand (2002) described a similar continuum, without explicit mention of the SOC. In this study they use the terminology of speaker involvement, or "the degree to which the present speaker is implicitly involved in the causal relation" (214). An utterance is placed on the continuum according to its level of speaker involvement.

The components of speaker involvement (or distance between the speaker and the SOC) include the volitionality of the consequent, the status of the SOC in terms of person and whether that person is implicit or explicit, the use of subjective markers, and the time frame of the causal event.

Cases of volitional content causality are considered subjective because it is the intentionality of the speaker or actor that is "the ultimate source of the causal event" (Pander Maat and Sanders 2000: 64). Pander Maat and Degand (2002) defined a volitional consequent as one in which the speaker or the SOC makes a decision to act.

Epistemic causality is considered to be subjective as well because the consequent occurs in the mind of the speaker or SOC who has drawn a conclusion based on the information presented in the antecedent. A crucial difference between epistemic and volitional causality, according to Pander Maat and Sanders (2000), is that in the case of epistemic causality the SOC is most likely also the speaker. In cases of volitional content causality there is greater variation; the SOC is often someone other than the speaker.

Cases of non-volitional content causality are considered to be objective because the antecedent and the consequent represent real-world events, neither the event in the antecedent nor the event in the consequent involve the mental work or the intention of the speaker or actor. In these cases the consequent is not caused by the speaker, and the relationship is perceived of as fact (Pander Maat and Sanders 2000: 65).

Other markers of subjectivity are considered because they help determine whether there are differing levels of subjectivity between two utterances involving the same type of causality. Person is an important component of the notion of subjectivity as described in both of these studies. First-person implicit forms representing the SOC were considered the most subjective because there is no difference between the speaker and the SOC. Implicit third-person forms referring to the SOC represent the greatest distance between the speaker and the SOC and therefore are the least subjective. Pander Maat and Sanders (2000) also took into consideration whether other explicit signs of subjectivity are present in the segments. These include deontic or epistemic modality as well as words or phrases that express the opinion of the speaker or SOC.

Finally, all of the authors concerned considered the time frame of the segments to be an important factor in determining the subjectivity of a causal relation. They claim that a causal event that takes place at a time other than the moment of speech is considered to be less subjective. The examples that they give only compare past and present tense, however (Pander Maat and Degand 2002: 215; Pander Maat and Sanders 2000: 67).

Through their corpus-based analysis of twenty-five tokens of each connective, Pander Maat and Sanders (2000) found, as mentioned above, that Sweetser's (1990) domain theory could not account for the use of the Dutch causal connectives *daardoor, daarom,* and *dus* because multiple forms could express content relations and multiple forms could express epistemic relations. They therefore investigated the relationship between subjectivity and the three forms. They categorized the forms as to whether they were used in cases of epistemic causality, dividing this further into whether the SOC was first person or third and whether the SOC was implicit or explicit. The cases of content causality were divided based on whether the action in the consequent was volitional or not. They also recorded the timeframe of the segments and the presence of additional subjective markers.

The authors found that this theory of subjectivity was able to account for the variation of these Dutch connectives with *daardoor* being maximally objective, *dus* maximally subjective, and *daarom* in the middle. Although they found that both *daardoor* and *daarom* were used in content causality relations, the difference between them lies in the fact that *daardoor* is used most frequently with non-volitional relations and *daarom* is used to connect volitional relations. Although *dus* and *daarom* were both used in epistemic relations, *dus* was categorically used with an implicit first-person SOC. *Daarom* was used with implicit first person as well as explicit first-person and third-person SOCs.

Similar results were found by Pander Maat and Degand (2002) for French. They found that the connectives *donc* and *dès lors* are the most subjective, while *de ce fait* is the least subjective. *C'est pourquoi* falls in the middle.

Because the Spanish PT and PLT and the Dutch and French connectives discussed above involve similar functions and were found not to correlate significantly with the cognitive domain, exploring PT and PLT from a subjectivity point of view was a logical next step in the investigation of their variation. In section 4 I will describe the data and the methodology used to study the relationship between discourse variant and subjectivity.

4. Methodology

All examples utilized in this chapter are taken from a corpus built from the website *20minutos.es*. This website features a variety of content such as news, celebrity tabloids, and blogs. The data is considered to be representative of

Peninsular Spanish because the website is written for a Peninsular Spanish audience. This is made obvious by the advertisements and the focus of the reports. In addition, there is another version of the website, *20minutos.com*, that is marketed toward a Latin American audience. The corpus was compiled specifically from three blogs featured on this site. The blogs are written by Spanish authors and their subject matter is quite different. The first is called *Madre reciente* and is written by a young mother and is generally directed toward parents and those looking to become parents. The second is titled *La gente de Rosy Runrún* and is a celebrity tabloid blog featuring information about the lives of Spanish celebrities and the opinions of the blogger. The final blog utilized in the corpus is *El ojo de Gran Hermano*, which is dedicated to the television reality show *Gran Hermano*.

All instances of PT and PLT were extracted from the main text and the commentary associated with these blogs as of June 2013. The tokens were found utilizing a Google site search that was saved via the program Evernote. This allowed each token to be isolated while maintaining the results of the initial Google search. Any tokens that were spam, quoted from another source, or written by self-identified non-Spaniards were excluded. Each token was initially coded for a variety of features. That of most relevance to the current chapter is causality type. For this study, only the tokens extracted from the commentary of the blogs are considered to avoid undue influence of speaker effect. This left a total of 493 tokens, 211 of which were PT and 282 of which were PLT.

In order to determine whether subjectivity plays a role in the variation of PT and PLT, I first looked at the instances in which they were used to introduce segments related to the previous by content causality. Recall that Sinnott (in press) had found that PT and PLT were both utilized in this condition. As noted above, the content domain can be split between volitional and nonvolitional consequents, volitional being more subjective than nonvolitional due to the involvement of the speaker or subject of consciousness in the causal relation. Because volitional is more subjective, we would expect to find a positive correlation between the use of PLT and volitional consequents if PLT is in fact used in more subjective environments.

To gauge the distribution of the discourse markers with relation to volitional vs. nonvolitional content causality, fifty tokens were extracted from the corpus. These fifty tokens consisted of twenty-five tokens of PT and twenty-five tokens of PLT that connected segments related by content causality. The data were randomly extracted from the corpus using a random selection generator in Microsoft Excel. Following Pander Maat and Sanders (2000), all tokens that did not include a verb in the second segment, such as seen in (5), were excluded.

(5) *es un termino "tecnico" y* **por tanto** *complejo*
'It is a "technical" and **por tanto** complex term.'

Each of these tokens was coded to enable comparison of the data according to the dimensions of subjectivity as described by Pander Maat and Sanders (2000) and Pander Maat and Degand (2002). Each token was coded for the following categories: volitionality, subject of consciousness/actor of second segment, subjectivity of first segment, subjectivity of second segment, tense of first segment, and tense of second segment. Each of the categories utilized is explained further below.

Following Pander Maat and Sanders (2000), a token was considered to be volitional if an intentional action was presented in q. An example is seen in (6). In this example the situation presented in p, that there was only a public school, caused the parents to engage in the intentional action in *q* of putting their son in that school.

(6) *solo hay el cole público,* **por lo tanto***, allí lo apuntamos*
'There is only the public school, **por lo tanto** we enrolled him there.'

An example of a nonvolitional token is seen in (7). In this example, the speaker states that men have no recourse in the legal system when it comes to maintaining custody of their children. The lack of regulations in their favor causes this situation and there is no intention on the part of the men to be defenseless. In fact, the hearer is led to understand that the men are completely helpless in this matter.

(7) *hay un vacío legal total al respecto y los hombres se hayan,* **por tanto***, en total indefensión*
'There is no legal help in that matter and men find themselves, **por tanto**, completely without a defense.'

The subject of consciousness was recorded for each case of volitional causality. Since there is no SOC in nonvolitional causality, grammatical person of the first segment was recorded. As discussed above, the SOC might be the speaker or it might be another party. In (8) I present an example in which the SOC corresponds with the speaker in that the speaker is the person completing the action entailed by the verb in the second statement. This does not necessarily correspond to a grammatical person, as seen in (9). In this case, it is again the speaker whose point of view is expressed. Therefore, the speaker is the SOC.

(8) *soy consciente que eso no es lo más habitual,* **por lo tanto** *aún lo valoro más*
'I'm aware that this isn't the most normal thing to do, **por lo tanto** I value it even more.'

(9) *si alguien se enfada por eso es que no me respeta, y* **por lo tanto***, no me interesa*
'If someone gets mad at me it is because they don't respect me, and **por lo tanto**, they don't matter to me.'

Again following Pander Maat and Sanders (2000), subjective segments were those that were presented in accompaniment with epistemic modality, deontic modality, or lexical items that conveyed an opinion or perspective. See, for example (10), in which the evaluative *me da igual* appears in both the first and the second segments.

(10) *termine pensando que realmente a mi me da igual lo que sea y que* **por lo tanto** *también me da igual saberlo*
'I ended up thinking that it really didn't matter to me what it is and that **por lo tanto** it didn't matter to me to know what it is either.'

Example (11) demonstrates a case in which the timeframe of the causal relation differs from the time of the speech act. As described above, this results in a more objective consequent because it is removed from the speaker in time. Verb tense was coded as past, present, future, or conditional.

(11) *pedí la epidural y me la pusieron mal* **por tanto** *sentía la mitad del cuerpo y en consecuencia dolor*
'I asked for an epidural and they administered it wrong **por tanto** I felt half of my body and as a result pain.'

By looking at these aspects of the utterances in the database, I will be able to determine the relationship between subjectivity and discourse marker election. The relationships that were found will be discussed in the following section.

5. Results and Discussion

In this section I will walk through each category mentioned above, beginning with volitionality. I will begin by addressing the principle hypothesis of this chapter—that PLT is utilized more frequently in volitional relations due to their higher level of subjectivity and, in turn, PT is utilized in nonvolitional relations due to their lower level of subjectivity.

The statistically significant distribution of volitionality and discourse marker is shown in table 4.1. Beginning with PLT, we find that 60% of tokens are volitional, demonstrating that PLT is used more frequently in volitional causality than in nonvolitional causality. When looking at PT, the results are more impressive, with 88% of PT tokens occurring within nonvolitional relations.

Looking from the perspective of volitionality, 79% of volitional tokens contain PLT while only 32% of nonvolitional cases utilize PLT. It is clear from this distribution that PLT is the more frequent option to link segments related by volitional content causality. In fact, it seems highly unlikely for PT to be used at all in this type of utterance. Recalling that volitional relationships are more subjective, it appears that PLT is marking the more subjective relations and PT the more objective relations, supporting the principle hypothesis. Both PLT and PT are used in nonvolitional relations, suggesting that neither form marks nonvolitional relations. I would argue as well that neither form marks volitional relations. PLT merely occurs more often in volitional contexts due to the subjectivity of the relationship. The subjectivity in turn renders more likely the desire for greater argumentative force.

While these results are statistically significant, the question remains as to why PLT is being used in nonvolitional relations at all and, in turn, why PT is used in some volitional relations. In order to explore this, we will look at the results from the other markers of subjectivity included in this study.

Each occurrence of PT and PLT in volitional contexts was coded for the SOC and each occurrence in nonvolitional contexts was coded for grammatical person. I will start with the volitional tokens; their distribution is shown in table 4.2. While there are scarcely enough PT examples to make any conclusions, I will discuss the data we have. PLT is the more frequent marker to occur in conjunction with the more subjective first-person speaker SOC. Out of twelve total first-person SOCs, eleven are accompanied by PLT and only one by PT. PLT also occurs nearly four times more frequently with first person than it does with third person. This offers further support for the idea that PLT tends to be utilized in subjective causal relations. Looking more in depth at the PT data, we see that PT's only occurrence

Table 4.1
Distribution of Volitionality and Discourse Marker

	Volitional	Nonvolitional
PLT	15	10
PT	4	21

Chi-square = 10.2716. P-value = 0.001351.

Table 4.2
Distribution of SOC and discourse marker in volitional contexts.

	1st	3rd	Passive
PLT	11	3	1
PT	1	2	1

with first person actually occurs at a time when the speaker is speaking on behalf of another generalized person, as seen in (12). Performing the voice of another renders the example less subjective because it increases the distance between the speaker and the subject of consciousness, which, one might argue, is actually the voice of the other.

(12) *Entiendo lo de "soy su madre y le conozco muy bien y por eso sé lo que quiere" o, aún más sincero, "soy su madre y **por tanto** nhago loq ue quiero con mi hijo."*
'I understand the idea that "I'm his mother and I know him well and so I know what he wants" or the more honest, "I'm his mother and **por tanto** I do what I want with my son."'

Due to the lack of PT volitional examples, an exploratory search was made through the entire corpus. Each volitional content causal relation containing PT was extracted and coded for person. Once again, if the second segment did not contain a verb, the utterance was not included. Out of sixty-four total PT content tokens, twenty-four (37.5%) were volitional, which makes up less than 5% of the entire corpus. The low frequency further demonstrates the tendency for PT to be used in nonvolitional relations rather than volitional ones. The SOC distribution of these twenty-four tokens is seen in table 4.3. With this broader view of the rare cases in which PT is used in volitional tokens, we see that the SOC distribution, while not as drastic as that seen in table 4.2, slightly leans toward the less subjective third person and passive environments. Taking a look at grammatical person within the nonvolitional content tokens, we see the distribution shown in table 4.4. This distribution also demonstrates a tendency for greater use of PT in less subjective environments. Sixty-eight percent of third-person segments are introduced by PT while first-person segments show no preference for one discourse marker over the other. A notable feature is that the only second-person segments

Table 4.3
Distribution of SOC within PT volitional tokens from entire corpus.

	1st	3rd	Passive
PT	10	13	1

Table 4.4
Distribution of person and discourse marker in nonvolitional contexts.

	1st	2nd	3rd	Passive
PLT	3		7	
PT	3	2	15	1

as well as the only passive statement are introduced by PT. Overall neither SOC nor grammatical person seem to play a great role in the distribution of PT and PLT. While it is true that most first-person SOCs or grammatical persons are introduced by PLT, it is also true that more first persons are found in volitional causal relationships. We have already seen that PLT is most frequent in volitional contexts. The interaction between these factors does not provide us with definitive information.

The exploration of PT and PLT along with overt markers of subjectivity did not prove statistically significant because these markers were overall rarely used within this content data. Regardless, PLT did co-occur more frequently than PT with other subjective markers in all segments. There are one hundred segments in the data. Of these, seventeen contained overt subjectivity markers. Out of seventeen total subjectivized segments, thirteen (77%) were accompanied by PLT. In addition, of the instances in which both segments were subjectivized, all three were accompanied by PLT (see table 4.5). However, once again, these overtly subjective markers tend to occur most often in volitional contexts. The remaining category to explore is the tense of the verb. Table 4.6 presents the timeframe expressed in the second segment of each data point. Each timeframe is divided into volitional and nonvolitional consequents. Present is by far the most frequent timeframe used in the corpus, therefore the distribution of discourse marker and volitionality within present tense reflects that of the overall distribution seen in table 4.1. Because of the low frequency of other tenses within the corpus, little else can be said regarding tense distribution. When not accounting for volitionality, the distribution of tense and discourse marker is almost 50/50. For example, out of thirty-five present-tense tokens, eighteen contained PLT and seventeen contained PT. A similar result is seen for past and present. This suggests that tense does not have a strong impact on connective choice and that there is no interaction between tense and volitionality.

This data has shown that volitionality affects the distribution of PT and PLT, supporting the principle hypothesis presented in this chapter. Other

Table 4.5
Overt subjectivity markers among segments.

	Subjective 1st segment	Subjective 2nd segment	Both segments subjective
PLT	7	6	3
PT	4	0	0

Table 4.6
Distribution of tense and discourse marker.

	Past		Present		Future		Conditional	
	V	NonV	V	NonV	V	NonV	V	NonV
PLT	2	2	12	6	1	2	0	0
PT	0	3	4	13	0	4	0	1
Total	2	5	16	19	1	6	0	1

subjectivity markers that were shown to affect the distributions of causal connectives in other languages did not correlate directly in this case. SOC and grammatical person both interacted with volitionality and tense did not show an effect.

It is interesting to note that PT is most sensitive to the volitionality of the causal relationship. PLT tokens are divided 60%/40% between volitionality types but PT tokens are divided 12%/88%. This is similar to other distributions discussed in Sinnott (in press) in which she found that PT was more sensitive than PLT when it came to domain distribution. In that study, 54% of PT tokens appeared in conjunction with content causality vs. 46% in epistemic. Meanwhile only 36% of the PLT tokens occurred in content contexts and 64% in epistemic. The range of difference between domain and PT was only 4% then, while the range for PLT was 28%. This difference in sensitivity is logical when analyzed within the greater context of this variation. As stated above, this particular study is a continuation of work begun by Sinnott. The hypothesis of that study was that PLT was used to exert more argumentative force, or to strengthen the relationship between the antecedent and the consequent. If this were the case, she hypothesized that PLT would appear more frequently in epistemic as well as in argumentative contexts. That was found to be true on both accounts.

In the current study I set out with the hypothesis that if PLT exerts greater argumentative force, it will likely be utilized in more subjective contexts.

Evidence has been presented to suggest that this is also true. Now, a speaker always has a choice whether or not to strengthen the relationship between the antecedent and the consequent that they are expressing. In certain cases, such as when there is no argument involved and when the context is rather objective, the speaker probably doesn't feel a need to "convince" the listener that the consequent they are presenting is valid. Thus these cases see a high rate of use of PT.

From the other point of view, PT does not exert any extra argumentative force; as a result, it is rarely used in these highly subjective contexts. PLT, on the other hand, offers a little more freedom. While it is likely that a speaker will want to increase the force of their arguments in the cases described above, it is also true that they might choose to do so in cases where, from an outsider's perspective, it might not seem as necessary. On the other hand, what might look to an outsider as a viable context in which to use PLT and add argumentative force might not be deemed as such by the speaker. The speaker's intention will be the most powerful determiner in the use of PT vs. PLT and, if this is able to be judged, one would need to look to a great deal of the surrounding context in order to determine these intentions.

Further research may help pinpoint what additional reasons a speaker might have for choosing one marker over the other when the general pattern is not followed as well as how they might be recognized in discourse. It is likely that they will involve subjectivity in some way, however, as Traugott and Dasher say, "an expression is neither subjective in and of itself; rather the whole utterance and its context determine the degree of subjectivity" (2002: 98). Therefore, we may not be able to rely on purely linguistic evidence alone.

6. Conclusion

In this chapter I have contributed a new perspective to the study of variation of Spanish discourse markers. Specifically, I have provided evidence to support the hypothesis that the distribution of the causal connectives PT and PLT correlates with the volitionality of the consequent in a relationship of content causality. In volitional contexts, PLT is utilized at a greater rate than PT. In nonvolitional contexts, the use of PT exceeds that of PLT. Due to the relative subjectivity of these two consequent types, I argue that PLT is likely to be used to express causality in a subjective causal relation. This aligns with previous findings that PLT contributes additional argumentative strength to an utterance in which it is used.

These findings contribute to our growing understanding of the variation of discourse markers. *Por tanto* and *por lo tanto* are situated among a group of discourse markers whose use has already been shown to rely on the subjectivity of an utterance. In addition, the results presented here further demonstrate previous insight into the variation of the two markers as conveyors of differing levels of argumentative strength.

As Sanders (2005) stated, more empirical study of further sets of discourse markers needs to be undertaken in order to further our understanding of just how sensitive they are to subjectivity. This, in turn, will contribute to our understanding of the notion of subjectivity. Further research is needed on PT and PLT specifically as well. We do not yet understand all of the reasons for which a speaker might choose to strengthen the argumentative force of the consequent. As the study of discourse markers grows, we begin to understand the subtle differences between them and how, through variation, they are able to express the slightest differences in pragmatic or cognitive meaning on behalf of the speaker.

PART III
Linguistic Attitudes and Discourse Analysis

5

Linguistic Attitudes in Argentine Spanish
(De)queísmo, DOM, and the Subjunctive

Mark Hoff and Rosa María Piqueres Gilabert

1. Introduction

The present study is concerned with three morphosyntactic variables found in Argentine Spanish—*(de)queísmo*, the use of differential object marking (DOM) with inanimate direct objects (DOs), and the use of the present subjunctive in place of the imperfect subjunctive in subordinate clauses introduced by a past tense main clause. Though these variables have been documented as occurring in Argentina, their place in the speech community and the ways speakers view their use have not yet been adequately described. The present investigation seeks to determine the social stratification, if any, of both the "standard" and "non-standard" variants of these morphosyntactic variables. Furthermore, we hope to examine speaker attitudes toward uses of these variants in terms of traditional matched-guise semantic scales. The overarching goal of our work here is to demonstrate the application of the tools available to linguists for the analysis of Spanish morphosyntactic variation, taking advantage of recent theoretical and methodological advances in the field. Additionally, this study endeavors to challenge, improve, and stimulate linguists' understanding of concepts central to the study of speaker attitudes, specifically, and of sociolinguistic variation, more generally.

2. Previous Literature

2.1. *(DE)QUEÍSMO*

(De)queísmo is defined in Schwenter (1999: 65) as the use of the preposition *de* after verbal constructions introducing sentential complements in cases where normative grammar does not prescribe its use. According to Schwenter (1999), *dequeísmo* and *queísmo*, often treated in linguistic literature as two phenomena, actually comprise one variable, as they are regulated by the same factors. Schwenter's quantitative variationist analysis of *(de)queísmo* revealed that the most important factor conditioning *de* use was the person of the subject in the main clause. *De* was used least with first-person and most with third-person subjects. These results suggest that *de* may function as an evidentiality marker that allows speakers to commit to or distance themselves from the content being communicated, especially when this information comes from a third party. In essence, greater distance between the verb and the complementizer *que* (created by the insertion of *de*) iconically represents greater distance between a speaker and his/her statement. Kanwit (2012: 1) corroborated this theory, presenting discourse-based data showing that Venezuelan speakers tended to use *de* to "provide a mitigating buffer prior to emotionally-charged propositional content."

The following examples demonstrate this difference, with third-person subjects favoring *de* use and first-person subjects disfavoring it. Examples (1) and (2) represent *queísmo* and normative use of a pronominal verb with *de* (*enterarse de que*), respectively.

(1) *Luego me enteré* **que** *el funeral había sido privado.*
'Later I found out that the funeral had been private.'

(2) *... cuando la gente se enteró* **de que** *era el 14 de junio ...*
'... when the people found out it was June 14th ...' (Schwenter 1999: 71)

Schwenter's (1999) treatment of *(de)queísmo* is particularly relevant to the current study as it included data from Argentine Spanish. Bentivoglio and Sedano (2011) also testified to the presence of *(de)queísmo* in Argentine Spanish, reporting that its use has increased in that region in the latter half of the twentieth century. Furthermore, Boretti de Macchia (1989), Fontanella de Weinberg (1987), Kovacci (1992), Rojas (1980), and others have described the use of *(de)queísmo* in several provinces of Argentina, including Tucumán, Santa Fe, Corrientes, and Buenos Aires.

Although Schwenter (1999) considered only linguistic variables, Kanwit (2012) found that, in the context of Caracas, upper class speakers favored *de* use while speakers from the lower class disfavored it. The middle class neither favored nor disfavored the use of *de* (.50). Kanwit proposed that the upper class's favoring of *de* may be related to hypercorrection and a desire to present oneself as highly educated. A very similar pattern of use by social class is seen in Guirado (2006). As for speaker sex, neither Kanwit nor Guirado found significant effects, although in both studies women used *de* slightly more than men. Speaker age was significant, however; in Kanwit's statistical analysis, older speakers favored *de* use, whereas younger speakers disfavored it.

2.2. DIFFERENTIAL OBJECT MARKING (DOM) USE WITH INANIMATES

In modern Spanish, DOs may be marked with the preposition *a*. This preposition, which is a type of differential object marking known as accusative *a* and is generally associated with the marking of animate objects, has been the subject of an impressive body of variationist research (Tippets & Schwenter 2007; Tippets 2011, and many others). However, von Heusinger and Kaiser (2003), among others, have noted the use of accusative *a* with inanimate direct objects in Spanish and concluded that factors such as animacy, definiteness, and specificity cannot fully explain the variation in the use and nonuse of *a*. Both Barrenechea and Orecchia (1977) and Tippets (2011) have identified Argentine Spanish as a dialect in which particularly high rates of inanimate direct object marking are seen.

As for the motivation behind the DOM of inanimates, Bossong (1985) stated that cross-linguistically *a*-marking may be related to questions of information structure; Laca (2002), speaking of Spanish specifically, argued that *a*-marking may be related to topicality in discourse. Hoff (2014) performed a quantitative analysis using an online questionnaire in which Argentine participants rated cases of marked and unmarked inanimate direct objects. The results of this analysis demonstrated that for these participants the use of accusative *a* with inanimate direct objects, while not preferred over normative marking, is widely accepted. As part of a complementary qualitative analysis, Hoff provided real-life cases of *a*-marked inanimates from a variety of sources and registers (social networking sites and blogs, TV shows, novels, government-issued signage, etc.). The present study aims to identify the social role of the DOM of inanimate DOs in terms of speakers' awareness and evaluations of its use in Buenos Aires Spanish.

Examples (3) and (4) illustrate the *a*- marking of topical inanimate direct objects in both pre- and post-verbal positions:

(3) Me   parece   que **a**   esa   película   ya   <u>la</u>   <u>vi</u>.
    To.me   it.seems that A   that   movie   already   CL   I.saw[1]
    'It seems to me that I've already seen that movie.'   (Hoff 2014)

(4) Vos   no   <u>las</u>   cumplís   **a**   <u>las promesas</u>
    You   no   CL   you.keep   A   the promises
    'You don't keep your promises.'   (Hoff 2014)

In example (3), a member of an online forum is responding to a post about a popular new movie. The topic of the movie is highly accessible in the discourse context and the commenter indicates this topicality in his own discourse via the use of accusative *a*. In (4), which comes from the hit TV show *Farsantes*, a newlywed couple is discussing promises they made to each other before getting married. The utterance in (4) appears in the midst of this discussion, with multiple mentions of promises coming both before and after, thus *promesas* is highly topical and is therefore *a*-marked.

2.3. PRESENT SUBJUNCTIVE IN PLACE OF IMPERFECT SUBJUNCTIVE

While prescriptive grammars have long maintained that a verb in a subordinate clause must be conjugated in the same tense as the verb in the principal clause (for example, [+past, +past]), some grammars, such as the Royal Spanish Academy (Real Academia Española 2009) have changed their positions in recent years. This change is appropriate considering that many varieties of Spanish, especially in the Americas, permit more temporally flexible uses of the subjunctive as "standard" (such as [+past, -past]) (Carrasco Gutiérrez 2000; Obaid 1967; Rojo 1976; Sessarego 2008; Suñer & Padilla-Rivera 1987, among others).

---

1. Glosses are presented as follows: IOCL refers to an indirect object clitic, CL refers to a direct object clitic, accusative *a* appears in bold, and the *a*-marked DO and its coreferential clitics are underlined.

Rojo (1976) identified two possibilities of defining the sequence of tenses of the subjunctive mode in Spanish—the principle of *consecutio temporum* and a more flexible system based on the temporal sense of the construction rather than its grammatical tense. The principle of *consecutio temporum* allows (6), as prescriptive grammars have historically done, but rejects (7) as ungrammatical because of the lack of temporal agreement between the main and subordinate clauses.

(6) *El médico recomendó que la niña no comiera tantos dulces.*
    [+past]   [+past]

(7) *El médico recomendó que la niña no coma tantos dulces.*
    [+past]   [-past]
    'The doctor recommended that the girl did/does not eat so much candy.'
    (adapted from Suñer & Padilla-Rivera 1987: 639)

Carrasco Gutiérrez (2000) argued that cases such as (7) are acceptable because of a double-access interpretation. In other words, there are two deictic axes that depend on speaker and listener interpretation—the axis of the action in the principal clause and the axis of the moment of the speech event. Therefore, if the action referred to (*comer* in the examples above) is posterior to the moment of speaking, the present subjunctive can be used.

Sessarego (2008) claimed that such structures are frequent and accepted in spoken Bolivian and Peruvian varieties, although his data showed [+past, +past] to be the preferred system in newspapers. Hoff (n.d.) presented a variationist sociolinguistic study of the variation between the present and imperfect subjunctive in subordinate clauses, when the principal verb was in the past. Based on questionnaire data from 125 young Argentines, Hoff concluded that [+past, -past] is not only an accepted option for these speakers, but rather the preferred system. Hoff also identified statistically significant dialectal differences—participants from the provinces of Entre Ríos and Buenos Aires favored the use of the present subjunctive in these cases while participants from Córdoba favored the imperfect subjunctive. Finally, Hoff found that men slightly favored the use of the present subjunctive, while women slightly disfavored it. These findings suggest that the use of the present subjunctive in cases where traditional grammarians prescribe the imperfect subjunctive is an excellent candidate for a study of speaker attitudes and social evaluations.

2.4. ATTITUDES

In recent years an increasing interest in determining the attitudes of speakers toward specific phenomena in their own language has emerged (Blanco de Margo 1991; Blas Arroyo 1995, 1999; Cooper & Fishman 1975; Lafford 1986; Lambert, Hodgson, Gardner & Fillenbaum 1960; Piqueres Gilabert & Fuss 2016; Rissel 1989; Sarnoff 1966; Wölck 1973). However, it has been noted that there is disagreement among researchers as to the most appropriate operationalization for this concept. Most researchers have followed the mentalist approximation to attitudes (Agheyisy & Fishman 1970; Cooper & Fishman 1975), which considers attitudes as a mental interior state and as a variable that plays a role in the stimulus that affects the individual and the response to the stimulus (Agheyisy & Fishman 1970: 138). These authors also frame the methodology used in studies regarding attitudes within three different instruments: questionnaires, interviews, and direct observation, the latter being the preferred method.

Milroy and Milroy (1985) represents a key work on the analysis of attitudes and the notion of prestige and socioeconomic status. This study determines the variable of prestige from the socioeconomic status of speakers, which is considered crucial in language variation since speakers with higher or lower social prestige will promote language change. Several studies involve the variable of prestige in their analyses of speaker attitudes toward different variants within a specific speech community (Lafford 1986; Matus-Mendoza 2004; Risell 1989). Risell (1989) and Matus-Mendoza (2004) examined /r/ assibilation in Mexico. Both researchers determined that assibilation was tied to prestige within Mexico, although not among Mexicans who live abroad, where assibilation was not considered a prestigious linguistic feature.

Much of this research has been conducted with the aim of describing the varieties of Spanish spoken in regions where contact between different languages exists (Blas Arroyo 1995; González Martínez & Blas Arroyo 2011; Piqueres & Fuss 2016; Wölck 1973). Wölck (1973) employed two Quechua-Spanish bilinguals to test whether stigmatization existed concerning the indigenous culture, using a rating-scale with the following adjectives: low vs. high class, educated vs. uneducated, urban vs. rural, ugly vs. pretty, weak vs. strong, and kind vs. unkind. The results provide evidence of the lower-class (Quechua) speakers obtaining better affective judgments, but the higher-class (Spanish) speakers receiving better general rankings. This suggests that Peruvians have an affective attachment to Quechua, though the language is also stigmatized.

These results are similar to those obtained by González Martínez and Blas Arroyo (2012), which showed that the Catalan spoken in Castellón has lower prestige than Spanish, the mainstream language in Spain. On the other hand, Blas Arroyo (1995) conducted research on the Catalan-Spanish language contact context in Spain, paying close attention to the Spanish spoken by bilingual speakers and comparing evaluations of different Catalan varieties. In Blas Arroyo (1995), participants rated Catalan-Spanish speakers with adjectives that fit within three different scales (following Ryan & Carranza 1975): personal competence and socioeconomic status, personal integrity, and social attractiveness. His results suggest that interlocutors who speak the Valencian variety receive higher rankings for social attractiveness, personal competence, and socioeconomic status than those who speak the Catalan variety, but Spanish interlocutors are ranked highest on all three scales.

Piqueres Gilabert and Fuss (2016) approached the study of attitudes focusing on Spanish interference in the Catalan spoken in La Plana (Castellón, Spain) by means of an oral perception test. Three specific morphosyntactic variables (expletive *que*, partitive *de*, and the preposition *a*) were analyzed, and the results suggest that participants notice the "non-standard" use of the preposition *a* and thus provide low rankings concerning personal attractiveness and socioeconomic status for this variant. Nevertheless, bilingual speakers from this region do not seem to be entirely aware of the other two variables.

In the present study, the authors will analyze speech community attitudes toward three different pairs of morphosyntactic structures (the use of *(de)queísmo*, DOM with inanimates, and present subjunctive) in order to see if stigmatization exists and how it is revealed by means of a perception questionnaire. In this way, the researchers expect to shed some light on the topic of language attitudes, specifically regarding the different variants in the speech of Argentine speakers that have been identified by previous researchers.

2.5. MATCHED-GUISE TECHNIQUE

For research directed at linguistic attitudes among speakers, the matched-guise technique is the methodology most utilized in recent studies (Blas Arroyo 1999; Campbell-Kibler 2006; Díaz-Campos & Killam 2012; Piqueres Gilabert & Fuss 2016). Lambert et al. (1960) pioneered this methodology with members of a bilingual community by having the same speakers read aloud several sentences in two different languages. The purpose of this instrument was to make participants believe that each of the sentences came from a different speaker (despite that there are fewer speakers than recordings), and participants listened to evaluate the speakers following different adjective scales (e.g., good vs. bad, poor vs. rich, unfriendly vs. friendly, and unintelligent vs. intelligent). Consequently, listeners attributed psychosocial judgments to speakers according to the language used. This methodology has also been used to determine attitudes when evaluating different variants of the same linguistic variable in one language (Díaz-Campos & Killam 2012).

In Lambert et al. (1960), sixty-four English-dominant speakers and sixty-six French-dominant speakers evaluated bilingual speakers following a differential semantic scale. A differential semantic scale is conceived as a method to evaluate the speaker's subjective or emotional reactions with the purpose of describing the affective dimensions of concept organization in a linguistic variety (Hernández Campoy & Almeida 2005). This study showed that the minority language (French in this study) tended to obtain lower rankings than the majority language (English) and that stereotypes play an important role when testing attitudes among a specific speech community. Confirmation of the validity of the matched-guise technique is the number of studies conducted in bilingual regions that follow this methodology (Blas Arroyo 1995; González Martínez & Blas Arroyo 2011; Piqueres Gilabert & Fuss 2016; Woolard 1984; Woolard & Gahng 1990).

Woolard (1984) and Woolard and Gahng (1990) studied the attitudes of Catalan participants toward the speech of Catalan-Spanish bilingual speakers, including native and non-native Catalan speakers as the recorded subjects. Results showed that speakers that used Catalan were given higher rankings while those that used Spanish were ranked lower. This demonstrates the diglossic status of Catalan and Spanish in the province of Barcelona where Catalan is more prestigious and thus is associated with higher socioeconomic levels. Piqueres Gilabert and Fuss (2016) used female and male interlocutors for the first time to test Clopper, Conrey, and Pisoni's (2005) claim that the interlocutor's gender does not affect the appropriate categorization of dialects. Indeed, no voice effect was found but the researchers did find varying degrees of stigmatization according to the morphosyntactic variable tested. On the other hand, Casesnoves and Sankoff (2004) considered how education influences attitudes toward Valencian and Spanish. They found that the notion of nationalism is essential when analyzing these linguistic attitudes, given that the most nationalist participants tended to be more competent in Valencian. Moreover, those participants holding more moderate views with respect to nationalism considered Spanish to be prestigious.

With respect to monolingual regions, Díaz-Campos and Killam (2012) conducted a study, also employing the matched-guise method, that assessed the attitudes of Venezuelan participants when two male and two female speakers deleted intervocalic /d/ and final /r/. The main objectives of this research were to determine if stigmatization existed among Venezuelans regarding these phenomena. The authors measured intelligence, professional capacity, and attraction and kindness. The results obtained suggested that deletion is not always a stigmatized feature among Caracas speakers: although /r/ retention was considered positive, both /d/ elision and retention were judged as neutral. Although strong claims about attitudes could not be made, the authors stated that stigmatization regarding /r/ deletion does exist.

González Martínez and Blas Arroyo (2011) and Piqueres Gilabert and Fuss (2016) used various pairs of adjectives for different semantic scales: personal attractiveness, social attractiveness, and socioeconomic status. The present study follows Blas Arroyo's semantic scales (1995) using four pairs of adjectives for three semantic scales: personal competence and socioeconomic status, personal integrity, and social/personal attractiveness. Díaz-Campos and Killam (2012) and Piqueres Gilabert and Fuss (2016) utilized four sentences for the same variable (two of the variants are expected to be stigmatized). Nonetheless, the present study includes only two sentences per variable in order to avoid fatigue and participants' realizing that speakers are repeated throughout the task to ensure that the results are as reliable as possible.

3. Research Questions and Hypotheses

This study measures attitudes with respect to "standard" and "non-standard" variants and aims to reaffirm the validity of the matched-guise method as applied to morphosyntactic variation in three different variables from the Spanish spoken in Buenos Aires. Our research is guided by the following questions:

1. Do any of the variants analyzed show social stratification by their rankings? And will variants traditionally considered "non-standard" be ranked equally in all the morphosyntactic patterns analyzed?
2. Which variants will be ranked highest with respect to the following three semantic scales: personal competence and socioeconomic status, personal attractiveness, and personal integrity?

Our hypotheses are the following:

1. We anticipate that the variants analyzed will show social stratification depending on whether the recorded stimulus contains a "non-standard" element (Blas Arroyo 1995; Díaz-Campos & Killam 2012). Thus, "standard" variants will receive higher rankings than "non-standard" variants in the personal competence and economic status sphere. We also expect that certain morphosyntactic variants will not be ranked as negatively as others, given their integration into the speech of this specific region (Piqueres Gilabert & Fuss 2016). Consequently, as Blas Arroyo (2011) affirmed, there is an acceptance scale among speakers: variants that are highly integrated into the language (despite their being "non-standard") will receive higher rankings. It is because of their more extensive use in everyday language that we predict that the use of present subjunctive in place of imperfect subjunctive and DOM of inanimates will obtain more positive rankings than *(de)queísmo*.
2. We expect that listeners will generally assign higher personal competence and socioeconomic status to "standard" variants. We anticipate that speakers who employ "non-standard" variants will receive more negative rankings, as Woolard (1984) and Woolard and Gahng (1990) demonstrated, although this is expected to vary according to the social integration of the linguistic feature. As previous studies have shown that younger speakers tend to evaluate "non-standard" patterns and minority languages in a positive manner concerning personal attractiveness (González Martínez & Blas Arroyo 2011), we predict that listeners will do the same. Following these predictions, we anticipate that "non-standard" variants will receive more positive rankings than "standard" variants concerning personal integrity (González Martínez & Blas Arroyo 2011).

4. Methodology

4.1. PARTICIPANTS

Two groups of participants were involved in this study. Group 1, comprised of four native speakers of the Buenos Aires variety of Spanish, born and still living in this province, served as the source of the recordings to be used in the matched-guise instrument. The first, Pepe, was born in the Autonomous City of Buenos Aires, in the neighborhood of Caballito. He currently lives in the province of Buenos Aires in the small town of Navarro, but attends a university in Luján. He is twenty-one years old and identifies as middle or upper-middle class. Juan is from Ramos Mejía, located in the district of La Matanza in Greater Buenos Aires. He is twenty-five years old and belongs to the middle class. Amparo is from Caballito in the Autonomous City of Buenos Aires. She is eighteen years old and has lived her entire life in this neighborhood of the capital. She identifies as belonging to the middle class and has just begun college. María is from the district of Quilmes in Greater Buenos Aires. She is twenty-four years old, is currently attending university, and considers herself middle class. These speakers belong to the same social strata (middle or upper-middle class, as defined by level of education and family income and confirmed by the speaker him/herself) and have similar educational backgrounds. Furthermore, they belong to the same generation and the same general geographic region.

Group 2 consists of twenty-four native speakers of Buenos Aires Spanish, who although they may have experience with foreign languages, identify as monolingual. All participants were born in and have lived the majority of their lives in the province of Buenos Aires, receiving primary and secondary education there as well. Participants range from eighteen to thirty years of age, which can be loosely defined as college-aged in the Argentine context. Reasonable efforts were made to ensure that participants had no personal ties to, and therefore would not recognize, the recorded speakers of Group 1.

4.2. INSTRUMENT

The main task that participants completed requires listening to recordings of sentences for the following morphosyntactic variables: *(de)queísmo*, DOM of inanimate objects, and present subjunctive in place of imperfect subjunctive. Each speaker from Group 1 recorded two sentences for each of the variables; one with the "standard" structure and another with the "non-standard" structure. Following previous research (Campbell-Kibler 2006; Piqueres Gilabert & Fuss 2016), the same sentence with a different morphosyntactic item is used for each variable in order to ensure there is no effect due to different lexical items. As in Piqueres Gilabert and Fuss (2016), each sentence is evaluated according to two different pairs of adjectives, making the task shorter for participants and to avoid voice quality effects in participant responses. However, the researchers decided to shorten the instrument, since in Piqueres Gilabert and Fuss (2016) it seemed that participants experienced boredom and may not have completed the task as faithfully as researchers would have liked. Therefore, the instrument employed in this study includes a total of twenty-four recordings (4 speakers × 3 variables × 2 variants). Furthermore, including both males and females as stimulus providers grants researchers more possibilities to avoid voice quality effects, given that comparisons among speakers are less likely to occur.

Together with the recordings, a matched-guise questionnaire composed of differential semantic scales with values from 1 to 6 was used. Ranking 1 corresponds to the most negative value of the adjective while ranking 6 is the most positive. For the present study, researchers follow the attitudinal categories used by Blas Arroyo (1995), which include personal competence and socioeconomic status, personal integrity, and social attractiveness. The adjectives employed for the differential semantic scale are unintelligent vs. intelligent and poor vs. rich for the category of personal competence and socioeconomic status, good vs. bad for personal integrity, and unfriendly vs. friendly for personal attractiveness. At the end of the questionnaire, participants were provided with a blank form where they were invited to express any thoughts or concerns about the sentences they had heard.

To control for the place of birth and residence of participants, a background questionnaire was also administered. By this means, the researchers were able to dismiss any data irrelevant to the purpose of the study, and only participants whose first language was Argentine Spanish and who were both born in and currently living in the province of Buenos Aires were considered.

4.3. ANALYSIS

In order to evaluate the average of participants' rankings, the researchers used the computer software package SPSS (2010), comparing the dependent variable of linguistic choice between "standard" and "non-standard" variants and controlling the random and fixed effects in a mixed model analysis (Díaz-Campos & Killam 2012; Piqueres & Fuss 2016). This analysis allowed the authors to obtain attitudinal averages among different speakers and the averages among the different variants included in the instrument. Statistical tests were performed to determine the following: general evaluations about the different morphosyntactic variants, evaluations given to different speakers to observe potential voice quality or gender effects, and evaluations according to the attitudinal categories previously described: personal competence and socioeconomic status, social attractiveness, and personal integrity.

5. Results

The results are presented in the following manner, following Piqueres Gilabert and Fuss (2016): first, we show the general evaluations of each morphosyntactic variable (*(de)queísmo*, DOM, and present vs. imperfect subjunctive); next, we provide figures demonstrating any gender and/or voice quality effects; finally, evaluations according to the four speakers (Pepe, Amparo, Juan, and María) and the three attitudinal spheres (personal competence and socioeconomic status, personal integrity, and personal attractiveness) are presented.

In Figures 5.1, 5.2, and 5.3 the general evaluations for the variants of each morphosyntactic variable are shown. Twenty-four participants evaluated six sentences according to two different adjective scales (1 sentence per variant and per speaker). In Figure 5.1 the average evaluation for *de que* was 3.688, while the "standard" variant received an evaluation average of 3.724. Despite the "standard" variant of the *(de)queísmo* phenomenon's obtaining higher evaluations, this difference is not significant $F_{(1, 358)} = 0.128$, $p = 0.721$. In the case of DOM with inanimate objects, a statistically significant difference does exist between the use and the non-use of the preposition *a* $F_{(1, 358)} = 24.741$, $p = 0.000$ (Figure 5.2). Surprisingly, in this case speakers evaluated the "non-standard" variant more positively, with a mean of 4.411 (while the "standard" variant received a mean evaluation of 3.698). The difference between the present and imperfect subjunctive (Figure 5.3) is not statistically significant $F_{(1, 358)} = 0.217$, $p = 0.642$. As is the case for DOM, here the "non-standard" variant, present subjunctive, obtains higher evaluations (mean = 3.734) than the "standard" variant (mean = 3.688). Another unexpected result is related to voice quality effects (Figure 5.4). The mixed model analysis revealed a statistical difference between all speakers $F_{(3, 1123)} = 69.152$, $p = 0.000$ (Pepe-Amparo, Pepe-Juan, Pepe-María, Amparo-Juan, Amparo-María, and Juan-María). However, no gender effect among speakers was found $F_{(1, 1125)} = 0.031$, $p = 0.861$ (Figure 5.5). With respect to the evaluations for each variant among different speakers, it is observed in Figures 5.6, 5.7, and 5.8 that some of these differences are statistically significant. Concerning the *(de)queísmo* variable, Pepe and Amparo

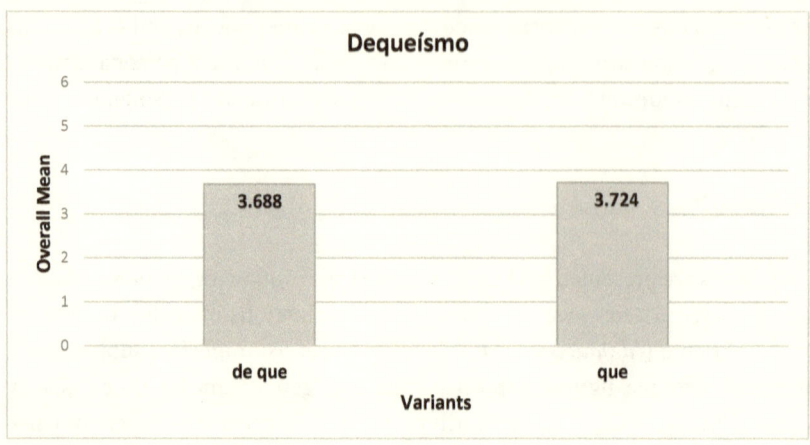

Figure 5.1
Presence and Absence of *De* (*(De)queísmo*).

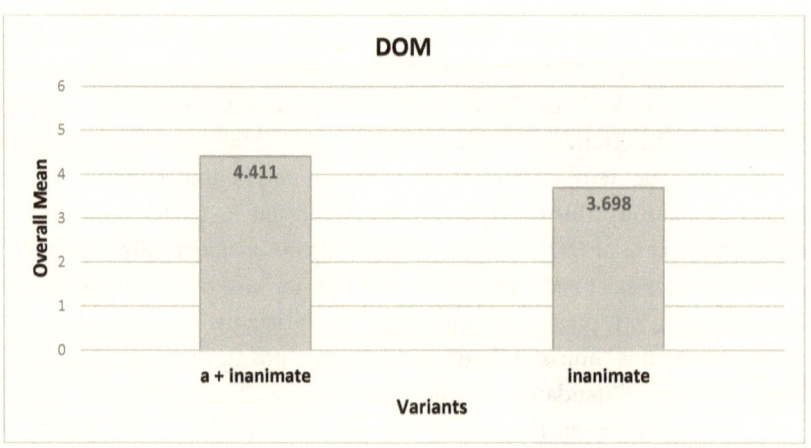

Figure 5.2
Presence and Absence of *a* (DOM) with Inanimate Objects.

do not show a significant difference between the presence or absence of *de* (Pepe F [1, 71] = 1, p = 0.321, Amparo F [1, 71] = 0.016, p = 0.9). Yet Juan and María do show significant distinctions between the two variants (Juan F [1, 71] = 4.511, p = 0.037, María F [1, 71] = 5.205, p = 0.026). In addition, the overall difference between the "standard" and the "non-standard" variants of *(de)queísmo* is significant F (3, 353) = 3.231, p = 0.023. In general, it can be seen that the "standard" variant (absence of *de*) obtains higher

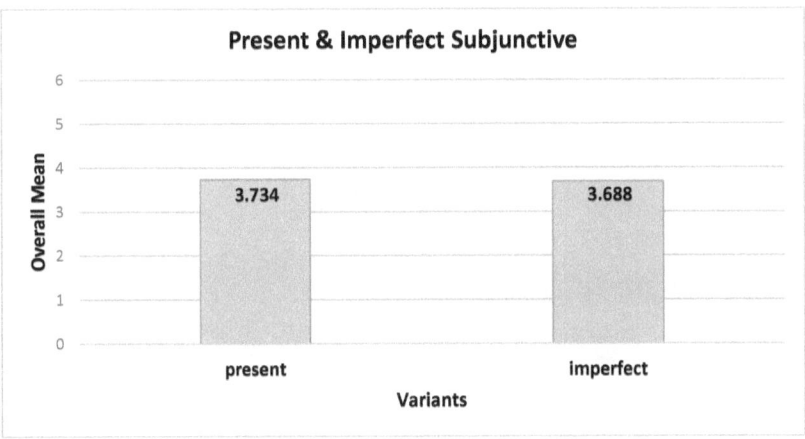

Figure 5.3
Present and imperfect subjunctive evaluation.

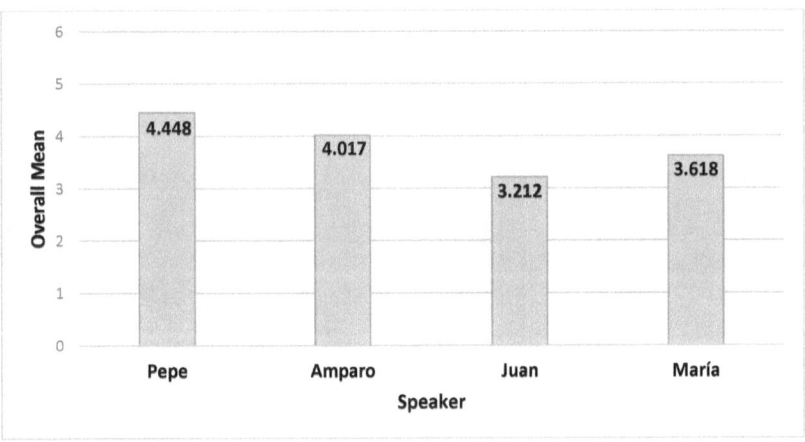

Figure 5.4
Voice quality effect.

evaluations than the "non-standard" variant. Concerning the DOM variable (Figure 5.7), only Pepe shows significant results for its variants F (1, 71) = 1.54, p = 0.000. However, the evaluative differences between the "standard" and "non-standard" variants for Amparo, Juan, and María's evaluations are not significant (Amparo F [1, 71] = 0.719, p = 0.339; Juan F [1, 71] = 0.286, p = 0.594; María F [1, 71] = 1.54, p = 0.219). The overall difference between these two variants is, however, significant F (3, 353) = 55.419, p = 0.000. Unlike

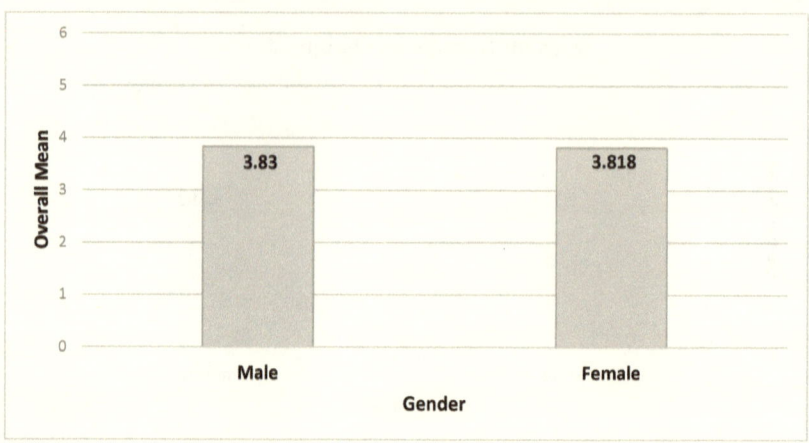

Figure 5.5
Overall gender effect.

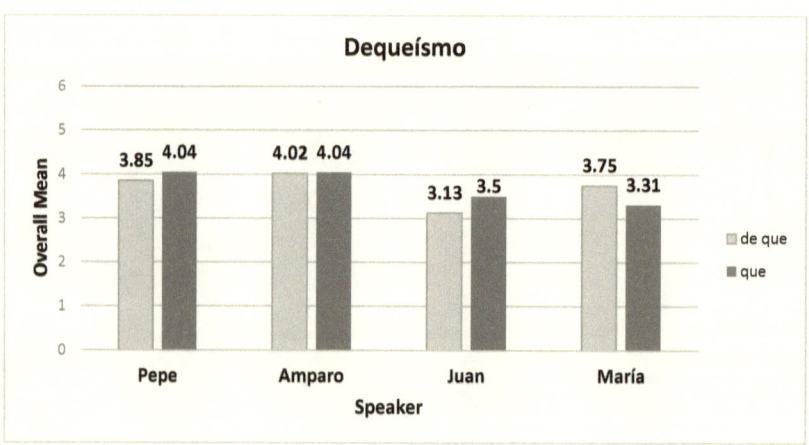

Figure 5.6
Evaluations for presence and absence of de ((de)queísmo) among speakers.

the (de)queísmo variable, for the DOM and present vs. imperfect subjunctive variables, specific trends are unclear given the diversity of evaluations. In the case of the present and imperfect subjunctive variable (Figure 5.8), only Juan shows a significant distinction between the "standard" and "non-standard" variants $F (1, 71) = 8.195$, $p = 0.006$. Pepe, Amparo, and María obtain non-significant results (Pepe $F [1, 71] = 2.878$, $p = 0.094$; Amparo $F [1, 71] = 0.896$, $p = 0.347$; María $F [1, 71] = 0.737$, $p = 0.394$). Moreover,

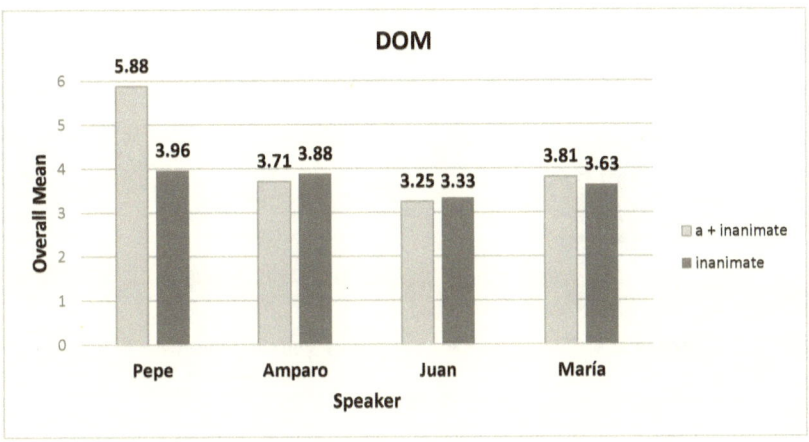

Figure 5.7
Evaluations for presence and absence of *a* (DOM) among speakers.

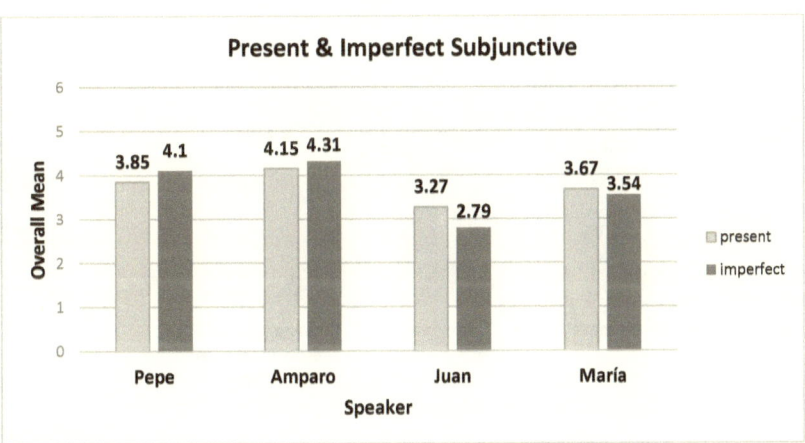

Figure 5.8
Evaluations for present and imperfect subjunctive among speakers.

the overall difference between these variants is significant $F(3, 353) = 3.314$, $p = 0.02$. Finally, the variants are analyzed with respect to the attitudinal spheres personal competence and socioeconomic status, personal integrity, and personal attractiveness. For *(de)queísmo*, the differences between the evaluations that have been assigned to the two variants are not significant in any of the three spheres (Figure 5.9), and it seems that listeners evaluate the "standard" and "non-standard" variants equally positively. Therefore,

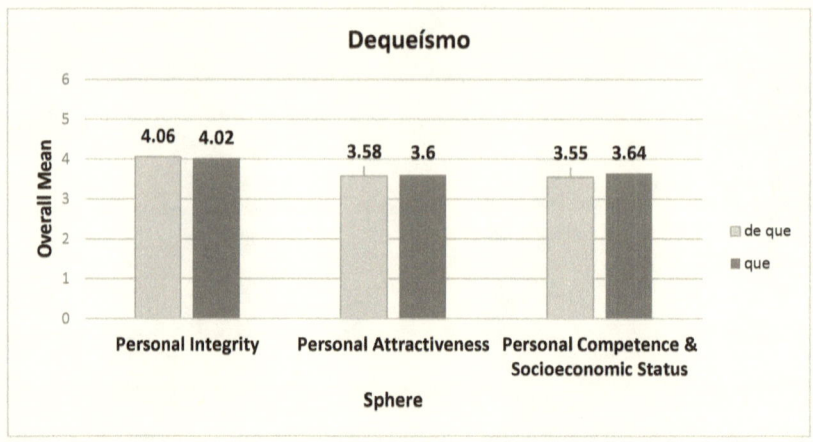

Figure 5.9
Evaluations for presence and absence of *de* (*(de)queísmo*) among spheres.

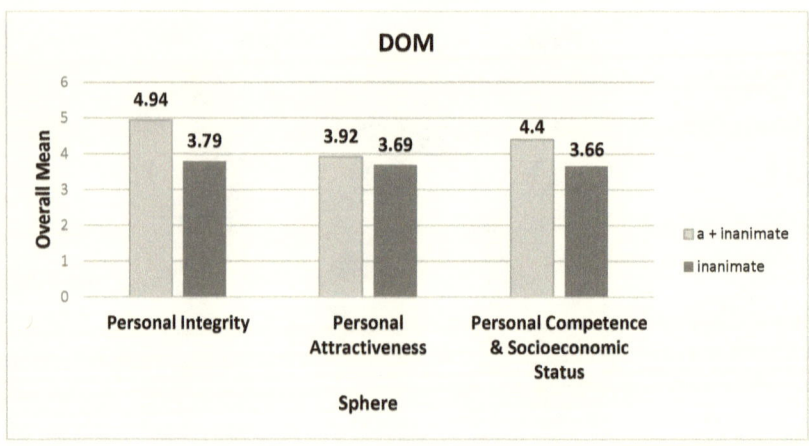

Figure 5.10
Evaluations for presence and absence of *a* (DOM) among spheres.

the mixed model analysis determines that the personal integrity $F(1, 71) = 0.051$, $p = 0.822$, personal attractiveness $F(1, 71) = 0.009$, $p = 0.927$, and personal competence and socioeconomic status spheres $F(1, 167) = 0.329$, $p = 0.567$ are not statistically significant. In the case of DOM (Figure 5.10), two spheres are significant in our analysis: personal integrity $F(1, 94) = 10.05$, $p = 0.002$ and personal competence and socioeconomic status $F(1, 167) = 11.239$, $p = 0.001$. On the other hand, personal attractiveness does not seem to

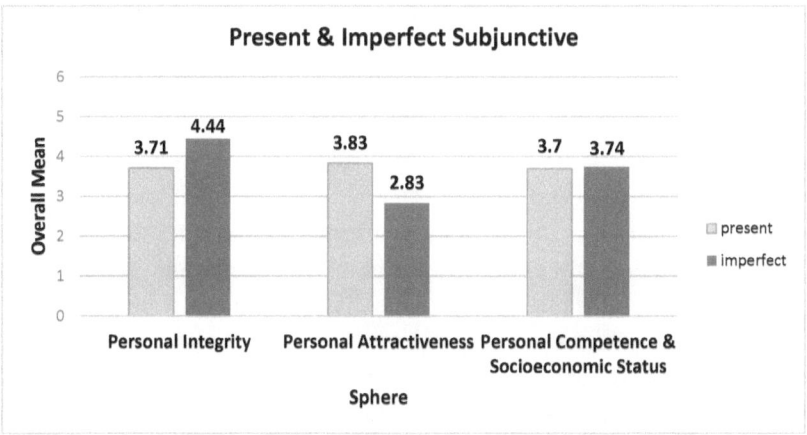

Figure 5.11
Evaluations for present and imperfect subjunctive among spheres.

be significant $F(1, 71) = 1.673$, $p = 0.2$. Still, in all spheres, listeners provided more positive evaluations for the "non-standard" variant *a* + inanimate. In the last figure (Figure 5.11) it can be observed that listeners evaluated the imperfect more positively for the spheres of personal integrity and personal competence and socioeconomic status. However, they evaluated the use of the present with higher values in the personal attractiveness sphere. While the personal competence and socioeconomic status sphere is not significant $F(1, 167) = 0.12$, $p = 0.729$, the personal integrity $F(1, 71) = 10.917$, $p = 0.001$, and personal attractiveness spheres $F(1, 71) = 23.667$, $p = 0.000$ show statistically significant differences among variants. These results suggest that participants are not conscious of these phenomena or alternatively that the variants examined here, in spite of their traditional treatment as representing "non-standard" language use, are not stigmatized among young Bonaerenses.

6. Discussion

The results of the mixed model statistical analysis presented here provide novel perspectives regarding speech community awareness of and attitudes toward *(de)queísmo*, the DOM of inanimates, and the present versus imperfect subjunctive. Although the existence of these morphosyntactic variables is attested to in previous works, little is known of the social evaluations associated with their use, particularly in the context of Buenos Aires. These insights respond to the call of authors such as Díaz-Campos and Killam (2012) for research related to the ability of sociolinguistic variables to trigger attitudinal reactions. As these authors acknowledge, there is a need in the field for perception studies of variables that may exist below the level of speaker consciousness (Díaz-Campos & Killam 2012). Our results suggest that *(de)queísmo* and the present versus imperfect subjunctive fit this description in that the difference in evaluations between the "standard" and "non-standard" variants of these variables was not significant. That is to say, participants seemed not to perceive the difference between the "standard" and "non-standard" variants and did not, therefore, consider these notions when evaluating the speakers. Interestingly, DOM with inanimates, perhaps the phenomenon that has received the least attention in the linguistic literature, did show statistically significant differences between the presence and absence of the preposition *a*. In fact, participants evaluated those recordings containing this non-normative object marking more positively than their "standard" counterparts. While empirical data regarding the frequency of use of DOM with inanimates is lacking, it may be that this phenomenon has come to be considered part of the norm in Buenos Aires Spanish.

A further contribution of these data is related to the attitudinal spheres of personal competence and economic status, personal integrity, and personal attractiveness. Although it has traditionally been believed that speakers using "standard" variants receive more positive evaluations of personal competence and economic status and that those who produce "non-standard" variants are evaluated more positively in terms of personal integrity and personal attractiveness, the results of the present study suggest that such a conceptualization may require further investigation as it does not seem to hold in many cases. In the case of DOM, for example, it is the "non-standard" use of accusative *a* that is most positively ranked in all three attitudinal spheres. Therefore, in these data, participant evaluations are seen to be quite complex, depending not only on the perceptual salience of a linguistic variable, but also on the speech community's unique attitudes, both conscious and unconscious, toward that variable. Similar results were obtained in Díaz-Campos and Killam (2012), where the elision and retention of /r/ and /d/ also defied this traditional understanding of attitudinal spheres within the matched-guise method.

The discussion that follows will relate the most important findings of the present study to the research questions and hypotheses as originally posed. First, responding to the question of whether any of the variants analyzed show social stratification by their rankings, it was shown that, in the case of *(de)queísmo*, both the "standard" and "non-standard" variants were evaluated equally positively, with no significant difference between them. This suggests that no stigmatization for *(de)queísmo* exists in this speech community, as young Bonaerenses in the present study perceive no difference between variants. For DOM, the "non-standard" variant is ranked more positively in all three attitudinal spheres, although only personal integrity and personal competence and socioeconomic status were significant. It appears, then, that participants are conscious to some extent of the use or non-use of inanimate *a*-marking and that this consciousness does translate to social attitudes toward other members of the speech community. With regard to the present versus imperfect subjunctive, the "standard" variant of the imperfect was evaluated more positively for personal integrity and personal competence and socioeconomic status, although only the sphere of personal integrity was significant. The use of the present subjunctive was ranked more positively for personal attractiveness, which represented a significant difference. Such a division between attitudinal spheres indicates that social stratification exists for this variable as well. If these data are representative of Buenos Aires Spanish, then those speakers who utilize the imperfect subjunctive in contexts such as the stimulus phrase tested here will be viewed by their peers as more honest and perhaps more intelligent and/or wealthy, whereas those who use the present subjunctive will be seen as more friendly. Regarding this research question, then, the original hypothesis was only partially confirmed, as those stimuli containing "standard" variants were not consistently evaluated more positively than those containing "non-standard" variants. However, as previously discussed, these evaluations are subject to the awareness participants have of variants, as well as the extent to which variants are incorporated into the norm of a specific speech community.

As for the question of "non-standard" variants and their ranking, it is clear that the evaluations are not equal across variables. Whereas the "non-standard" variant of *(de)queísmo* was not distinguished from the "standard" variant, evaluative distinctions were made between the "standard" and "non-standard" variants of DOM and the present versus imperfect subjunctive. Yet the patterns of evaluation were not the same for both variables. In the case of DOM, the "non-standard" variant was evaluated more positively in all three attitudinal spheres (although only two were statistically significant), whereas the present subjunctive was evaluated more positively for personal attractiveness but not in terms of personal integrity or personal competence and socioeconomic class. Although the original hypothesis did correctly predict that the present subjunctive and the "non-standard" DOM of inanimates would be evaluated more positively than the "non-standard" variant of *(de)queísmo* due to more extensive daily use and greater incorporation in the Buenos Aires speech community, in the case of the present versus imperfect subjunctive, the present subjunctive received more positive evaluations in only one of the three attitudinal spheres, that of personal attractiveness.

In addition to those questions where participants were asked to listen to recordings and evaluate speakers, an open-ended question was also provided for participants to make any additional comments and voice their opinions or concerns about the instrument. Less than half of participants opted to make such comments, and the vast majority of those that commented made mention of prosodic differences between speakers or the difficulty in determining someone's social class or intelligence based on such limited stimuli. Only one individual made mention of a difference between phrases, noting the difference between the "standard" and "non-standard" variants of *(de)queísmo* and calling the use of *de que* an "error." The fact that only one participant noted this difference, and that several participants said they didn't understand why they were repeatedly asked to listen to the same sentence, corroborates the assertion that participants do not perceive the use of "standard" and "non-standard" forms in the case of these particular variables. This finding suggests that linguists' perceptions of variants as "standard" or "non-standard" may not always align with a speech community's own evaluation of variants. However, additional information regarding the social status of all three morphosyntactic variables in the specific context of Buenos Aires is needed to complement the attitudinal data presented here.

7. Conclusions and Further Research

The present study has provided quantitative evidence of the attitudes of young speakers of Bonaerense Spanish toward three morphosyntactic variables whose social evaluations had not yet been fully described. In addition, the results presented here provide further evidence of the utility of the matched-guise technique for the examination of morphosyntactic features. In the present study, statistically significant voice effects were present for all four speakers. While other authors, such as Campbell-Kibler (2006) and Díaz-Campos and Killam (2012), have experienced similar effects in varying degrees, voice effects are difficult if not impossible to foresee and avoid and therefore may be considered a disadvantage within the matched-guise methodology. Still this technique allows linguists to examine speaker attitudes toward variation in a fine-grained and sociolinguistically appropriate way. In the present study, the matched-guise methodology allowed us to highlight subtle speaker reactions to "standard" and "non-standard" variants and is thus a promising avenue for future research on linguistic variables speakers may not be aware of or that are not easily classified in terms of prestige or stigma.

Future studies should examine native speaker attitudes in other speech communities of the Spanish-speaking world regarding these and other morphosyntactic features. Further research is also needed regarding the frequency, domains of use, and factors conditioning the variation of both DOM with inanimate direct objects and the present versus imperfect subjunctive. The variable use of the accusative *a* to mark topicalized inanimate DOs has received particularly little attention, thus a better understanding of its linguistic and extralinguistic constraints may shed light on its positive evaluations in all attitudinal spheres as obtained in the present study, an unexpected finding from a prescriptive point of view. Regarding instruments employing the matched-guise technique, additional means of ensuring that speaker recordings are similar in terms of pitch, speech rate, and tone should be explored in order to avoid voice quality effects. Finally, additional research is needed regarding native speaker awareness and unawareness of linguistic variables, as a complete understanding of speaker attitudes cannot be achieved without such information.

Acknowledgments

We would like to thank Manuel Díaz-Campos for his guidance and support throughout this research and the Indiana Statistical Consulting Center for their valuable advice. Any errors are our own.

6
Voseo Vocatives and Interjections in Montevideo Spanish

María Irene Moyna

1. Introduction

This study presents a comprehensive contrastive description of two vocative particles in Montevideo Spanish, *che* and *bo*, including their possible syntactico-pragmatic value and the sociolinguistic and attitudinal factors determining their use. Briefly put, like other Río de la Plata varieties, Montevideo Spanish has a vocative form *che* 'hey!,' but it also features a second vocative, /bo/ (spelled *bo* or *vo*) 'id.,' which is restricted to Uruguay and etymologically related to the *vos* pronoun.

Whereas *che* has been described in some detail (Bertolotti 2011), the current analysis provides the first thorough description of *bo*, a vocative and interjection which has until now only been mentioned sporadically and tangentially (Bertolotti 2010: 85; 2011: 36, for Uruguay, Rivera-Mills 2011: 100, for Salvadorans in the United States). The description is illustrated with data from online forums and discussion groups, since the register of computer-mediated communication provides the necessary conditions for the appearance of *bo*. The marginal status of *bo* in the scholarly literature contrasts with the extensive descriptions of *vos*, the informal singular pronoun with which it is etymologically related (Behares 1981; Bertolotti & Coll 2003; Elizaincín & Díaz 1981; Fontanella de Weinberg 1970, 1971, 1976, 1977, 1979, 1987, 1992, 1993, 1996; Moyna & Ceballos 2008; Mendoza 2005; Páez

Urdaneta 1981; Rona 1967; Siracusa 1977; Steffen 2010; Weyers 2009, 2012). Given the historical link between *bo* and the pronoun *vos*, this analysis is an important piece in the overall description of the second-person paradigm of Montevideo Spanish.

This study sought to ascertain who claims to use which form with what type of addressee and in what situation. Additionally, the social distribution of the two vocative particles was analyzed through surveys of reported usage in Montevideo (n = 367) and through explicit attitude interviews (n = 17). *Bo* was reported more frequently among young male speakers, when the addressee was also a young male and when the interaction was impolite. Older female respondents rejected the *bo* vocative as inappropriate, whereas younger speakers of both genders showed either neutral or positive attitudes. The quantitative results were corroborated by the qualitative data. The *bo* vocative is thus shown to retain pragmatic features that the pronoun *vos* has lost in Río de la Plata Spanish (henceforth RPS), but which are still apparent in other dialects (e.g., Chile, Torrejón 1986, 2010).

The study shows one specific way in which language form and language usage are inextricably linked. In particular, it demonstrates the connection between the aspects of morphology that are of interest to theoretical linguistics (grammatical category, core/periphery relations) and those that are the central concern of sociolinguistics (variation by social affiliation and situation) in a process of change. Structurally, the study shows a connection between second-person pronouns and other grammatical elements, such as particles with vocative or expressive function outside the scope of the sentence. The study of *bo* thus shows a formal pathway of change, as a sentence constituent (the subject pronoun) gives rise to a vocative element. Moreover, the analysis of the sociolinguistic distribution and spread of innovative vocatives at the expense of older ones shows the origin and development of subtle identity markers in areas that are close geographically and culturally but separated by national boundaries.

The chapter is structured as follows. Section 2 presents some background on vocatives and interjections, considered in general and for the specific case of RPS. This section also presents new data on the distribution and meaning of *bo* in Montevideo Spanish, as well as evidence of awareness and attitudes of speakers toward its usage. Section 3 presents the quantitative and qualitative methodology employed to analyze the variation between *che* and *bo,* including the survey sample, questionnaire items, data collection and quantification, as well as the attitude interview questions, format, transcription, and coding procedures. Section 4 presents the results for both the quantitative and qualitative portions of the study. Section 5 discusses the results and Section 6 concludes the study by presenting some areas for future enquiry.

2. Vocatives

2.1. BETWEEN SYNTAX AND PRAGMATICS

Vocatives have been defined as particles with appellative function (Bühler 1934), that is, whose purpose is to invite a person to assume the role of addressee (Lyons 1977). In Andersen's (2012) taxonomy, vocatives are classified mainly on the basis of Jakobson's (1960) conative and phatic functions, often with an admixture of expressive elements. Andersen includes three types of conative vocatives, namely, openers, which invite the addressee to be an interlocutor; summons, which request the addressee's presence; and calls, which seek to find the addressee through verbal contact (cf. alerters in Alba-Juez [2009] and calls in Zwicky [1974]). Additionally, Andersen describes phatic vocatives, whose overall purpose is to continue the communication by creating an atmosphere of solidarity and empathy (Zwicky's [1974] addresses). This second group can be subdivided into two types, depending on whether they show the speaker's continued communicative intent or assure the addressee of the speaker's attention.

In terms of the structures that can be used as vocatives, many possibilities have been identified, including second-person pronouns, proper names, or noun phrases that denote the addressee's age (child, young lady, Sp. *pibe* 'child,' *viejo* 'old man') profession (professor, doctor, coach), or rank or title (sergeant, Sp. *jefe* 'chief'). In some languages it is possible to employ descriptive predications, such as locative or sociative descriptions ('you in the back row,' 'you with the water gun') (Andersen 2012: 138).

The vocative function is associated in some languages with specific nominal morphology such as affixation or declension. However, it has been noted that the so-called vocative "case" is quite different from other types of nominal case: the vocative is not a sentence constituent, nor is it governed by a verb or preposition as other cases are (Daniel & Spencer 2009). Structurally, vocative noun phrases have restrictions and particularities that distinguish them from argument noun phrases, such as their incapacity to co-occur with articles and their accentual and other phonetic distinguishing features (Moro 2003). Their structural isolation from the sentence is marked prosodically, since vocatives are both preceded and followed by pauses (Alonso Cortés 1999; Downing 1969; Moro 2003; Schaden 2010; Zwicky 1974).

In syntactic accounts, vocatives are often attributed to a functional projection defined by a deictic feature (Espinal 2013). Some analyses include the vocative phrase in its own functional domain, the Role Phrase, extending the computations of core syntax to the left-edge domain through a Speech Act Shell (Hill 2007). This extension recognizes that although the vocative may appear as peripheral when one considers sentence syntax, at the pragmatic level it occupies a central position (Andersen 2012: 156).

Finally, vocatives often have sociolinguistic value, since they provide information about the speaker's attitudes toward the discourse and the addressee (Zwicky 1974) and are thus closely related to politeness (Alonso Cortés 1999: 2037). With few exceptions, vocatives are an explicit expression of the familiar register and casual conversational style (Andersen 2012: 153).

2.2. VOCATIVES IN RPS

For the specific case of RPS, several previous studies have noted the existence of *che* 'hey!', the most common informal vocative particle in the dialect (Bertolotti 2010; Malmberg 1964; Rona 1963; Rosenblat 1962), spread over a *Sprachbund* that extends into Paraguay and Brazil. Those studies focus on etymology, in particular whether *che* can be traced back to Spanish (Rosenblat 1962) or indigenous (Guaraní) roots (Bertolotti 2010; Rona 1963), a matter that is orthogonal to the present analysis. Of interest here are the grammatical functions of *che*, which Bertolotti (2010) summarizes as follows: (a) a determiner of a noun phrase, *che Juan* 'hey, Juan'; (b) an appositive to the second-person pronoun *vos*, *che vos* 'hey, you'; (c) a particle outside the clause ¿*vamos, che?* 'shall we go, then?'; and (d) an interjection indicating annoyance, ¡*Che!* 'C'mon!'

In Montevideo the story does not end there. Alongside the pan-RPS *che* there is another form, /bo/, variously represented with the spelling *vo* or *bo*, which has received a great deal less scholarly attention. In contrast to *che*, whose origin has been disputed, the origin of the vocative *bo* is transparently the pronoun *vos*. Thus, the *Diccionario del Español del Uruguay* tersely defines *vos* as "forma de la segunda persona del singular que cumple función de sujeto, **vocativo** o término de complemento" ('second-person singular form that has the function of subject, **vocative**, or prepositional complement'; my translation and emphasis) (Academia Nacional de Letras

2011: 558), conflating the vocative and pronominal categories under a single entry and spelling. The phonological similarities between both items and their common semantic features of second-person singular informal deixis strongly support this analysis. One could also note the parallels in non-*voseante* dialects of Spanish, which frequently employ the second-person singular pronoun *tú* as a vocative particle: ¡*Tú! ¿Qué miras?* 'You! What are you looking at?' In what follows, I assume no further evidence is needed that the *bo* vocative particle is etymologically related to the pronoun.

In spite of the commonalities between the *vos* pronoun and the *bo* particle, they can also be distinguished by a number of phonological, intonational, and syntactico-semantic features, as shown in 2.1. The first difference is segmental. Standard Montevideo Spanish is a weakening dialect where final /s/ is frequently aspirated in specific contexts such as before a pause (1a) or before a consonant (1b), but not before a vowel, even across word boundaries (1c). Total elision of syllable-final /s/ is possible only in non-standard speech and is highly stigmatized. By contrast, the vocative particle is invariably /bo/ and never exhibits a final consonantal segment, regardless of its phonetic context and speaker social variables (2). In other words, the vocative is the result of truncation, a process with parallels in other languages (cf. Andersen [2012] for Russian).

(1) a. *Te quiero a vo[s]/vo[h]*. (non-standard *vo*[ø])
'It is you I love.'
b. *Vo[h] comés demasiado*. (non-standard: *vo*[ø])
'You eat too much.'
c. *Vo[s] abrís la puerta*. (non-standard: *vo*[ø])
'You open the door.'

(2) a. ¡*No vengas, bo!* (*vo[s], *vo[h])
'Don't come, man!'
b. ¡*Bo* (*bo[s], *bo[h]) *Marcelo! ¡No te hagas el loco!*
'Yo, Marcelo! Don't act all crazy!'
c. ¡*Bo* (*bo[s], *bo[h]) *Alejandro! ¡No te hagas el loco!*
'Yo, Alejandro! Don't act all crazy!'

A second difference is intonational. The pronoun is a sentence constituent and, as such, not separated from its predicate (3), whereas the vocative has a special intonational contour, typically preceded and followed by pauses isolating it from other constituents (4). When it appears mid-sentence, it is flanked by parenthetical pauses (5) (Alonso Cortés 1999).

(3) ¿*Vos* *(#) tenés miedo?
'Are you afraid?'

(4) ¡*Bo*! # No seas cagón.
'Hey! Don't be a wimp.'

(5) No se puede creer #*bo*# que nunca llegues en hora.
'It's unbelievable, man, that you can never be on time.'

There are also syntactico-semantic distinctions between *vos* and *bo*. The *vos* pronoun is a sentence constituent that serves as an argument of the verb or is selected by a preposition. Thus, for example, the declarative sentence in (6) and the imperative sentence in (7) have *vos* pronoun subjects. On the other hand, the vocative particle *bo* is devoid of a thematic role. It may appear by itself (8), as a determiner to another nominal or adjectival vocative (9a, b), or itself selected by another vocative particle (10).

(6) ***Vos*** pensaste que yo era igual a todas y yo pensé que eras diferente a los demás. (Google)
'You thought I was the same as all the others and I thought you were different from the rest.'

(7) ***Vos*** dejate de joder y de mentirme. (Google)
'You stop messing around and lying to me.'

(8) ***Bo***, ¿qué te pasa? ¿Se te recalentó el motor? (Google)
'Hey, what's wrong with you? Did your engine overheat?'

(9) a. ***Bo***, Sergio, ¿sos algo de Claudio I.? (Google)
'Yo, Sergio, are you any relation of Claudio I.'s?'
b. ¡***Bo***! Petisa, ¡quién dijo que no tenemos glamour! (Google)
'Yo! Shortie, who said we have no glamour?!'

(10) **Che, bo**, gil, dame tu caravana. (Google)
'Hey, you, dummie, give me your earring.'

Another difference between the *vos* pronoun and *bo* vocative is number agreement. Whereas the pronoun *vos* is only possible with second-person singular verbs (11 a, b), the vocative can also have a plural addressee (12 a, b). The vocative exhibits overall semantic impoverishment, with parallels in other languages (Abreu de Carvalho [2013] for Portuguese).

(11) a. *¿**Vos** sos bobo?*
'Are you-2s stupid?'
b. *¿****Vos** son bobos?*
'Are you-2pl stupid-2pl?'

(12) a. **Bo**, *vengan a Uruguay.* (Google)
'Hey, come-2pl to Uruguay.'
b. **Bo**, *ya se enteraron. No lo puedo creer. No se puede tener un secreto acá en Uruguay.* (Google)
'Yo, you-2pl have heard already. It's hard to believe. One can't keep a secret here in Uruguay.'

Finally, *bo* can have expressive or mirative rather than appellative functions, in which case it is better described as an interjection (Alonso Cortés 1999: 4029). In other words, there are uses of the particle *bo* that do not require an addressee for the speech act to be felicitous, a process with parallels in other languages (Andersen 2012: 132). When thus used, *bo* conveys annoyance and may appear in positions other than the left margin (13).

(13) a. *¡**Bo**, qué calor!* (Google)
'Damn, it's hot!'
b. *Pero qué joda*, **bo**, *parece cosa de locos.* (Google)
'You must be kidding me, man, it's hard to believe.'
c. *¡No se puede creer*, **bo**! *¡Ustedes son capaces de todo!* (Google)
'It's unbelievable, man! You guys will stop at nothing!'

Speakers are acutely aware of the differences mentioned above between the vocative/interjection and the pronoun, even if they cannot articulate them explicitly. Their intuitions often manifest themselves as uncertainty about the spelling one should use to distinguish the two forms (14). In fact, online discussion groups sometimes offer fanciful origins for the vocative, such as a shortening of the noun *botija* 'young boy' (*Wikipedia*, Vo), which is used as a vocative in its own right (as are *pibe* 'boy,' *gurí* 'boy,' *valor* 'value, i.e., man,' *nene* 'kiddo,' and many other common human denotation nouns in RPS). Without wishing to support any of these rather improbable etymologies, they are worth mentioning because they provide evidence of the considerable semantic and formal distance between the vocative and the pronoun, even for laypeople. Because of the highly informal registers in which *bo* appears, it is written infrequently (15, 16), and even today its spelling has not stabilized. However, *bo* appears to be gaining ground over *vo* and is thus the orthography selected here.

(14) *¿Como se escribe **bo** o **vo**? Como buen uruguayo que soy, utilizo mucho esta palabra. Pero nunca me puse a pensar bien como es que se escribe.*
'How does one spell it, *bo* or *vo*? As any good Uruguayan, I use this word a lot. But I've never stopped to think how you spell it.' (Yahoo Argentina)

(15) *Che, **bo**, che bolichero / dame una grapa fiada, una prestada.* (Leo Maslíah, *Che Bo*)
'Hey, you, hey, bartender, give me a shot of grappa free of charge, front me one.'

(16) ***Bo** cartero por favor / no te hagas el loco y dámelo / una carta, una postal /que si no yo me pongo a llorar.* (El Cuarteto de Nos, *Bo cartero*)
'Hey, postman, please, don't mess with me and give me a letter, a postcard; if you don't, I'll cry.'

Let us now consider the place of origin of *bo*, the extent of its geographic spread, and the awareness that speakers have of this dialectal distribution. The Río de la Plata area has an undisputed center of linguistic innovation, Buenos Aires, which tends to be where changes are first attested. This should come as no surprise: the influence of large cities on mid-size cities is well documented for Spanish in the Americas (Lipski 2002). For the specific case of Buenos Aires and Montevideo, this influence has long been recognized by linguists (Bertolotti 2011) and decried by non-linguists (Kühl de Mones 1981: 48). However, *bo* is an exception: an innovation that originated on the eastern bank of the Río de la Plata and has, as far as we can tell, stayed there. This is confirmed by Buenos Aires speakers, who comment explicitly on the usage of *bo* (17) or make it a trope for Uruguayanness (18) and also by Uruguayans abroad, who have become aware of this peculiarity of their speech (19). In fact, some fictional accounts produced on the Argentine side of the river use *bo* to distinguish characters from Uruguay from their Argentine counterpart (20).

(17) *Estoy en Montevideo, donde todos dicen "**vo**" en medio de las palabras.... Mejor me voy a la rambla, **vo**.* (Zanoni 2006)
'I'm here in Montevideo, where everyone says "vo" in the middle of their words [*sic*].... I'd rather go walk along the seafront, yo.'

(18) *De uruguayo a uruguayo, de **vo**' a **vo**,' Lugano es una vieja y rubia debilidad de Francescoli.* (Cogan 2013)
'From one Uruguayan to another, from vo to vo, Lugano [a defender in the Uruguayan team] is an old blond crush of Francescoli's [former Uruguayan star, now soccer coach].'

(19) *En Uruguay es muy común que se utilice la expresión "**bo**" para dirigirnos a otra persona conocida. Es como decir "oye, Juan" o "che, Juan," decir "**bo**, Juan" es lo mismo. El "oye" no se utiliza en Uruguay.* (Univisión Foros 2010)
'In Uruguay it's very common to use the expression "bo" to address someone we know. It's like saying "oye, Juan" ("hey") or "che, Juan" ("yo"); saying "bo, Juan" is the same thing. We don't use "oye" in Uruguay.'

(20) U: *¡No se puede creer, **bo**, ustedes son capaces de todo! Pero no me importa. ¡Vas a morir!*
A: *¿Pero por qué, **che**, boludo? ¿Por lo de reshién? Uuuhhh, buchón, shacate la gorra, shacate.* (Weblogs *Clarín*)
'U: It's unbelievable, bo, you guys will stop at nothing! But it doesn't matter. You will die anyway!
A: But why, che? For what I just did? Wow, man, take off your cap!'

To summarize this section, the repertoire of Montevideo Spanish includes two very frequent vocative/interjective particles, *che* and *bo*. The former, which can be convincingly traced back to Guaraní (Bertolotti 2010; Rona 1963), is common across a vast *Sprachbund* that includes Argentinian and Paraguayan varieties and southern Brazilian Portuguese (*tchê*). On the other hand, *bo* shares enough semantic and formal features with the second-person pronoun *vos* that its etymology is not a matter of much serious dispute. However, its phonological and syntactico-semantic characteristics are distinct enough for speakers to recognize their categorial differences. There is also evidence that *bo* is a development of the eastern bank of the Río de la Plata and, as such, a Uruguayan innovation that acts as an identity marker for the smaller speech community in the face of the metropolis on the west bank.

Montevideo speakers thus have two informal vocative/interjective particles to choose from, *che* and *bo*. The rest of the chapter is devoted to ascertaining the social and pragmatic conditions determining variation between them. In the next section I present the methodology followed by the quantitative and the qualitative analyses.

3. Methodology

3.1. QUESTIONNAIRE

The quantitative data for the present study come from a large-scale survey carried out in Uruguay between July and August of 2012. A paper version of the questionnaire was given to individuals and to groups in several educational institutions. An identical digital version was made available through *Survey Monkey* and disseminated through social networks by email and listservs.

The questionnaire included a sociolinguistic section followed by questions on second-person verbal usage. The social variables of participants were ascertained through a set of questions about age, gender, provenance, and socioeconomic class. This was followed by thirty-four questions worded as situations, where participants were given options to choose what they would say. Only four of the survey questions inquired specifically about the usage of vocative forms relevant to this study. These questions presented parallel situations that differed in the gender of the hypothetical addressee and the degree of politeness, so that, for both male and female addressees, one of the items presented a neutral situation, while the other was impolite (cf. Appendix 1).

Possible answers included a *bo* variant, a *che* variant, and a third variant meant to convey formality (*oiga*). Participants were given the option of choosing up to two forms or to fill in their own responses if none of those given reflected their usage.

3.2. PARTICIPANTS

In all, 579 Uruguayan participants completed the survey; of those, 367 were from Montevideo and are thus considered here. The sample was divided by gender and age (18–30, 31–40, 41–50, 51 and older). Although some social information was obtained, the sample was quite homogeneous in educational attainment; as a consequence, class was not considered as a variable.

It must be noted that establishing provenance is not always straightforward, since Uruguayan society is quite mobile (Veiga 2010: 41); in view of that, three questions in the survey helped ascertain whether respondents were from Montevideo. The first inquired about place of birth, the second about the location where the respondent had lived the longest, and the third about current residence. Respondents were considered to be from Montevideo if they had been born and resided there for most of their lives. People who had moved to Montevideo before the age of eighteen were also included. For highly mobile respondents (only 1.6% of the sample), Montevideo was considered their provenance if it was their place of longest residence.

3.3. QUANTIFICATION OF RESPONSES

To calculate the usage of each form, totals were calculated for each of the four questions. In the tabulation, *bo* was coded as B, *che* answers as C, and *oiga* answers as O. If a participant chose two possible categories, those answers were coded as mixed and identified with the specific combination selected (i.e., B, C; B, O; C, O). This was considered preferable to splitting each answer between the two variants chosen, given that it was a clearer and more faithful representation of the degree to which respondents were aware of variability.

Filled-in answers were considered equivalent to the response that employed the same vocative category. Thus, for example, if the answer written contained *bo*, it was coded as B. A subset of the filled-in answers could not be used, either because they did not contain any vocative or because they employed neither of the two options (e.g., ¡M'hijo, otra vez! 'Child, again, really?!).

3.4. STATISTICAL ANALYSIS

For the statistical analysis, categorical data analysis methods were used. It was assumed that class was uniform across respondents, given the limited variation in educational attainment in the sample. The method used was a chi-square test of associations, which tested the use of *bo* and *che* in each type of context (neutral vs. polite), for each addressee and for each speaker age group. To ascertain the effect of speaker gender on vocative choice, odds ratios were calculated for each addressee/pragmatic context combination. Results were considered statistically significant at p-values equal or smaller than 0.05.

3.5. ATTITUDE INTERVIEWS

To supplement the snapshot provided by the survey, attitude interviews were carried out between July and August 2012. Of a total of forty-seven interviewees, this study reports exclusively on the seventeen respondents from Montevideo. Participants were selected using a snowballing technique, starting with friends, neighbors, and acquaintances who then provided contact information for other potential interviewees. The sample was again quite homogeneous socially, with mostly middle-class speakers.

Interviews typically lasted between thirty minutes and an hour; most of them were individual, but on one occasion two participants were interviewed together. Each interview included questions about usage and attitudes about second-person singular forms in general, with some items focused specifically on the vocative particles *che* and *bo*. Although interviews were planned in advance, the questions were asked at different points, following the natural flow of the conversation.

All interviews were recorded on a Marantz PDM 620 digital recorder and saved as audiofiles. These were then transcribed in their entirety by a professional transcription service (*Caption Synch* at *automaticsync.com/captionsync/*). Each transcription was then checked and corrected for accuracy by a Spanish native speaker familiar with the variety and by the researcher. Only thirteen interviews had usable information concerning *bo/che*. Of those, six interviewees were men and seven women; four were between eighteen and thirty, four between forty-one and fifty, and five over fifty-one. Five were professionals or retired professionals, four were university students, and four were employees or business owners (cf. Appendix 2).

The participants' answers were coded for information on the following items: meaning attributed to *bo* and *che*; claiming of *bo/che*; perceived distribution by speaker gender, age, class, and geographical provenance; attitudes; and awareness of the provenance and identity status of vocative forms.

4. Results

This section presents the results for both the reported usage and the qualitative interviews, starting with the quantitative data and moving then to the analysis of interview responses.

4.1. REPORTED USAGE SURVEY

Survey data showed that the presence of vocatives (either *bo* or *che*) was perceived as more informal and less polite than their absence (Figure 6.1) and was influenced both by situational context and interlocutor. Participants claimed that they used vocatives less frequently in neutral contexts than in impolite contexts and less when addressing females than males. Overall, vocative claiming was highest (71.1%) in impolite speech addressed to males and lowest (54.2%) in neutral speech addressed to women. The differences were statistically significant (Chi-square = 22.6987; p < 0.0001).

In situations when respondents claimed they would use vocatives, *che* was the most frequent across contexts and addressees. It was much more frequent than *bo* in neutral contexts (79.8% when addressing men, 92% when addressing women). *Bo* reporting more than tripled in impolite contexts for male addressees (12.6% to 46.7%) and for female addressees (6% to 19.6%). These

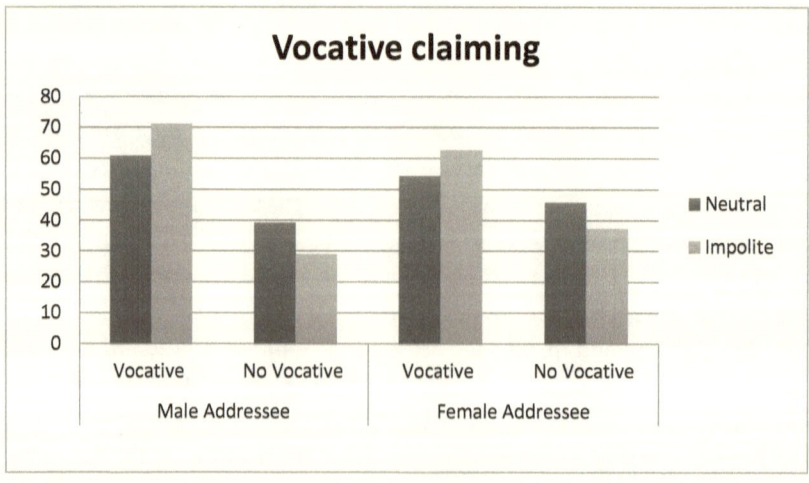

Figure 6.1
Percentage of vocative claiming in neutral and impolite contexts, for male and female addressees (n = 1468).

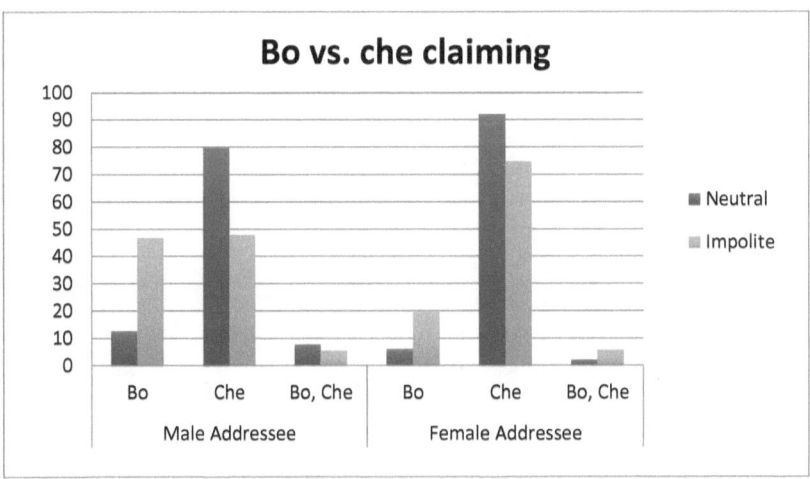

Figure 6.2
Percentage of *bo/che* claiming in neutral and impolite contexts, for male and female addressees (n = 913).

differences were statistically significant (chi-square = 142.6806; p < 0.0001). The gender of the respondent also influenced vocative choice. The odds of *bo* usage by male participants were always higher than for women participants, regardless of addressee gender and pragmatic context. These differences by participant gender were statistically significant for male addressees in neutral contexts (odds ratio = 3.01; p < 0.001), for male addressees in impolite contexts (odds ratio = 2.18; p < 0.01), and for female addressees in impolite contexts (odds ratio = 1.93; p < 0.05), but not for female addressees in neutral contexts (odds ratio = 2.39; p = 0.90) (see Appendix 3). Finally, age of participants also affected vocative choice. The youngest respondents were most likely to claim *bo* usage exclusively or in combination with *che* (32.2% and 8%, respectively). There was a steady decrease in *bo* claiming as age increased (32.2%, 24.6%, 15.5%, and 8.6%), with a corresponding relative increase in *che* claiming. This difference was statistically significant (chi-square = 58.5143; p < 0.00001).

4.2. ANALYSIS OF ATTITUDE QUESTIONNAIRES

The attitude questionnaires confirmed and complemented the quantitative data by providing details about the meanings of *bo* and *che*, the interviewees'

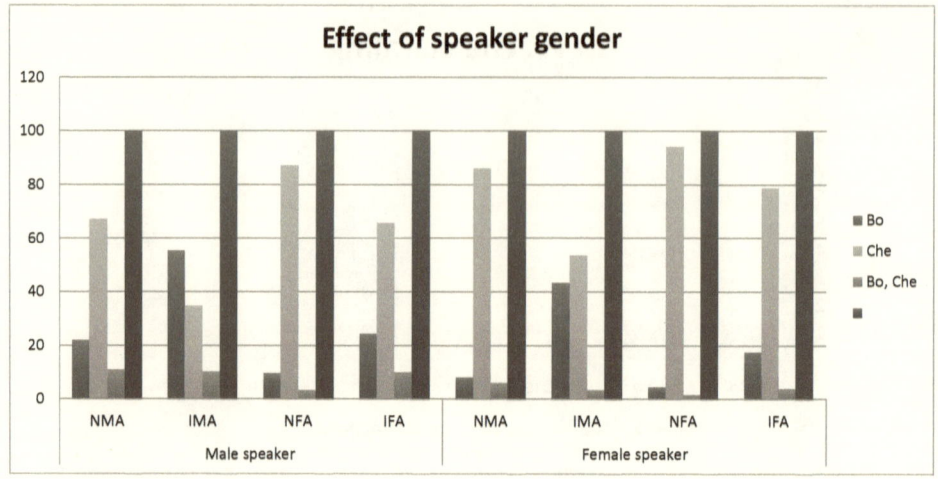

Figure 6.3
Percentage of *bo/che* claiming by gender of speaker in neutral and impolite situations, for male and female addressees (n = 913). Key to table: N = Neutral, I = Impolite, MA = Male Addressee, FA = Female Addressee.

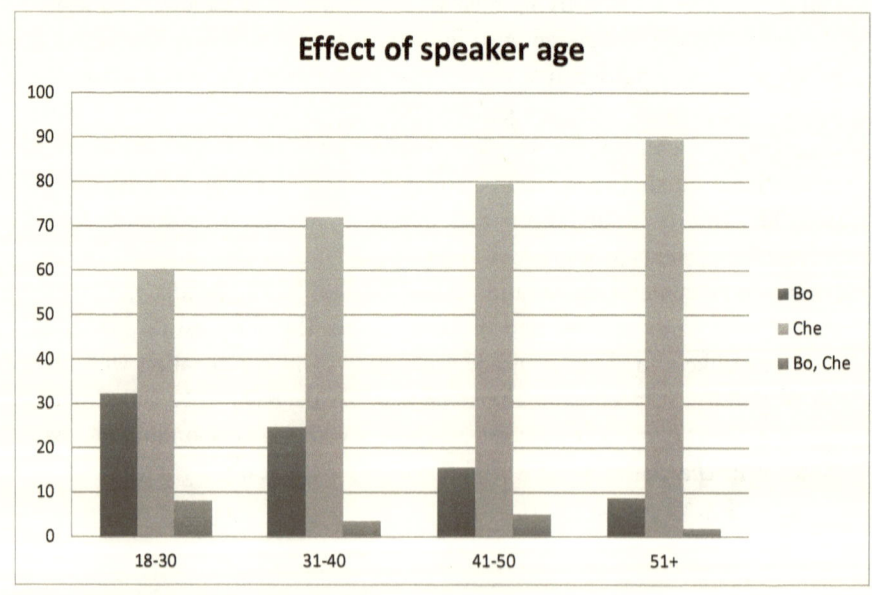

Figure 6.4
Percentage of *bo/che* claiming by age of speaker (n = 913).

own usage of both forms, their impressions about sociolinguistic distribution, register, their attitudes, and their hypotheses about the provenance of these particles. When pertinent, I indicate differences by participants.

In terms of the meaning of *bo* and *che*, most speakers did not give explicit definitions, nor were they able to differentiate between the two semantically. However, some speakers did make explicit distinctions between the vocative functions of *che/bo* and the pronoun *vos* (21). Others emphasized the expressive function of *bo* over the purely vocative (22).

(21) *Pero ese no es el **vos**, ¿eh? . . . Es como un llamado de atención; hay algo que yo quiero decirle especialmente a ella. . . . . Y yo le digo "Ay, **che**, Cristina."*
'That's not the same as *vos*, OK? . . . It's like a call for attention; there is something I want to tell her especially. . . . And I tell her "Oh, hey, Cristina."' (F, 51+, retired professional)

(22) *El **bo** lo uso al final, sin ningún tipo de—No tiene mucho significado, como el po de los chilenos. . . . El **che** lo uso antes de una frase para llamar la atención del interlocutor.* (M, 41–50, university professor)
'I use *bo* at the end, with no . . . it doesn't have much meaning, like the Chilean *po* . . . I use *che* before a clause to call the attention of my interlocutor.'

Most interviewees were not explicit about their usage of vocatives, although some admitted that they had become aware of such usage indirectly through comments by others (23). Typically, women were ready to accept that they used *che* more than they were willing to admit to using *bo*, except those of the youngest generation (24, 25). Only one person expressed negative attitudes toward both *che* and *bo* (26).

(23) *Yo ni siquiera me di cuenta que los usaba. Y mi primo que ahora cumplió cinco, me dice . . . "Ceci, ¿por qué me decís **che**? Yo no me llamo **che**."* (F, 18–30, university student)
'I hadn't even noticed that I used it. My little cousin who just turned five asked me . . . "Ceci, why do you call me *che*? My name is not *che*."'

(24) *Yo creo que a veces lo uso el **che**. . . . Pero no lo considero una cosa mal. [El **bo**] jamás en la vida.* (F, 51+, retired teacher)
'I think I do use *che* sometimes. . . . But I don't think there's anything wrong with it. [*Bo*] never in my life.'

(25) *Yo uso el **bo** mucho y el **che** también.* (F, 18–30, university student)
'I use *bo* a lot and *che* also.'

(26) *El **bo** no es apropiado nunca. . . . Para mí no, y el **che** tampoco. A no ser que hablen del Che Guevara.* (F, 41+, podiatrist).
'*Bo* is never appropriate. . . . At least for me, and neither is *che*, unless they are talking about Che Guevara.'

Regarding awareness of the sociolinguistic distribution of both forms, the most recurrent comment was that *bo* is more masculine, an observation that emerged in six out of the thirteen interviews (27). Other comments highlighted the possible preponderance of *bo* among working-class speakers (28). Interviewees also mentioned the situations or registers where *bo* would be appropriate or inappropriate (29) and gave other indications of its patterning with informal registers.

(27) *Antes se usaba más . . . capaz que era más machista el **bo**, ¿no? más varonil, pero hoy creo que las mujeres lo usan igual.* (M, 41–50, professional musician)
'It used to be . . . maybe *bo* used to be more masculine, right? More of a male thing, but now I think women use it as much.'

(28) *[Lo asocio] con un medio de una clase media tirando abajo, más bajo. . . . De planchitas.* (M, 51+, retired teacher)
'[I associate it with] middle class, more like a lower class. . . . Something ghetto.'

(29) *[El **bo**] es más de muchachones de la esquina, de cuando hablan de fútbol y toman mate.* (F, 51+, retired teacher)
'*Bo* is something used by youths who hang around on street corners talking about soccer and drinking mate.'

The vocative form *bo* elicited the strongest negative attitudes. Of the ten people who gave some kind of opinion, all the women (a total of six and most of them older than forty) expressed negative views (*una cosa espantosa* 'something terrible,' *horrible* 'horrible,' *feo en el oído* 'harsh to the ear,' *agresivo* 'aggressive, uncouth'), and they were especially critical of its use by women. By contrast, only one of them remembered having been chastised for using *che* (30). The four men who expressed views were more evenly distributed: one of them admitted not liking it when women used *bo*, but also observed that this view was typical of people of his middle-aged generation. Another expressed a more neutral view, and the two younger speakers made comments that were more positive than negative, suggesting that *bo* has covert prestige in this group (31).

(30) *Un día yo llegué del liceo y le dije a mamá, "**Che**, mami!" y me dijo "**Che** no." Y de ahí me quedó que el **che** no va.* (F, 51+, retired teacher)
'One day I came back from school and I said to my mom, "*Che*, mom!" and she said, "Not *che*." And that's where I got the idea that *che* was not OK.'

(31) *El "**che, bo**" es . . . rompe los esquemas tradicionales de clases sociales. . . . Quiero decir que lo puede utilizar, por ejemplo, un hijo de estanciero, como lo puede usar un hijo de recolector o de reciclador de una zona periférica.* (M, 18–30, university student)
'That "*che, bo*" is . . . it breaks the traditional social barriers. . . . I mean to say that it can be used, for example, by the son of a rancher and by the son of a garbage collector or a recycler that lives in the periphery.'

Interestingly, only one interviewee expressed any awareness of the geographical distribution of *bo* and its function as an identity marker for Uruguayans (32). Not surprisingly, it was someone who traveled frequently to other countries in the region as part of his job. In other words, whereas participants were very sensitive to the social and situational value of *bo* within Uruguay, they were for the most part oblivious to its value as a regional marker for their linguistic community outside national borders.[1]

---

1. This lack of awareness is likely to have changed recently (mid-2014), since a well-known Argentine comedian, Peter Capusotto, created a character called James Bo (named after the Ian Fleming special agent). James Bo is a Uruguayan spy who has purportedly infiltrated the Argentinian secret service. One of his speech mannerisms is an exaggerated use of /bo/, anticipated in his very surname. This program is aired in both Argentina and Uruguay, and it may mark the starting point of a growing recognition among Uruguayans of the role of *bo* as an ethnic identifier.

(32) *Muchos de los porteños, esa es una cosa que nos diferencia. . . . Estee, que te dicen "Imitame a un uruguayo" y te dicen "Vamo arriba, **bo**." . . . El **bo** no lo usan. . . . Ellos usan el **che**.* (M, 41–50, professional musician)
'For many people from Buenos Aires, this is our distinctive trait. . . . They say, "Imitate a Uruguayan for me" and they say, "Let's go, *bo*." . . . They themselves don't use *bo*. . . . What they use is *che*.'

In the next sections, I summarize and discuss the implications of this study. Additionally, I present some possible objections to the methodology employed and show that in spite of its limitations, the analysis provides solid groundwork for future studies in this heretofore untapped area of research on second-person address in RPS.

5. Discussion

The quantitative results show that the presence of both vocatives, *bo* and *che*, is perceived as colloquial by Montevideo speakers in the sense that in neutral questionnaire items, more participants refused to select either of the two forms. Of the two vocatives, *che* was the more neutral. It was the most frequent response for all items, but even more so when the addressee was a woman and when the situation did not suggest impatience or other triggers of impoliteness. The only case where *bo* was chosen as frequently as *che* was in the subset of responses where the participant was a man, the hypothetical addressee was also a man, and the tone was impolite. Finally, age also influenced *bo/che* alternation: the younger the participant, the higher the frequency of *bo*. This suggests that *bo* and *che* are competing in Montevideo Spanish, with the former gaining ground over the latter.

These results were confirmed by the attitude comments, especially as they pertain to usage by speaker gender. The strongest negative views toward *bo* were expressed by middle-aged or older participants, especially women, and they were directed especially toward the usage of the form by women. In the youngest generation *bo* was seen as less gender-marked and less negatively evaluated across the board. The older generations show that attitudes toward *bo* are a manifestation of stigma that the pronoun *vos* no longer has in RPS, but which is still alive in other dialects, such as Chilean (Torrejón 1986, 2010).

Another pertinent observation is that *bo* is not perceived by the vast majority of Montevideo speakers as a distinctive feature of their dialect. This was apparent in the data collected online, where the Uruguayanness of *bo* is always noted by foreigners in Montevideo or Uruguayans living abroad. It was confirmed by the fact that only one of the thirteen interviewees had anything to say about its geographic distribution, and this person had been faced with this realization while in Argentina. It is too early to say, but the recent use of *bo* in Argentine media as a stereotyping feature of Montevideo speech may heighten self-awareness among Uruguayan audiences.

A more general observation is in order about the connection between formal and social aspects of language, which is consistent with the overall objectives of this volume. Although we tend to study grammatical categories (e.g., the contrast between pronoun and vocative particle) separately from the social conditions of language use, this study shows that these are in fact inseparable and much is gained by considering them together. Thus, the semantic closeness between the pronoun and the vocative undoubtedly made it possible for the former to give rise to the latter. However, there were also social conditions that fueled the transition, such that what started as a stigmatized vocative form with covert prestige among males was then generalized to both genders. Note that in settling on an invariable form for the vocative (*bo*), speakers chose the most stigmatized variant of the pronoun (/-s/-deleting *vos*), so that in crystalizing the semantic distance between both forms, they indirectly reflected the social origins of the process.

In closing, one should mention some possible methodological shortcomings of this study. The use of surveys and explicit attitude questionnaires to gather information about reported usage poses some interpretive issues, especially with stigmatized vernacular forms that participants may be unwilling to acknowledge. However, the survey format has been used in second-person studies profitably before (Mendoza 2005; Rona 1967; Johnson & Grinstead 2011) and offers many advantages. First, it is a fast and economical way to reach a large number of respondents in a short period of time. Second, once responses are collected, they are easy to process and to compare across respondents. Third, the survey allows for a controlled presentation of possible linguistic and pragmatic contexts. As for explicit attitudinal questionnaires, they may make it difficult to obtain accurate answers from speakers who hold negative attitudes toward *bo*, *che*, or both. That being said, the high degree of agreement between the data obtained through both techniques in the present study serves to demonstrate the robustness of the findings.

6. Conclusions and Future Directions

There are several ways in which the present analysis could be expanded and strengthened. For example, the information gathered from these questionnaires could be supplemented using other types of techniques, such as oral elicitation based on hypothetical situations (cf. Baumel Schreffler 1989, 1995), recordings of actual usage in authentic contexts (cf. Moser 2003, 2008), contemporary literary sources (cf. Behares 1981), and various kinds of semi-structured activities (cf. Fontanella de Weinberg 1979). The matched-guise technique of Lambert et al. (1966) would offer the advantage of controlling for specific features in the items tested and also of employing deception, which allows researchers to tap into implicit attitudes of which participants themselves may not be aware.

Additionally, data obtained here through reported usage questionnaires could be strengthened with the use of authentic speech, which would serve to confirm, expand, and nuance them. One of the advantages of employing these techniques would be the possibility of collecting data from working-class respondents, who are less likely to participate in a written survey and/or offer reflective metalinguistic comments.

Finally, a question not addressed in the current study, but of interest nonetheless, is the historical depth of the presence of *bo* in Montevideo Spanish. This may be a complex matter to establish, given the oscillation in the orthography of the vocative (*bo* is a recent spelling, and *vos* can be of ambiguous status) and the absence of written evidence for a very vernacular form. However, realistic drama from previous historical periods may offer some possible sources for further investigation.

Acknowledgments

I have to thank Magdalena Coll, Lindsey Cordery, A. Cruz Cabral (Cruzca), Jorge Hipogrosso, Soraya Ochoviet, and Juan Sader for their help with data collection. My most heartfelt thanks go to all the participants who took time out of their busy lives to share their linguistic intuitions with me.

Appendix 1: Questionnaire items analyzed in this study

1. Usted está con un grupo del trabajo esperando a un nuevo compañero en el restaurante. Cuando entra, ustedes lo ven, pero él no los ve a ustedes. Usted lo llama desde la mesa:
   a. ¡Che, Diego, estamos acá!
   b. ¡Bo, Diego, estamos acá!
   c. ¡Oiga, Diego, estamos acá!
   d. Otra forma: _____

   Translation: You are with a group of friends from work, waiting for a new colleague at a restaurant. When he comes in, you see him, but he doesn't see you. You call him from the table:
   a. Hey, Diego, we are here!
   b. Hey, Diego, we are here!
   c. Hey, Diego, we are here!
   d. Something else: _____

2. Usted está jugando a la baraja con su compañero de siempre pero él se distrae y muestra las cartas. Ya lo ha hecho otras veces y por su culpa han perdido varias manos. Usted se impacienta y le dice:
   a. ¡Che, idiota, otra vez estás mostrando las cartas!
   b. ¡Bo, idiota, otra vez estás mostrando las cartas!
   c. ¡Oiga, idiota, otra vez está mostrando las cartas!
   d. Otra forma: _____

   Translation: You are playing cards with your friend but he becomes distracted and shows his cards. He has done it before and has caused you to lose several previous games. You become impatient and say:
   a. You fool, there you go again showing your cards!
   b. You fool, there you go again showing your cards!
   c. You fool, there you go again showing your cards!
   d. Something else: _____

3. Usted está con un grupo del trabajo esperando a una nueva compañera en un bar. Cuando ella entra, ustedes la ven, pero ella parece perdida. Usted la llama:
   a. ¡Che, Julia, estamos acá!
   b. ¡Bo, Julia, estamos acá!
   c. ¡Oiga, Julia, estamos acá!
   d. Otra forma: _____

   Translation: You are with a group of coworkers waiting for a new female colleague at a café. When she comes in, you can see her, but she looks lost. You call her:

a. Hey, Julia, we're here!
   b. Hey, Julia, we're here!
   c. Hey, Julia, we're here!
   d. Something else: _____

4. Usted está preparando la comida con la ayuda de su hija, pero ella se distrae y se le pasan los fideos. Ya lo ha hecho otras veces y han tenido que tirar la comida por eso. Usted se impacienta y le dice:
   a. ¡Che, pasmada, otra vez se te pasaron los tallarines!
   b. ¡Bo, pasmada, otra vez se te pasaron los tallarines!
   c. ¡Oiga, pasmada, otra vez se le pasaron los tallarines!
   d. Otra forma: _____

Translation: You are preparing dinner with your daughter, but she loses track of time and the noodles are overcooked. She's done this before and you've had to throw out food because of this. You grow impatient and tell her:
   a. You twit, you overcooked the noodles again!
   b. You twit, you overcooked the noodles again!
   c. You twit, you overcooked the noodles again!
   d. Something else: _____

Appendix 2

Table 6.1
Demographic data for the participants of the attitude interview.

	Gender	Age	Occupation
Marcelo	male	18–30	University student
Elia	female	51+	Retired professional
Mariela	female	41–50	Massage therapist
Roberto	male	41–50	Professional musician
Cecilia B.	female	18–30	University student
Dora	female	51+	Retired teacher
Mario	male	51+	Retired teacher
Cecilia S.	female	18–30	University student
Alejandro	male	18–30	University student
Andrés	male	41–50	University professor
Alberto	male	51+	Shop keeper
Sonia	female	51+	School janitor
Marta	female	41–50	School janitor

Appendix 3

Table 6.2
Odds ratio for *bo* claiming by male and female speakers, for each context (neutral vs. impolite) and gender of addressee (male vs. female).

Context and Addressee	CMH Odds Ratio for *bo* (OR_Male/OR_Female)	P-value
Neutral, male addressee	3.0087	0.000983***
Impolite, male addressee	2.1778	0.005058**
Neutral, female addressee	2.3889	0.89657
Impolite, female addressee	1.9335	0.036194*

7

Genre and Register Variation
Academic Conference Presentations in Spanish in the United States

Carolina Viera

1. Introduction

Conference presentations (CPs) are instrumental in the academic sphere, since they provide a space in which academics disseminate their ongoing research, interact with their colleagues, and position themselves in their professional community (Swales 2004; Ventola, Shalom & Thompson 2002; Rowley-Jolivet & Carter-Thomas 2005). Unique to the academic community of Hispanic studies in the United States is the fact that texts can be produced either in English or Spanish, therefore, both languages are promoted as a viable means of academic communication. Additionally, scholars who deliver presentations in Spanish in the United States speak a wide array of Spanish dialects, come from different countries, and have diverse educational backgrounds (Viera Echevarria 2014). Therefore, even though this professional community resembles other Hispanic studies discourse communities in the world, it differentiates itself from them through its active bilingualism and dialectal diversity. In sum, conference presentations in Hispanic studies in the United States are cultural products inserted in a bilingual and multidialectal academic discourse community. Within this diverse community, CPs need to be constructed in a way that are recognized as a particular text type or *genre* by all members of the community, therefore, governed by similar stylistic, lexico-grammatical, and discursive conventions that result in specific language choices. As a consequence, we can reasonably expect linguistic variation in CPs that are delivered in the context of the United States.

Swales (2009: 6) stated that members of the academic community should be aware of the idiosyncratic changes that *genres* suffer depending on the context. This is of particular importance for what he calls "occluded genres, i.e., those that are hidden and out of sight to all but a privileged and expert few." Even though there is vast literature that focuses on the writing mode, variation in oral discourse has been understudied in the field of academic language. Until recently, few studies have focused on understanding the way in which speakers construct their oral texts when presenting at academic conferences (Hood & Forey 2005; Räisänen 1999; Rowley-Jolivet & Carter-Thomas 2005; Ventola, Shalom & Thompson 2002). In the context of the United States, research on academic oral texts in Spanish is concerned primarily with oral proficiency of students of Spanish (Achugar 2003, 2009; Valdés & Geoffrion-Vinci 1998), whereas there is little information regarding advanced levels of the language.

This chapter discusses the findings of the first comprehensive study of Spanish oral conference presentations in the United States and claims that discourse analysis of such texts, informed by the Genre and Register theoretical framework (Bhatia 2004; Biber & Conrad 2009; Bolívar 2005; Ciapuscio 2005; Eggins 1994; Martin 1994, 1997; Martin & Rose 2008; Moris & Navarro 2007; among others), might expand our understanding of the social interaction of this Spanish-speaking academic community and provide a powerful tool to determine the way in which Hispanists working in the United States adapt their academic texts to this bilingual and multidialectal context. Additionally, this chapter discusses the use of discourse analysis techniques as a suitable methodological approach to better understand variation in oral academic language.

1.1. THEORETICAL FRAMEWORK

Sociolinguistic studies have long shown that language is a cultural artifact that varies according to social contexts, social interactions, and the ultimate communicative purpose of the message (Firth & Palmer 1968; Halliday & Matthiessen 2014; Hood 2010; Hood & Forey 2005; van Dijk 2008). Among other factors, effective communication is marked by the ability of interlocutors to develop appropriate interpersonal relations through language in a given context. It is precisely because of the crucial role language has in establishing interpersonal relations that it is fundamental in shaping distinctive discourse communities (Swales 1990; Davies 2005). In the academic world, different professional communities have developed linguistic and discourse features that strengthen professional ties among members, including specific jargons, text organization, and citation conventions (MLA, APA, etc.), as well as even more subtle grammatical and lexical items, such as verb modality and discourse markers (Konzet 2012; Hyland 2000; Ventola, Shalom & Thompson 2002). In this sense, the appropriate use of academic genres within a particular discourse community signals membership in a professional group but also pragmatic knowledge and an advanced level of proficiency in the language.

Research has also shown that the same professional discourse community would differ in the use of language depending on the country involved, and the language used (Robles Garrote 2013; Rowley-Jolivet & Carter-Thomas 2005; Swales 2009; Vassileva 2002). Considering the above, it is reasonable to think that academic discourse communities that use Spanish in the United States would have developed a set of language conventions that sets them apart from other academic discourse communities of the Hispanic world. As Achugar (2008: 23) claimed: "Language has either a constitutive or ancillary character with respect to social activity. As a social practice, language is the activity of meaning construction." Therefore, the users of a language engage in meaningful social practices that shape the structure and discourse characteristics of the texts that are created within a community. In this sense, texts are idiosyncratic of the spaces where they circulate and will vary according to users and contexts. Academic contexts would favor a particular type of text—one that allows abstract operations, generalizations, identifications, the establishment of logical relations, and overall the communication of the scientific and argumentative research practices that are central to the academic professional community. Moreover, academic texts are intended to circulate within the community in order to build up their collective scientific knowledge. Since academic texts are intended for distribution in specific scientific communities, they rely heavily on the interpersonal functions of language (Halliday & Matthiessen 2014) and are strongly influenced by contextual sociocultural factors. Thus, academic texts would also reveal and express the inner discursive features of the community that creates them. Even though we might expect similarities among texts produced by members of the same macro-professional community, geographical and social context variation would be realized. Accordingly, CPs will vary linguistically to fit particular professional discourse community conventions and to conform to contextual prevailing cultural patterns.

According to Swales (1990), a *discourse community* is described as a group of people who is oriented toward a set of agreed public goals. This community has mechanisms of communication that vary according to the community, its members actively participate and provide feedback in regard to these common goals, has a specific technolect (specific lexis), and a set of textual genres, that is, abstract text varieties that can be recognized in a given culture (Biber & Conrad 2009). Textual *genres,* as Swales (1990: 58) pointed out, "are *exemplars* that share similarities in structure, style, content and intended audience" and should be easily recognized within the boundaries of a particular discourse community, however, they might slightly vary in structure and style when a different community is considered. Last, discourse communities have different types of membership ranging from novice to experts, with the latter being the most powerful, active, and knowledgeable participants.

The theoretical construct of the discourse community is applicable to the group of Hispanic studies scholars working in the United States, since they actively produce and exchange academic knowledge in the fields of Hispanic literature, cultural studies, and linguistics through a series of written and oral textual genres in designated spaces. Written and oral texts created within this professional community are characterized by a technical lexicon that serves the purpose of an adequate description of the community's research topics. The production and circulation of these texts is regulated by linguistic and discursive conventions that are the result of members' agreements. Thus, knowledge and appropriate use of these conventions signals membership. The community is organized hierarchically, ranging from experts to novices, with the most prolific producers of knowledge ranked as experts and graduate students ranked as novices (Viera Echevarria 2014: 55). Therefore, if we consider conference presentations as a textual genre, we should expect some degrees of variation depending on the professional community in which the CP is delivered but also depending on the presenter.

In order to study the discourse produced in CPs, and, eventually, the cultural patterns embodied in such discourse, the theory of Genre and Register offers a sound theoretical and methodological research framework for the study of text variation according to context. First, this theory of discourse analysis has been favored by many scholars around the world and has led to a vast array of studies that can be replicated with proven methodological techniques. Second, research findings informed by this theory have been successfully implemented in educational contexts (Martin & Rose 2008), therefore, the applicability rate of the theory is one of its advantages.

According to this theory, members of a given community engage in social activities that are mediated and instantiated in language, that is, expressed in the language, thus, susceptible to analysis. Martin and Rose (2007: 8) pointed out: "we learn to recognize and distinguish the typical genres of our culture, by attending to consistent patterns of meanings as we interact with others in various situations." Therefore, genres have a predictable structure and knowledge of this structure constitutes cultural knowledge in itself. As members of a discourse community, ". . . we organize our messages in ways that indicate how they fit in with the other messages around them and with the wider contexts in which we are talking or writing" (Thompson 2014: 28). However, heterogeneous communities or emerging discourse communities (Swales 2009) might represent challenges for their members as coexisting, different structures are possible. The way a text is organized around a particular communicative goal is central to the construct of genre. It is for this reason that genres are usually defined as "a staged, goal-oriented social process" (Martin & Rose 2007: 8). Following this definition, genres can be analyzed when it is possible to determine their different structural stages, also called steps or moves. This information is vital for the novice who wants to participate in a discourse community, as only through practice or explicit teaching we are able to grasp the culturally adequate.

However, not only are texts organized in a patterned structure, but they are also created with a specific *register*. As Burns, Joyce, and Gollin (1996: 6) claimed: "Commonly in second language teaching, register has been described as a feature of language which is linked to the person being addressed, and the choices have ranged between formal and informal." Indeed, *the system of register* implies the different configurations language adopts to serve the purposes of the social activity in which it is deployed, the relationship among participants of this activity, and the medium in which it is used. Every text has lexical, grammatical, and discursive configurations that are dependent on the type of activity that is constructed through language. Thus, in systemic functional linguistics (SFL), one of the discourse analysis schools that works within the Genre and Register theory and largely informs this study, "discourse analysis interfaces with the analysis of grammar and the analysis of social activity" (Martin & Rose 2007: 4). The analysis of particular features of language reveals the preferred grammatical and discursive options that participants of a certain community make when constructing a text to fit contextual situations, and, once again, knowledge of the way in which text register varies is gained through participation in the discourse community or through explicit teaching only.

In connection with register analysis, it is important to consider that CPs are oral monological texts created to be delivered in formal settings, or at least less conversational settings than a spontaneous dialogue among friends. It has been proposed that text types vary along an orality/literacy continuum, with spontaneous conversational speech on one side and formal scientific writing on the opposite side of such a continuum (Colombi 2006; Halliday 1990; Halliday & Matthiessen 2014). Although this idea has been contested for those who disfavor descriptions of language based on dichotomist divisions (Tannen 1985; Murray 1988), the general consensus is that the mode in which language is conveyed and the specific context of the situation would be expressed in specific linguistic features (Biber 2006; Chafe 1987; Halliday 1990; Parodi 2007). Determining where in the continuum CPs can be found is an important descriptor and shows the way CPs might vary among different discourse communities. Potentially, CP presenters have a set of linguistic options when creating their texts. They might choose to create formal or informal texts, dense and packed with academic abstract lexicon, or with more or less dialogic features. These linguistic options imprinted in the fabric of the text reveal the *tone* that the presenters instill in their texts, therefore, the way they perceive the relationship with the intended audience and discourse community as a whole. A CP that resembles a spontaneous friendly conversation shows a presenter who prioritizes establishing a strong rapport with the audience as opposed to a speaker who focuses on the academic content of the message.

Table 7.1 summarizes some of the language features that have been found relevant to register analysis when describing spontaneous conversational oral texts versus formal written texts and that were used in this study.

2. Methodology

The corpus of collected data analyzed in this study comprises thirty-two oral presentations from nine different conferences held in four U.S. states. Each presentation was thirteen to twenty minutes in length and was video recorded and then transcribed. Presentations were given in Spanish by scholars who work or study in the fields of Hispanic literature (18) and linguistics (14) in the United States. Presenters were seventeen professors of Spanish, who were considered *experts* in this study because they presumably have presented at several conferences before and had a better knowledge of possible discourse community conventions. The corpus also includes the presentations given

Table 7.1
Language features by text type.

	Conversational spontaneous	Formal writing
Fluency	pauses; errors; reformulation; repetition; false starts; hedges; fillers	no errors; standard language syntax; coherent and cohesive
Mode	direct interaction; dialogic; unplanned; subjective; focuses on processes (actions)	synoptic information; monologic; planned; objective; focuses on products (nouns)
Tenor	involvement; cooperative; focuses on participants	detachment;non-cooperative; focuses on information, descriptions and results
Lexical and grammatical features	deictic expressions; first- and second-person pronouns; colloquial expressions; conversational discourse markers; material verbs	minimum use of deictic expressions; impersonal expressions; technical language; formal connectors; relational and mental verbs
Grammatical intricacy	complex group of joined simple; digressions	nominalization; lexically dense

by fifteen graduate students of Spanish, who were considered *novice* for the purpose of this study. The majority of participants were native speakers of Spanish (28) and four participants spoke Spanish as a foreign language. This disparity was not sought out but it reflects the fact that non-native speakers of Spanish tended to present in English in the conferences where this corpus was collected. Indeed, English was the chosen language among Hispanic scholars of this corpus as well (Viera Echevarria 2014: 106). Only the oral text produced by the presenter was considered for the analysis, that is, written texts in PowerPoint presentations that were not read aloud or oral text included in audio or videos were disregarded. This methodological decision has proved to be erroneous, due to the actual multimedia nature of CPs and relevant discourse information might have been lost in the analysis.

After transcriptions, the text of each individual CP was segmented into structural stages and labeled following a series of steps adapted from Eggins and Slade (1997) and Taboada (2004):

a. Determination of main goals of the presentation;
b. Determination of recurrent structural stages according to main communicative goals;
c. Labeling according to items a) and b);

d. Determination of obligatory and optional stages in the genre;
e. Devising a structural formula;
f. Lexico-grammatical analysis at the clause level to determine recurrent main language features that can be associated with register in each structural stage;
g. Computer-assisted analysis that corroborated and provided further evidence to support findings yielded by manual analysis.

The software used with that purpose was *UAM Corpus Tool* version 2.8 (O'Donnell 2008) and AntConc 3.2.4 (Anthony 2013). Two small corpora of written oral presentations were used for comparative purposes. Automatic analysis following corpus linguistics methodology (Baker 2010; McEnery & Wilson 2001) was used to find *frequent words* and *keywords* of the corpus along with the calculation of the number of occurrences of discourse markers and language features present in oral spontaneous speech: errors, pauses, fillers, hedges, and question tags (Biber 2006; Chafe 1987; Halliday 1990; Parodi 2007).

For the determination of obligatory stages in the generic structural formula, the following criteria, which follows Navarro (2011), were used: a) 26% to 50%, *occasional*; b) 51% to 75%, *frequent*; and c) 76% to 100%, *obligatory*. These criteria, however, proved to be methodologically inaccurate because of the inherent variability of the oral text, which most often needs to be modified because of unexpected circumstances. For this reason, I suggest that the percentage of occurrence be lowered in future studies in the following way: a) 26%–46%, *occasional*; b) 47%–70%, *frequent*; and c) 71%–100%, *obligatory*.

3. Results

Manual and automatic analysis together allowed for determining the linguistic and discursive features that are characteristic of the CPs of this study.

3.1. GENRE ANALYSIS

The genre analysis showed that literature and linguistics create two different genres. Literature texts are characterized by *argumentative texts* that work around a thesis statement, whereas linguistic texts are usually *reports* of research findings. Therefore, oral presentations from these two fields have different generic structures since they have different purposes. However, both disciplines create texts that follow the same macrostructure, which is shown in the following structural formula that follows Eggins and Alcántara (2002). In this formula "^" represents sequential order, parenthesis represent optional elements, and "{" signal the beginning and end of generic structure elements:

Macro-structural formula: {opening ^ introduction ^ development ^ (conclusion) ^ closure}

As shown in the previous formula, CPs differ from written papers in the macro-stages of *opening* and *closing* (Rowley-Jolivet & Carter-Thomas 2005; Hood & Forey 2005; Viera Echevarria 2014). These two macro-stages are distinctive structural elements of this particular genre and have an important interpersonal goal that consists of establishing a connection with the present audience (opening) and with the discourse community as a whole (closing). The genre analysis showed that expert presenters (professors) favored interpersonal stages and when time was limited, they chose to include a *closing* over the *conclusion* stage. *Conclusions*, as opposed to *closings*, are the logical ending of the content information on which the conference focuses. Thus, this discourse community, when delivering CPs, seems to prefer interpersonal structural elements of the presentation to informational content. The most frequent *openings* in this corpus are *greetings*, *acknowledgment* to the work of the chair and organizers, and *exordium*. The acknowledgment is the preferred genre used for the *opening* macro-stage in this corpus. The *closing* is constructed differently in literature than in linguistics. Literature presenters tend to reserve the most eloquent and poetic type of language for this stage, creating a literary climax for their analysis, one that surely is intended to remain in the memory of the audience. Linguistic presenters resort to a form of epilogue that resembles the *peroratio*: an ending that highlights the importance of the presented study for the professional community or society as a whole.

Two interesting findings were found in the corpus as a whole (both disciplines): a) presenters only occasionally included a functional stage that serves as an outline for the presentation in their introductions, and b) presenters frequently choose not to explicitly state their thesis statement in their introduction but constructed it as they developed their texts. Thus, texts are usually of the inductive-deductive type, that is, a combination of both rhetorical techniques. However, the tendency to reveal the thesis statement in a completed way is greater in linguistics. The way in which texts are constructed in connection with the thesis statement should be explored in future studies to better understand if it reveals a feature of this particular discourse community.

Regarding discipline-specific generic structure, the following generic formulas show the results for the *frequent* and *obligatory* functional stages for literature and linguistics:

Literature: {(acknowledgement) ^ topic presentation ^ social and historical context ^ (literature review) ^ thesis statement ^ analysis ^ (evidence) ^ (conclusion) ^ epilogue}

Linguistics: {(semiotic spanning with the panel) ^ topic presentation ^ literature review ^ (niche) ^ research questions ^ (thesis statement [explicit]) ^ (theory) ^ (methodology) ^ research process [narration] ^ results ^ conclusion ^ epilogue ^ (acknowledgment)}

The analysis also showed that experts tended to create texts with fewer functional stages that correspond with the obligatory stages shown in the previous formulas. Interestingly, when considering the entire corpus, it is evident that experts relied less on citation and the literature review, which is a typical trait of academic writing. However, linguistic scholars did include a *literature review* as an obligatory stage of their presentation.

In conclusion, genre analysis showed the preferred functional stages in which members of the professional discourse community considered in this study organized their texts when giving an individual oral presentation on a panel. It was possible to establish the importance of interpersonal functional stages that imprinted the oral text with the necessary immediacy of the situational context and to determine differences in organization for the two disciplines represented in this corpus.

3.2. REGISTER ANALYSIS

One of the main goals of register analysis was to determine the way in which oral texts vary from written academic texts in this discourse community. Additionally, it was of interest to establish the tenor of the members' relationship as expressed by patterned structures in the language used when presented. Thus, the degree of formality or informality was analyzed as well as the resources that the presenter used to strengthen membership in this professional community. The usage of English is a parameter that, if present, might reveal that scholars of this discourse community construct a bilingual professional identity and insert their texts into a bilingual context. Last, since the texts of this corpus belong to the academic sphere, it was necessary to corroborate if the lexical and grammatical characteristics, normally described for academic texts that confer a greater degree of technicality and abstraction (Banks 2008; Colombi 2006; Cubo de Severino 2002; Halliday 2001; Martin 2001; Schleppegrell 2004), were present in the texts of this corpus. In connection with these goals, this section discusses the major findings of this research.

In this corpus, CP texts vary according to the discipline, with literature CPs tending to be more formal and usually based on a written text that is read aloud, whereas linguistic texts are more prone to being spontaneous texts built on base of a PowerPoint presentation. However, overall, most texts were classified as *formal* and *semiformal* and only seven were classified as *spontaneous-dialogic*. All of the seven were from linguistics and from presenters that completed their university studies mostly in the United States. These spontaneous texts presented all the language features described for conversational dialogue (see chart in introduction), including errors, false starts, and disfluencies that affect the general text cohesion. *Formal* texts (fifteen presenters) are characterized by a presenter who detaches herself from the audience and does not interact in any direct or indirect form with it. Passive voice and impersonal structures are recurrent along with a focus on processes and objects rather than actors. *Semi-formal* texts (ten presenters) are planned, usually written, and that are at moments abandoned and adapted spontaneously to better fit the immediate communicative situation. In most cases, these inserted spontaneous segments are elaborations, the addition of further examples, and the establishment of connections with what was presented in the panel or conference. In all cases, language changed to a more colloquial, interactive, and less abstract type (Viera Echevarria 2014: 342). In this sense, spontaneous speech transforms the text into one that is more cooperative with the process of understanding of the audience and becomes a discursive resource by which the presenter positions her text as part of the collective production of knowledge of her professional community. It is of no surprise, then, that experts were the ones who preferred this type of text. It is clear after the analysis that, regarding mode and tenor, CPs are hybrid texts that, even when planned and based on the written mode of language, respond to the immediate presence of an audience and contextually unexpected situations. Orality features are present in most of the samples of this corpus, and if we consider that experts favor the insertion of spontaneous segments into their planned texts, it is possible to conclude that CPs in this discourse community value presenters that are able to transform their texts in order to cooperate with an audience who is, indeed, other members of the presenter's professional community.

Regarding *technicality*, automatic analysis with *UAMCorpusTool* and *AntConc* software yielded that linguistic texts use more technical terms than literature ones. However, a closer look at the *keyword* analysis reveals that literature uses words normally occurring in everyday speech, like *memory*, *democracy*, and *story*, but assigns them a technical sense that is only understood within the professional community. However, the whole corpus cannot be described as a high, technical one, in accordance with what Swales (2004) finds for oral academic texts in English. Therefore, oral texts in this corpus are constructed with a lower degree of technicality than their written counterparts, like research articles. However, *UAMCorpus Tool* shows an overall lexical density of 70%, which signals that abstractions and nominalizations are present even in CPs that are spontaneous texts. Considering that Matsuda et al. (2012) have found similar lexical density in a written corpus from the humanities field, it is possible to conclude that the texts in this corpus, although exhibiting less technicality and oral features of the language, are nevertheless academic and condense the information into nominalizations. Therefore, CPs are more abstract texts than conversational samples.

At the discursive level, several communicative resources aimed to establish and strengthen an indirect dialogue with the audience were found in most texts. *Formal* texts deploy rhetorical questions and softening of their assertions via modalization, that is, the use of grammatical structures, such as modal verbs, that make claims less categorical (Hyland 2000). Semi-formal and spontaneous texts resort to question tags, hedges, and even direct conversation. Humor is also a recurrent feature in this corpus, present in fifteen presentations: nine experts and six novices. Through the incorporation of humor as a discursive resource, the presenter narrows the distance with the audience and aims at the coconstruction of meaning (Hood & Foley 2005).

Finally, the usage of English in the analyzed presentations is not a peripheral aspect in this corpus. Indeed, 65% of participants used English when they included quotations that were not translated into Spanish, or when they used specialized language or technolect. Presenters usually included both the Spanish and English word as if the English word might further clarify the meaning. Interestingly, none of the four speakers of Spanish as a second language, who were dominant in English, integrated this language into their presentations. This last finding calls for further research, however, as this corpus shows that many presenters who use Spanish in CPs in the United States assume a bilingual audience, able to understand non-translated quotations, and seem to resort to English to further comprehension on technical terms that constitute the discipline's technolect. In this regard, English is used with an interpersonal function to preserve the authentic voice of the individual quoted or to acknowledge that the production of collective scientific knowledge in this community is oftentimes carried out in English. Furthermore, the use of English in this community constitutes one of the many strategies speakers deploy to make their discourse more comprehensible for the audience, thus, English seems to be perceived as a linguistic resource to enhance communication in a bilingual academic setting.

4. Conclusions

Since texts are cultural products that depend on contextual circumstances, discourse analysis techniques, as the ones discussed previously, provide a powerful methodological approach to the study of language variation. Analysis showed that the Hispanic scholars who participated in this study modified their texts to follow specific discourse community conventions. Markedly, texts varied in structure and register according to the discipline considered, which shows that novice presenters should be aware of discipline-driven variation when creating their texts. In this sense, the present study offers the most favored generic structure for both literature and linguistics and the preferred stages in which discourse usually unfolds in Hispanic studies CPs. Analysis also shows that interpersonal stages are paramount for this type of text in this community. Once the generic structure of CPs has been determined, contrastive studies with other professional communities would provide details with regard to linguistic variation in the Spanish spoken in academic settings.

Regarding *register*, when the whole corpus is considered, it is clear that informality and more dialogic texts are not favored by most scholars. This finding should not be overlooked since it has been claimed that there is a growing tendency toward more conversational and informal styles in academia (Fairclough 1994; Frober-Adamo 2002; Wineburg 2004). If this finding is representative of a major trend, it seems that this particular community resists the aforementioned register change toward informality and colloquiality in academia. Conference presentation texts also varied depending on the type of membership that the presenter had in the discourse community. *Expert* members resorted to language and discursive strategies to boost interpersonal equal relationships among members of the academic community.

Considering the continuum of writing/orality (see Table 7.1), CP texts in this corpus are eminently oral, however, they also exhibit features that are usually present in formal academic written texts. In this respect, literature texts exhibit the linguistic characteristics associated with written texts to a greater extent than linguistics. Technicality is likewise constructed differently in both disciplines. However, analysis showed that the majority of the CPs in this corpus were lexically dense and characterized by the presence of discipline-specific technical terms. Last, the usage of English by many speakers indexes a Spanish speaking community that works in a bilingual setting. In this sense, Hispanic scholars in this community portray themselves as bilingual speakers and signal that the professional community discourse is usually constructed in both languages.

The present study has shown that rather than a homogeneous phenomenon, academic language is subject to linguistic variation due to contextual factors. In order to study such variation, discourse analysis tools and the Genre and Register theory have proven useful to establish the language features that are susceptible to change and that could be the focus of further comparative studies among Spanish-speaking professional communities.

PART IV
Variation in the Minimalist Program

8

A Feature-Geometry Account for Subject-Verb Agreement Phenomena in Yungueño Spanish

Sandro Sessarego

1. Introduction

This chapter investigates subject-verb agreement phenomena in Yungueño Spanish (YS), an Afro-Hispanic language spoken in the Department of La Paz, Bolivia (Lipski 2008b; Sessarego 2011a, 2011b, 2014a). In line with the main purpose of the current volume, this chapter combines linguistic theory and empirical data collection to cast light on the processes of variable subject-verb agreement that characterize the speech of a little-studied Afro-Andean community. In order to better understand why YS presents the aforementioned variability, a few words on its history and social context are due.

African slavery was introduced in Bolivia from the very beginning of the Spanish conquest, in the first decades of the sixteenth century. It lasted until 1826 when, soon after independence from Spain, slaves were declared free. However, in practice, until the Land Reform of 1952, black Bolivians did not really acquire freedom. In fact, the abolition of slavery implied that their legal condition passed from the status of "slaves" to the one of "forced peons." In practice—in the majority of the cases in Bolivia, and elsewhere in Latin America—this actually worsened their standards of living (cf. Sessarego 2013b for Bolivia; Sessarego 2014b, 2014c for similar scenarios in Ecuador and Peru).

The Land Reform of 1952 provided black Bolivians with small pieces of land to grow their produce and gave them access to education and mobility. The introduction of schools in these rural communities combined with the possibility of traveling to urban centers to look for better-paying jobs resulted in the systematic decline in use of YS by black Yungueños in favor of the more prestigious regional variety of Spanish, Highland Bolivian Spanish (HBS) (cf. Sessarego & Gutiérrez-Rexach 2011; Sessarego 2012). Currently, only a few hundred elderly Afro-Bolivians speak the traditional dialect, while the younger generations tend to speak varieties of Spanish that have almost completely converged with HBS (Lipski 2006a, 2006b; Sessarego & Ferreira 2015).

Traditional YS presents a number of morpho-syntactic features that are also commonly encountered in the majority of the Afro-Hispanic languages of the Americas (AHLAs) (Sessarego 2013a) and that deviate systematically from their respective counterparts found in other native varieties of Spanish. Due to these structural characteristics, in the literature it has been claimed that YS may be seen as the byproduct of a process of decreolization of a previous pidgin or creole language (Lipski 2006a, 2006b, 2008; Perez 2015). On the other hand, a different view on the origin of YS has suggested that this dialect, as well as many other AHLAs, may be seen as the result of L1 acquisition (nativization) of advanced L2 grammars, without necessarily following the prototypical creole life cycle according to which pidgins became creoles and then eventually decreolized (Sessarego 2013a, b, in press a).

Far from solving the current debates on the origin of YS, the primary objective of this research is to analyze quantitative and qualitative aspects of YS verbal morpho-syntax and provide a formal account for the results. Nevertheless, in so doing, this work also adds further fuel to the ongoing discussion. This study integrates current assumptions on agreement operations (Pesetsky & Torrego 2007; Preminger 2011) with proposals on the nature of default values and feature geometry (Harley & Ritter 2002). In particular, the morpho-syntactic phenomena encountered in YS are seen as the result of a trans-generational conventionalization of a non-target-like mastery of the syntax/morphology interface (Slabakova 2009). The presence in YS of seemingly L2 features is analyzed within a model of contact-induced cross-generational language acquisition, which has been proposed in Sessarego (2013a) to account for the nature of a number of other AHLAs.

This article consists of eight sections. Section 2 is an overview of the main morpho-syntactic features shared by YS and the AHLAs. Section 3 summarizes the qualitative findings of previous studies (cf. Lipski 2008b;

Perez 2015) on YS subject-verb (dis)agreement. Section 4 describes the data collection and the methodology adopted in this research, and section 5 provides the quantitative results obtained by performing statistical runs on the data. Section 6 proposes a formal framework to account for the emergence and conventionalization of default values in YS, and section 7 discusses the results. Finally, section 8 contains the conclusions.

2. On the Nature of YS and Her "Sisters"

YS presents, in line with the majority of the AHLAs, a number of morphosyntactic features that differentiate this vernacular from other native dialects of Spanish and align it with varieties of Spanish spoken as second languages (Montrul 2004). According to several authors (Megenney 1993; Perl & Schwegler 1998; Álvarez & Obediente 1998; among others), such features may be seen as the traces of a previous creole stage for the AHLAs, which would have decreolized in recent years due to contact with regional varieties of Spanish. Similar claims have also been made for YS, for which a Hispanic pidgin origin has been suggested (Lipski 2008b: 186). In fact, all of the "creole-like" elements reported for the AHLAs can also be encountered in this Afro-Bolivian dialect, as Table 8.1 shows. The presence of the aforementioned elements in the AHLAs and in other Hispanic and Lusophone contact varieties spoken around the world made some researchers propose that such grammatical patterns might have developed from a single Afro-Portuguese pidgin/creole vernacular. De Granda (1968b, 1970) was among the first linguists to adopt this model (the monogenesis hypothesis) to account for these shared linguistic features. He suggested that several AHLAs, as well as the Spanish creoles from the Philippines and the Portuguese creole spoken in Macau, had to derive from a common proto-Afro-Portuguese pidgin, which would have developed on the West African coasts through the contact of Portuguese sailors and African populations in the 15th and 16th centuries. In his view, such a contact variety would have spread around the world through the following phases of the European colonial expansion. For this reason, De Granda stated (1968b: 202–3):

> *No parece, sin embargo, factible... la producción independiente de procesos de simplificación, exactamente coincidentes, en ámbitos geográfica y socioculturalmente tan alejados como son África, Asia,*

Table 8.1
Five commonly reported Afro-Hispanic features traditionally ascribed to a previous creole stage.

Phenomenon	AHLAs	YS
Use of non-emphatic, non-contrastive overt subjects	• *Yo tando muy pequeña yo conocí a una señora.* 'When I was young I met a woman' (Barlovento Spanish, Megenney 1999: 117). • *Cuando yo ta la congreso, yo neglo, yo va dicí…* 'When I go to the congress, I am black, I am going to say…' (Afro-Peruvian Spanish, Lipski 1994b: 208).	• *Claro yo como fue chico yo no acorda vela.* 'Of course since I was a child, I do not remember about candles' (Lipski 2008b: 101). • *Yo no acorda, yo fue huahua eje tiempo; chico yo fue, algo yo acorda, yo acorda cuando…* 'I do not remember, I was a child then, I was small, I remember something, I remember when…' (Lipski 2008b: 100).
Invariant verb forms for person and number	• *Yo sabe [sé]* 'I know'; *yo tiene [tengo].* 'I have'; *yo no pue [puedo]* 'I cannot' (Afro-Puertorican, Álvarez Nazario 1974: 194–95). • *Tú jabla [hablas] y no conoce [conoces].* 'You speak and you do not know' (Afro-Cuban Spanish, Guirao 1938: 3).	• *Nojotro tenemos jrutita.* 'We have fruit' (Lipski 2008b: 107). • *Yo quiero comprá un carro.* 'I want to buy a car' (Sessarego 2011b: 51).
Lack of nominal gender and number agreement.	• *Tán chiquito puej mij nene[s].* 'My kids are so little' (Afro-Mexican Oaxacan Spanish, Mayén 2007: 117). • *Gente branco [blanca].* 'White people' (Cuban Bozal Spanish, Álvarez Nazario 1974: 189).	• *Mis buenos amigos mayores.* 'My good old friends' (Sessarego 2011b: 47). • *Nuestra cultura antigua.* 'Our old culture' (Lipski 2008b: 89).
Lack of subject-verb inversion in questions	• *¿Onde tú taba, mijito?* 'Where were you, my son?' (Barlovento Spanish, Megenney 1999: 118). • *¿Qué tú comes?* 'What do you eat?' (Caribbean Spanish, Lorenzino 1998: 36).	• *¿Qui lado oté cayó?* 'Which side did you fall on?' (Lipski 2008b: 135). • *¿Qué oté ta jugá?* 'What are you playing?' (Sessarego 2011b: 56).
Presence of bare nouns	• *Me metía en [el] pueblo con [los] trabajadores.* 'He put me in the village with the workers' (Chocó Spanish, Ruiz García 2001: 45). • *Porque [el] próximo pueblo puede ser Salinas.* 'Because the next town could be Salinas' (Chota Valley Spanish, Lipski 1987: 163).	• *El patrón vivía La Paz.* 'The owner lived in La Paz' (Lipski 2008b: 85). • *Los perros comen carne.* 'Dogs eat meat' (Sessarego 2011b: 48).

América y Oceanía. Este hecho sería tan extraño como la invención paralela de un mismo sistema alfabético en múltiples distantes puntos geográficos.

'Indeed, it does not seem possible ... to find the independent evolution of the same simplifications in regions that are as geographically and culturally apart as Africa, Asia, America and Oceania. This fact would be as strange as the parallel invention of the same alphabetic system in multiple and distant geographic locations.'

The monogenetic hypothesis has been subsequently revisited by Schwegler (1999), who reduces the number of "sister languages" born from the same Afro-Portuguese "mother." Thus, he suggests that not all the contact varieties mentioned by De Granda can be accounted for by this hypothesis, but that at least three AHLAs should be linked to it on the linguistic bases that all of them would share the Portuguese-derived subject pronoun *ele* 'he': Palenquero (Colombia), Chota Valley Spanish (Highland Ecuador), and nineteenth-century Bozal Spanish (Cuba) (cf. Sessarego 2013c, 2013d, 2014c for a different account). In a new study, Schwegler (2014) has added to the "family" also YS (Bolivia) and the ritual language of Palo Monte (Cuba). More recently, the Afro-Portuguese roots of YS have also been claimed by Perez (2015), who ascribes a variety of morpho-syntactic and prosodic features encountered in this dialect to a previous Portuguese creole stage. On the other hand, other studies have provided a different perspective on the origin and evolution of the AHLAs (Sessarego 2013a; Sessarego & Gutiérrez-Rexach in press; Sessarego & Ferreira 2016; Sessarego & Romero in press). These investigations have claimed that the so-called "creole like" features encountered in the AHLAs may be analyzed as advanced second-language acquisition strategies, not necessarily related to any previous creolization phase. In particular, for the YS case, a number of studies have concentrated on both the socio-historical and linguistic aspects of this dialect to suggest that this Afro-Hispanic contact variety was never a creole; rather, it may be better classified as the byproduct of the nativization of a conventionalized advanced second language (Sessarego 2011a, 2011b, 2013b).

Far from solving the current debates on the origin of YS and the other AHLAs, the present study focuses on one of the aforementioned "creole-like" features found—to different extents—in all of these varieties: variable subject-verb agreement. The analysis, which builds on the quantitative and qualitative data available for this phenomenon (cf. Lipski 2008b; Sessarego

2009; Perez 2015), is in line with current theoretical models on the nature of feature variability (Adger & Smith 2005) and the acquisition of L2 morphology (McCarthy 2008; Slobakova 2009).

3. Subject-Verb (Dis)agreement in YS: Qualitative Findings

As reported by Lipski (2006b: 23), traditional YS (1), in sharp contrast with Spanish (2), does not inflect verbs for person and number; rather, the only verb form used with all the subject pronouns is the third-person singular one.

(1) YS 'to dance'
   1SG *Yo baila*
   2SG *Oté baila*
   3SG *Ele baila*
   1PL *Nosotros baila*
   2PL *Otene baila*
   3PL *Eyu baila*

(2) Spanish 'to dance'
   1SG *Yo bailo*
   2SG *Tú bailas*
   3SG *Él baila*
   1PL *Nosotros bailamos*
   2PL *Ustedes bailan*
   3PL *Ellos bailan*

Lipski (2008b: 107) provided a number of naturalistic examples that illustrate this phenomenon (3). He compared his data on YS with those provided by Baxter (1997) for Helvécia Portuguese (HP), an Afro-Brazilian vernacular that presents parallel morpho-syntactic structures across its nominal and verbal domains. After an analysis of these two varieties, Lipski concluded that "a glance at the radically simplified VP and DP of the basilectal Afro-Yungueño dialect suggests that a full-fledged creole once existed here" (2006b: 37). Indeed, Baxter (1997: 271–75) also considered the variable agreement processes found in HP to be symptomatic of a previous creole stage (4) and stated that "the evidence..., albeit inconclusive, implicates creolization" (1997: 284).

(3) a. *Nojotro tiene [tenemos] jrutita.* 'We have fruit.'
 b. *Yo no entiende [entiendo] eso de vender jrutita.* 'I don't understand that [business] about selling fruit.'
 c. *Esus palo no sirvi porque se va yená jai di poliya [esos palos no sirven porque se van a llenar de pollilas].* 'Those trees are worthless because they will be filled with termites.'
 d. *Yo creció [crecí] junto con Angelino.* 'I grew up with Angelino.'
 e. *Eyu vivía [vivían].* 'They were living.'
 f. *Eyu salía [salían] mi avisá aquí.* 'They came to warn me here.'
 g. *Lu patrón siempre tenía [tenían] partera.* 'The landowners always had midwives.'

(4) a. *Eu vai [vou] embora.* 'I am leaving.'
 b. *Eu pisô [pisei] na pedra.* 'I trod on the stone.'
 c. *Eu pegô [peguei] minha boiada.* 'I took my herd.'
 d. *Eu pega [pego] Mário e mandou ele cortar.* 'I got Mario and told him to cut (it).'
 e. *Nascia uns cabelo un poquinho eu faz [faço].* 'A few whiskers would grow and I would shave.'
 f. *Eu (es)tá [estou] trabalhando, ai eu lembrei . . .* 'I was working, then I remembered . . .'

Baxter (1997: 281) concluded his study on HP by stating that first-person singular "is the first person number morpheme to be acquired." He also added that, since "the incorporation of 1sg. is more advanced in the present tense verb than in the preterite verb," there is evidence to suggest "the following acquisitional order: person-number in present tense > person-number in preterite." In a parallel fashion, Lipski (2006b: 29) suggested that first-person singular verb forms are the first to appear in YS, followed by first-person plural forms, and then eventually the other forms. He also pointed out that present tenses develop agreement before past ones, so that some speakers may show agreement with first-person singular and plural subjects in the present tense, but use third-person singular default forms in the past: *yo trabajo* 'I work,' but *yo trabajó [trabajé]* 'I worked.'

Lipski's and Baxter's observations have been more recently echoed by Perez (2015), who reports several other naturalistic examples attesting the lack of subject-verb agreement in traditional YS (5); she also notes that first-person singular subjects are overall more likely to show concord with the verb than other subjects and that past tenses show lower levels of agreement than present ones. In line with many traditional AHLAs studies, Perez (2015) ascribes these phenomena to a previous creole phase for YS.

(5) a. *Yo jue [fui] la chumi.* 'I went in the forest.'
  b. *Nohotro vinió [vinimos] buscá tío Ramón.* 'We came to look for uncle Ramón.'
  c. *Yo ta [estoy] yorando.* 'I am crying.'
  d. *Nohotro yora [lloramos], mi mamá yora.* 'When we cried, our mother cried.'
  e. *Yo tosta [tuesto] mi cajué.* 'I roast my coffee.'
  f. *Ante yo sabe [sé] escuchá.* 'Before, I used to listen.'
  g. *Cuando yo sinti [siento] aguacero.* 'Suddenly I felt the rain.'

4. Data Collection and Quantitative Methodology

In contrast with the aforementioned qualitative studies on YS, in Sessarego (2009), I have analyzed the subject-verb agreement phenomena found in this Afro-Bolivian dialect by adopting a quantitative methodology. In particular, internal (linguistic) and external (social) factors were evaluated to understand the dynamics of a trans-generational language change, which consists of the systematic substitution of invariant third-person singular forms with fully conjugated forms (Sessarego 2009: 117–18).

The fieldwork was conducted during July–August 2008. A total of 2,160 tokens were extracted from a corpus of twelve recorded interviews. All the speakers lived in the communities of Tocaña, Mururata, and Chijchipa, three villages in the municipality of Coroico, North Yungas. The informants were native speakers of the Afro-Bolivian dialect; they did not speak any other language spoken in Bolivia, such as Quechua or Aymara.

In carrying out the interviews, I followed a sociolinguistic methodology of data collection. The speakers were asked general questions concerning their communities; they were allowed to talk about any topic of their liking. The objective was—therefore—to overcome the observer's paradox (Labov 1972) in order to obtain more naturalistic data.

Gender, level of education, and generation were the external factors that guided the selection of the informants. Since gender has often been identified as a key factor in patterning language variation (Labov 1990), the categories male and female were adopted to code the tokens. The informant's level of education was also taken into consideration. In this case, speakers were divided in two main groups: literates vs. illiterates. Literate informants included the speakers who could attend school and—as a consequence— were exposed to formal Spanish. For this reason, I expected them to present more subject-verb agreement in their speech than those who did not have such an educational experience. The factor group generation consisted of three sub-groups, divided according to three age brackets: 21–40, 41–70, and 71+. Given that over the past six decades, after the Land Reform of 1952, Afro-Bolivians progressively experienced more access to the outside world, we may expect to observe a systematic increase in agreement rates across the three groups, with the oldest generation showing the lowest levels of concord and the youngest members presenting the highest ones.

My analysis also took into consideration internal/linguistic factor groups. As indicated in the previous section, Baxter (1997), Lipski (2006b), and Perez (2015) pointed out that concord seems to be more prominent with first-person singular subjects and with present tense. For this reason subject and tense were selected as linguistic factor groups. Since third-person singular subjects act as default forms, the subject categories initially identified for the subject factor group were as follows: first singular, second singular, first plural, second plural, and third plural. As for the tense factor, the categories contrasted for the statistical run were present vs. past.

5. Statistical Results

As far as the internal factors are concerned (see Table 8.2), it can be observed that the subject factor group is the most significant one (range 29) with second-person singular subjects strongly favoring disagreement (factor weight .73) and first-person singular subjects disfavoring it (factor weight .44) (Sessarego 2009: 114). During the statistical runs, third- and second-person plural subjects were collapsed since the latter category only contained twenty-three tokens and both types of subjects present the same verbal form in Spanish (i.e., *ustedes/ellos bailan* 'you/they dance'). The combined tokens provided a factor weight of .60 for the newly created category (second-/third-person plural subjects), while the remaining first-person plural subjects disfavored agreement phenomena by showing a score of .45. Overall, results appear to be in line with the observations of Lipski and Baxter who noticed that the first conjugated forms to emerge are those agreeing with first-person

Table 8.2
Variable rule analysis of the contribution of internal factors to the probability of lack of subject-verb agreement. (Total = 2160; Total Chi-square = 4.1881; Chi-square / cell = 0.5235; Log likelihood = −1217.213; Significance = 0.000; Input 0.261)

	Factor Weight	% Lack of Agreement	N	% data
SUBJECT				
2nd-singular	.73	43	193	9
2nd-/3rd-plural	.60	37	1102	51
1st-plural	.45	26	258	12
1st-singular	.44	21	607	28
	Range 29			
TENSE				
Past	.61	34	649	30
Present	.43	22	1511	70
	Range 18			

singular subjects. In Sessarego (2009: 215), I have also suggested that phonological processes may have played a role in patterning these results. In fact, YS presents cases of final /s/ weakening and elision; thus, this may provide an explanation for why second-person singular subjects showed the highest levels of lack of agreement (i.e., *baila(s)* 'you dance'). As Table 2 indicates, also the tense factor group turned out to be significant (range 18). Findings reveal that past tenses showed a higher level of disagreement (factor weight .61) than present ones (factor weight .43), a result that is in line with previous studies and that may also be partially driven by a frequency effect (Sessarego 2009: 215). As far as external factors are concerned, Table 8.3 shows that generation is the most significant factor group (range 77), with informants over seventy showing the highest levels of third-person singular invariant verb forms (factor weight .83) and the youngest generation (21–40) presenting an agreement pattern almost completely converging with the standard one (factor weight .06). Another significant factor group was education (range 25), with illiterate speakers favoring disagreement (factor weight .63) in contrast with literate ones (factor weight .38). On the other hand, the factor gender did not have any significant effect on the distribution of the data; indicating that men and women do not differ significantly in the use of subject-verb agreement (Sessarego 2009: 216).

Table 8.3*
Variable rule analysis of the contribution of external factors to the probability of lack of subject-verb agreement. (Total = 2160; total chi-square = 4.1881; chi-square/cell = 0.5235; log likelihood = -1217.213; significance = 0.000; input 0.261)

	Factor Weight	% Lack of Agreement	N	% data
GENERATION				
71+	.83	44	747	35
41–70	.73	34	716	33
21–40	.06	01	697	32
Range	77			
EDUCATION				
Illiterate	.63	40	1140	53
Literate	.38	12	1020	47
Range	25			
GENDER				
Male	[.51]	27	1071	50
Female	[.49]	26	1089	50

*The statistical results presented in this table slightly diverge from those reported for external factors in Sessarego (2009: 116). The reason for the difference has to do with the number of tokens analyzed, which were 2604 in the original table. As explained in Sessarego (2009: 113), 444 tokens had to be excluded from the statistical run since they belonged to the "present perfect" tense and showed no variation. Nevertheless, such a difference does not have any relevant effect on the data distribution and on the significance of the factors patterning the variation.

6. Theoretical Assumptions on the Nature of Agreement and Default Values

The language architecture assumed in this study is framed within the Minimalist Program. According to this program, the language faculty, the component of the human mind devoted to language, is defined by a small number of syntactic operations: merge, move, and agree (Chomsky 2000, 2001). The cyclical application of *merge* and *move* builds constituent structure. The operation *merge* selects two elements from the collection of lexical items (numeration) and assembles them. The operation *move* creates a copy of a certain element and merges it with a different part of the syntactic structure. The syntactic constituent must receive an overt form; this overt realization occurs at spell-out, where computations split and derive two independent representations, logic form (LF) and phonetic form (PF).

(6)

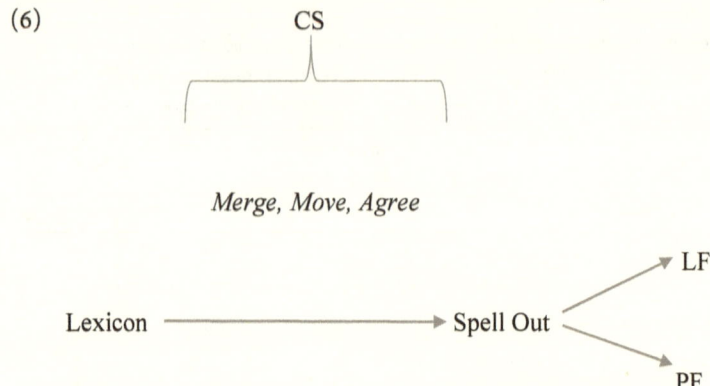

Agreement is the overt manifestation of the syntactic operation *agree*, which can be formally conceived as the relation between two different syntactic elements acting respectively as a probe and a goal. In order for *agree* to take place a series of requirements have to be met. Specifically, (a) the probe should display an unvalued feature corresponding to a value contained in the goal (activity condition), (b) the probe must c-command the goal, (c) they have to be sufficiently close to each other (locality condition), and (d) no other valued object should interfere with the probe-goal relation by being closer to the probe (minimality condition) (cf. Preminger 2011).

In line with Adger & Smith (2005), variable subject-verb agreement in YS can be seen as the byproduct of *agree*, where the items entering the syntactic numeration have variable uninterpretable feature specifications. Since the features under question are uinterpretable, they will be—by definition—invisible to logic form (LF), thus they will not affect the semantic interpretation of the construction. This allows us to account for variation and alternation between forms, without postulating competing grammars. Such a model is therefore also compatible with the idea that external and internal factors may play a significant role in such a lexical selection.

The evolution of morphological features in interlanguage grammars has been recently addressed by McCarthy (2008), who adopted a feature-geometry approach. At the core of this model stands the assumption that morphological features can be understood as geometrical combinations of natural class nodes (cf. Harley & Ritter 2002; Cowper 2005). According to this line of reasoning, more complex features involve more nodes, which, in turn, will be more difficult to process and acquire.

In a recent article, Slabakova (2009) has adapted this feature-geometry approach to the analysis of person and number features to investigate the evolution of subject-verb agreement in L2 German. Example (7) reproduces her graphic representation for number features. She conceives "singular" as the default value, while "plural" represents an increase in complexity, since it implicates an additional node. Along the same vein, (8) exemplifies person features. Here 3 is the default value, 1 is more marked—since it involves the [participant] node—and 2 is the most complex, since it also comprises the [addressee] node.

(7) Number features:
SG   PL
\#   \#
      |
      [>1]

(8) Person features:
3   1   2
π   π   π
     | |
     [Participant] [Addressee]

In a feature-geometry analysis of INFL in English and Spanish, Cowper (2005) offers an account of tense features that may be schematically represented as in (9), where past represents the more marked tense—since it involves the [precedence] node—while non-past (or present) represents the default value.

(9) Tense features:
Non-past   Past
ж   ж
           |
           [Precedence]

Not only can a feature-geometry account be used to predict the incremental evolution of interlanguage morphology (Slabakova 2009), but it can also be applied to the analysis of vernacular dialects and in particular contact varieties, which tend to show a set of recurrent morphological features (see for example Table 8.1 for the AHLAs), traditionally classified as simpler or less complex (cf. Sessarego & Ferreira 2016).

7. Discussion: Applying the Theory to the Data

If we apply current syntactic theory to our statistical results, the subject-verb agreement variation reported in section 5 can be accounted for by saying that in YS two different tense heads (T1 and T2) can be selected from the mental lexicon before entering the numeration. This analysis, *à la* Adger and Smith (2005), leads us to postulate that in one case (T1), the tense head is endowed with a full set of features (tense, case, number, and person), like in standard Spanish, while, in the other case (T2), the tense head does not bear features for number and person.

The overt result of the operation *agree* (and *merge*) between T1 and a subject pronoun will be a verb form conjugated for tense, number, and person (cf. Pesetsky & Torrego 2007), as shown in (11–12) for the verb *bailar* 'to dance' and the pronoun *nosotros* 'we.'

(10) T1 [tense:non-past, *u*case:nom, *u*num:, *u*pers:] ... pronoun [num:pl, pers:1, case:nom] → T1[tense:non-past, num:pl, pers:1] ... pronoun [num:pl, pers:1, case:nom]

(11) Spell-Out: *Nosotros bailamos*
We.NOM dance.PRESENT.I.PL

On the other hand, we can account for the non-agreeing configuration if we postulate that the probe (T2) is not specified for person and number features. In such a case, the application of *agree* will result in a verb form conjugated for tense, but showing default values for number and person (i.e., third-person singular).

(12) T2 [tense:non-past, *u*case:nom] ... pronoun [num:pl, pers:1, *u*case:] →
T2 [tense:non-past] ... pronoun [num:pl, pers:1, case:nom]

(13) Spell-Out: *Nosotros baila*
We.NOM dance.PRESENT.3.SG

Having provided an explanation for the variability found in the YS corpus by relying on Adger and Smith's (2005) model, an analysis of the YS data in light of the feature-geometry framework proposed by Harley and Ritter (2002) may help us understand why we encounter the attested linguistic patterns in the evolution of subject-verb agreement. Indeed, the selection of third-person singular as the default form follows from the fact that singular and third are the least marked values for number and person features (cf. 7 and 8). From this approach, it also follows that first-person subjects should be the first ones to develop agreement. This is not only confirmed by Lipski (2006b) and Perez (2015), who pointed it out in their qualitative analyses of YS verbal morphology; the quantitative findings reported in section 5 also indicate such a developmental path. Moreover, as predicted, second-person agreement turned out to be difficult to acquire. As far as number is concerned, again, empirical data align—to a good extent—with theoretical predictions. Indeed, first-person plural forms present lower levels of agreement (factor weight .43) than first-person singular ones (factor weight .63). At first look (cf. Table 8.2), the fact that second-person singular subjects presented the highest levels of lack of agreement (factor weight .73) may appear somehow counterintuitive, since their plural counterparts should—in theory—be more marked. Nevertheless, it must be considered that second-person plural tokens were quite rare in the corpus (only twenty-three tokens) and consequently they were collapsed with third-person plural ones. In addition, the fact that these two verbal forms are homophonous in Spanish may be taken as a factor facilitating their acquisition. Another factor that may have determined the high levels of subject-verb disagreement with second-person singular subjects is the presence of /s/ weakening and elision processes (i.e., *baila(s)* 'you dance'). As far as tense forms are concerned, the feature-geometry account correctly predicted that past forms would be more difficult to acquire since they imply a higher level of complexity. It should be pointed out that acquisition of present forms over past ones may have also been favored by their higher frequency in grammar.

As for the social/external factors, both generation and education turned out to be significant factor groups, while gender did not seem to significantly pattern the variation. Even though women are traditionally identified as those who lead the linguistic change and tend to adopt more standard-like forms (Labov 1990), the data here analyzed do not confirm such a scenario for the YS community, where both men and women present comparable levels of subject-verb agreement (factor weights .51 vs. .49). On the other hand, the statistical runs indicated that generation is the most significant factor group (range 77), thus showing that remarkable differences exist among the levels of agreement found across the age groups. In fact, the oldest generation, which represents the people who more than anybody else experienced the segregation of the hacienda system, appears to show the most conservative speech behaviors (factor group .83), while the youngest speakers, who had more access to outside society, present the highest levels of concord (factor group .06). Also education resulted to be a significant factor group (range 25). Indeed the illiterate group—as expected—shows higher levels of lack of concord (factor weight .63) than the informants who experienced some form of schooling (factor weight .38) and, consequently, had more exposure to standard Spanish.

At this point, we may wonder how a native dialect of Spanish, such as YS, can present structures that would be commonly encountered in L2 Spanish varieties (cf. Montrul 2004; McCarthy 2008). It appears that a non-target-like acquisition of the syntax/morphology interface characterized the evolution of the YS verb system. This generated L2 default patterns that were conventionalized in the local speech community. Such patterns were subsequently acquired as part of the L1 of following generations of YS speakers, thus they were nativized.

Recent proposals on the nature of language interfaces and second-language acquisition may provide us with insights into this issue. A number of interface frameworks have been proposed in the literature (cf. Jackendoff 1997, 2002; Burkhardt 2005; etc.); for the sake of simplicity, I adopt here the one based on the language architecture suggested by Reinhart (2006). As it can be observed in Figure 8.1, Reinhart envisions a system where syntax plays a central role and interfaces independently with the other modules forming the language faculty (3). The concept of interface has been very successful in contemporary SLA research, since it has been claimed that cases of non-target-like attainment are often related to linguistic constructions that require the contemporary mastery of different language modules (cf. White 2011 for a literature overview). A recurrent claim is that differences in term of acquisition challenges exist between internal and external interfaces (Sorace & Serratrice 2009), so that linguistic phenomena concerning the latter ones would be harder to acquire and master than those involving the former ones. Nevertheless, even in the realm of internal interfaces, not all of them are created equal, and some of them appear to be more challenging than others. For example, the syntax-morphology interface has been identified as the

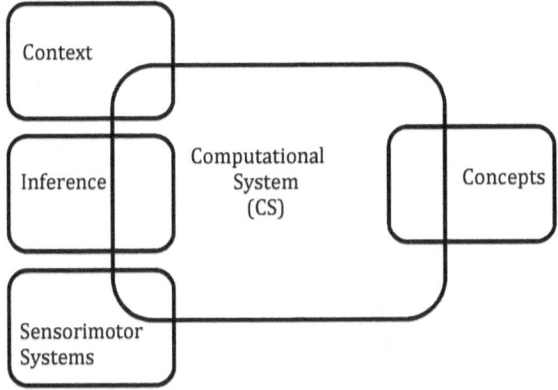

Figure 8.1
Reinhart's language faculty architecture.

"bottleneck" of acquisition (Slabakova 2009). Along these lines of reasoning, and considering the information we have about YS grammar and history (cf. Sessarego 2011b, 2014a), I analyze the aforementioned impoverished YS agreement patterns as the result of advanced SLA strategies. This proposal, therefore, diverges from the claims indicating that YS should be seen as the byproduct of (de)creolization. On the other hand, I wish to suggest that the prototypical creole life cycle, according to which pidgins became creoles and then eventually decreolized, probably did not apply to the Afro-Bolivian context, so that YS, as well as several other AHLAs, may be conceived as *the result of L1 acquisition (nativization) of advanced L2 grammars.*

As I have claimed elsewhere (cf. Sessarego 2013a), these contact varieties appear to have formed in social contexts in which the African-born slaves (*bozales*) achieved a relatively good proficiency in Spanish (the TL) and internalized a grammar (G1), which was neither a basic pidgin nor a creole, but a close approximation to Spanish. Their linguistic outputs (X) served as the primary linguistic data (PLDx) for the following generation of speakers, which acquired this vernacular natively (G2). Example (14) represents a graphic sketch of such a trans-generational contact-induced language transmission.

(14) a. Individual from Generation 1:
TLy → UG driving L2 acquisition → G1 → set of outputs X
b. Individual from Generation 2:
PLDx → UG driving L1 acquisition → G2 → set of outputs Z

As it can be observed, G2 consists of a native language (L1) that has been built on L2 input (PLDx). This is meant to account for the fact that in YS, as well as in many other AHLAs, it is possible to encounter impoverished agreement phenomena, along with other morphological reductions, that can be classified as nativized forms of advanced SLA strategies.

8. Conclusions

In line with the main spirit of the present volume, this chapter has applied formal syntactic models to the analysis of empirical data collected by means of sociolinguistic interviews. This study has—therefore—provided a formal perspective on YS variable subject-verb agreement by postulating the coexistence in this speech community of competing lexical and functional entries bearing different clusters of uninterpretable features (Adger & Smith 2005).

It has been shown that the evolution of agreement, which is developing cross-generationally, consists of the substitution of traditional third-person singular (default) forms with fully agreeing HBS ones. This approximation of the HBS variety is driven by the stigmatization attached to the former vernacular combined with the increasing exposure they have to the latter dialect. Contact with HBS augmented significantly after the Land Reform (1952), which freed Afro-Bolivians from forced peonage and introduced public schools in these rural villages. For this reason, generation and education were identified as significant factor groups.

Internal factors are also key to understanding the data. In particular, results confirm the prominence of agreement for present tense and first-person singular. Such a distribution has been accounted for by adopting a feature-geometry framework (Harley & Ritter 2002; Cowper 2005), which describes the representation of morphological features in terms of structural combinations of natural class nodes. Indeed, according to recent analyses on the evolution of morphological complexity in language acquisition (McCarthy 2008; Slabakova 2009), first-person singular subjects and present tense forms appear to be less complex and thus less challenging for acquisition.

Finally, the presence of seemingly L2 patterns in an L1 variety of Spanish has been analyzed within a model of cross-generational contact-induced language transmission (Sessarego 2013a), which accounts for the "nativization" of L2 forms in L1 grammars and appears to be suitable for explaining the nature of YS and a number of other AHLAs.

Agreement and Valuation of Phi-Features in Judeo-Spanish: A Cross-Generational Account

Rey Romero

1. Introduction

Studies in sociolinguistic variation typically focus on the distribution of one particular variant among the speaker population. Factors such as geography, age, gender, and social group are usually utilized as variables that help explain correlations in token distributions. This assumption, however, takes for granted that the entire linguistic population in question is operating the same version of underlying grammar, with variation ascribed to social or linguistic distribution factors. Although this may be the case in monolingual populations or in healthy and stable bilingual populations, situations of intergenerational language shift may pose a different scenario where semi-speakers, who acquired their heritage language under extreme circumstances of domain reduction and competition from the official or higher language, are possibly utilizing a different grammar altogether. This chapter aims to contribute to current variationist studies by providing a syntactic derivation component, through the Minimalist Program, that helps visualize the different distribution patterns in gender agreement between fluent and semi-speakers of Judeo-Spanish. These two groups are said to have acquired two underlying syntactic derivations, thereby resulting in the gender variation seemingly ruled by the age and proficiency continuum. However, because gender variation at the generational level and the syntactic level (parts of the

DP) follows a similar pattern in all three Judeo-Spanish populations, in spite of geographical location and contact languages, I believe that the Minimalist Program approach utilized in this study buttresses social variation with a fine-grained syntactic explanation. It is not meant to take away from social variables, but rather, the fact that these variables were powerful enough to entail a disruption in intergenerational transmission, creating a new underlying structure, at least in the DP.

Furthermore, this study entails an innovative contribution to Spanish variation since it utilizes data from endangered varieties of Judeo-Spanish (JS). Also known as Ladino, Muestro Espanyol, and Judezmo, among other nomenclatures, JS is the traditional and heritage language of several modern Sephardic communities. After their expulsion from the Iberian Peninsula in the late fifteenth century, Spanish Jews established new communities in the Ottoman Empire, the eastern Mediterranean, and the Balkans, were the Judeo-Spanish dialect developed and thrived for centuries. These Ottoman communities are often referred to as "Sefarad II," since the cultural, religious, and linguistic environment inherited from Spain or "Sefarad I" were rebuilt. Sephardic communities never experienced a compulsion to adopt Turkish, and the Spanish language became synonymous with Jewish identity and even enjoyed special economic status as a language for trade and commerce in Ottoman lands (Sachar 1994: 82–84). The situation changed dramatically centuries later, after World War I, as the dismemberment of the Ottoman Empire led to nation states with strong nationalistic linguistic policies, thereby forcing intergenerational language shift in favor of official languages such as Turkish, Bulgarian, and Greek. This period also witnessed considerable migration of Sephardim out of the former Ottoman lands and toward the United States, Latin America, Western Europe, and, a few decades later, to the nascent State of Israel (Sachar 1994: 101–2). These new communities are also identified as "Sefarad III" because Sephardim attempted to rebuild the social and communal patterns from their Ottoman communities. This study utilizes data from two communities of Sefarad II (Istanbul and the Prince Islands) and one from Sefarad III (New York City).

In addition to migration and strict nationalistic language policies, Judeo-Spanish populations also suffered the systematic deportation perpetrated by the Nazis and their collaborators in the Balkans. Entire communities, such as those of Monastir and Salonika, were annihilated and were never able to recover in the post-war period, and their Judeo-Spanish varieties are now considered extinct or extremely endangered (Benbassa & Rodrigue

2000: 176; Mazower 2004: 417–25). Even those communities that managed to remain stable after the Second World War and waves of migration are now also undergoing rapid language shift. A successful intergenerational transmission has not been achieved, due to extreme social pressure to adopt the coterritorial official language (Turkish, English, Hebrew, etc.), and there are no monolingual speakers. Judeo-Spanish is spoken by about 110,000, and most are sixty years or older (Lewis et al. 2014). The historical background and current status of the language in the Istanbul, Prince Islands, and New York communities relevant to this study will be discussed in section 2.

2. Judeo-Spanish in Istanbul, the Prince Islands, and New York City

Although separated by geography and migration patterns, all three communities present similar sociolinguistic characteristics and patterns of domain loss in favor of Turkish (Istanbul, Prince Islands) or English (New York City). The Jewish population in Turkey is mostly Sephardic and it consists of about 17,600 individuals, or roughly 2% of the total Turkish population (Della-Pergola 2010: 61), with the majority in the Istanbul metropolitan area and another significant population in Izmir. The Istanbulite community has managed to preserve Judeo-Spanish, albeit in peripheral domains. Judeo-Spanish is still used by some Sephardim in the home domain, to communicate with parents, grandparents, or other elderly relatives and sometimes with friends, as an in-group or code language (Romero 2012: 92–96). Judeo-Spanish is also employed when telling jokes or moralistic stories (*konsejas*), as the language for traditional music, and, on some occasions, as part of theater plays and other entertainments (Romero 2012: 97–98). However, Turkish remains the primary language, and it has even entered the religious domain, which had hitherto been exclusively reserved for Hebrew, Aramaic, and Judeo-Spanish (Romero 2012: 77). The community is actively pursuing a revitalization effort, and the weekly *Şalom*, which has one page in Judeo-Spanish, has now been joined by the monthly *El Amaneser*, which is completely in Judeo-Spanish. However, emigration out of Turkey has continued to reduce the community. Sporadic anti-Semitic attacks and anti-Jewish, anti-Israeli political rhetoric has impulsed new migration movements. A recent survey on Turkish Jewish populations revealed that most Turkish Jews live in the European side of Istanbul and that the community has experienced significant emigration to

Israel (and to a lesser rate to Western Europe and the Americas). About 10% of the population is under age fifteen, compared to almost 20% that is sixty-five and older (DellaPergola 2010: 51).

The Sephardic community in the Prince Islands is intricately connected with that of Istanbul. The earliest and largest Jewish community settled in Büyükada in the easternmost part of the archipelago toward the end of the nineteenth century and the beginning of the twentieth (Güleryüz 1992: 37–38). The Büyükada community and those that settled on two other islands in the 1950s and 1970s were actually Istanbulite Jews moving toward the periphery of the metropolitan area, an internal migration consequence of political struggles and anti-minority riots (Romero 2011a: 164–67). Although the Prince Islands community may be considered an extension of the Istanbulite community, the social and linguistic dynamics change during the summer months, as hundreds of Sephardim travel there from Istanbul and elsewhere in the Turkish Jewish diaspora. This provides an ideal opportunity for three generations of Sephardim, especially school-age children, to hear and practice Judeo-Spanish without the social pressure and stigma of the Turkish majority. Unfortunately, due to new economic and social demands, the influx of younger Sephardim to the Islands is diminishing (Romero 2011a: 177–82). Similar to Istanbul, Judeo-Spanish is spoken in the Prince Islands at home, but also in the beach resorts and in other entertainment activities such as songs and plays. The language is mostly spoken by the older generation, or when talking to elders who are less proficient in Turkish. It is also used as a code or in-group language. Several speakers remarked that up to one generation ago, Judeo-Spanish was the preferred language in the synagogue, but that now everything is in Turkish and Hebrew (Romero 2011a: 171–74). Additionally, Hebrew and French also compete for linguistic space. Hebrew is now spoken by many returning Sephardim who migrated and settled in Israel, and French is still spoken by a large percentage of the upper middle class (Romero 2011a: 176).

Although there has been a Spanish and Portuguese Sephardic community in New York City since the mid-seventeenth century, relevant to this study are the Judeo-Spanish immigrants from the former territories of the Ottoman Empire who arrived from the 1880s until 1921, when the U.S. Congress passed a law limiting the number of immigrants (Ben-Ur 2009: 193–94; Angel 1982: 17). The newcomers were fleeing dire post-World War I conditions and the nationalistic ethnic and linguistic policies imposed throughout the Balkans and Turkey. These Sephardim spoke a variety of Judeo-Spanish dialects, but they were able to rebuild a thriving Judeo-Spanish community with several newspapers, cafes, social clubs, religious institutions, and charity organizations (Angel 1982: 61–68). Most importantly, they lived closed to each other, mostly in the Lower East Side of Manhattan, forming a cohesive geographical community where Judeo-Spanish occupied most domains. However, similar to other immigrant groups, learning English became an economic asset, and, already in the 1940s, the dangers of acculturation were declaimed by several community leaders (Angel 1982: 164). Being a minority within a minority, Sephardim not only faced pressure to assimilate into American Society, but also into the larger Ashkenazic Jewish society (Angel 1982: 165). Sephardic-Ashkenazic "intermarriage" further contributed to the loss of Judeo-Spanish in the home domain, as new families opted English as the lingua franca. In the 1980s roughly 75% of New York Sephardim had married Ashkenazic partners, and this trend has continued, even marrying outside the Jewish religion (Angel 1982: 178). Lower birth rates, social mobility, motility into suburbia, and the lack of intergenerational transmission have replaced Judeo-Spanish in most of the domains it formerly occupied during the immigration period (Angel 1982: 177). The informants I interviewed represent a wide variety of Judeo-Spanish dialects (Bulgaria, Istanbul, Çanakkale) and are not part of a cohesive community. The majority is comprised of semispeakers, at best, who speak it sporadically with elderly family members, whereas the three most proficient speakers have found it useful in their current or former place of employment. Overall, all three communities display a dramatic loss of language domains, but, against all odds, after more than five hundred years since their expulsion from Spain, Judeo-Spanish has managed to survive, at least in the home and family domain.

3. Phi-Features in Endangered Languages

This study on gender agreement variation includes a Minimalist Program approach to explain variation inside the DP. According to this precept, gender agreement occurs as a result of feature valuation and checking (Chomsky 2001, 2002, 2006). The features in question are denominated phi-features, which represent an array of inflection processes such as person, number, gender, and possibly animacy and definiteness (de Dikken 2011: 857). In this research I will focus on gender agreement (masculine and feminine in Spanish) in the DP, and since their synonymy with phi-features is integral to this chapter, I will briefly explain their mechanisms in the Minimalist Program. Phi-features undergo a valuation process, which results in what is commonly known as adjectival or determiner agreement (Picallo 2008). This valuation process occurs through agree operation, defined as:

(1) AGREE
   a. An unvalued feature F (also known as a probe) on a head H at syntactic location α (Fα) scans its c-command domain for another instance of F (a goal) at location β (Fβ) with which to agree.
   b. Replace Fα with Fβ, so that the same feature is present in both locations. (Pesetsky & Torrego 2007: 4)

Once a probe has obtained the value from the goal, the former can now serve as the goal for another probe undergoing agree operation, thereby resulting in a single feature F shared by several positions (α, β, γ, etc.). In the instance of gender, a noun is specified in the lexicon as having an interpretable feature (i) of gender (G), with a value [*val*]. Following this structure, feminine nouns in Judeo-Spanish such as *mujer* 'woman,' *kaza* 'house,' and *kolor* 'color' come from the lexicon into agree operation as iG[*fem*], that is, the feminine value is interpreted for the gender phi-feature.[1] Elements with uninterpretable unvalued features then undergo agree operation and their features are valued as uF[*val*]. In the case of feminine gender, the result is gender agreement as uG[*fem*] with the feminine noun iG[*fem*]. This process in the DP is exemplified in (2):

(2) [$_{DP}$ una [$_{NP}$ kaza ermoza]
   uG[*fem*] ... iG[*fem*] ... uG[*fem*]
   'a beautiful house'

An interesting linguistic phenomenon occurs in the inflectional patterns, that is, valuation of phi-features, in endangered languages, especially in varieties spoken by semispeakers. Linguists such as Dorian (1973) noted "a dismal patchwork of inconsistencies" in the grammar randomly spread over East

---

   1. Although with few exceptions, Judeo-Spanish non-sex-differentiable or semantic residue nouns generally assign the feminine gender to nouns that end in -*a*, -*á*, and -*or*: *la komida* 'food,' *la udá* 'room,' *la golor* 'smell.' This gender assignment mechanism may yield feminine gender words in Judeo-Spanish that are masculine in Castilian and Latin American Standard Spanish. Examples of these are the following: Judeo-Spanish *la kalor* 'heat' and *la poema* 'poem,' which are masculine in standard Spanish. A great majority of nouns that end -*á* are borrowings from Hebrew and Turkish, stress-final languages. See Romero (2009) for a detailed analysis of gender assignment and lexical borrowings in Judeo-Spanish.

Sutherland Gaelic speakers (414). Some researchers suggest that variation in the inflectional patterns of endangered languages is the result of obligatory rules in the healthier variety of the language that become optional or simply fail to apply in speakers toward the lower end of the proficiency spectrum (Campbell & Muntzel 1989: 189). Andersen (1982) made the assertion that endangered languages or languages in shift will not exhibit the same number of morphological categories as the corresponding healthy variety (97). This entails that the inflectional morphology associated with such categories will undergo variation and change. Several studies have documented variation in phi-feature agreement in a wide variety of endangered languages. For instance, in person agreement, no Warlpiri speaker under the age of seventeen maintained all five pronominal forms (Bavin 1989: 280–81). For number, Ocuilteco has replaced its dual category with the plural inflection (Campbell & Muntzel 1989: 191–92). Moreover, several examples come from endangered varieties of Spanish (denominated "vestigial" by Lipski), such as Guamanian Spanish in (3) and Trinidadian Spanish in (4). The standard plural inflection is shown in brackets, following their original format in Lipski (1985: 972):

(3) *En estos días no hay escuela[s] español[as]*
'These days there are no Spanish schools.'

(4) *Ahora tiene casa[s] . . .*
'Now there are houses . . .'

Studies also demonstrate variation in phi-feature agreement in the valuation of uG[*fem*]. To illustrate, Dorian's (1981) research on East Sutherland Gaelic noted that semispeakers were substituting feminine agreement forms with those of the masculine, taken to be the default inflection (124–25). Lipksi's work on "vestigial" speakers of Spanish also provides additional examples of the lack of valuation of uG[*val*] with the feminine forms. The following examples come from Isleño Spanish, with the standard feminine gender inflection in brackets (Lipski 1985: 972):

(5) *Ehta décima fue composío[a] pol mi tío.*
'This decima was composed by my uncle.'

(6) *un[a] rata ansina.*
'a muskrat this (big).'

Lipski's research on the Spanish of transitional bilinguals in the United States yielded similar results, as informants were not consistent with feminine gender agreement (Lipski 1993: 161–62). The same phenomenon was observed in the Judeo-Spanish varieties analyzed in this study, Istanbul (7), Prince Islands (8), and New York City (9):

(7) *Yo tengo kaza viejo[a].*
    'I have (an) old house.'

(8) *Ay muncho[a]s kazas ermozo[a]s.*
    'There are many beautiful houses.'

(9) *Ay tantos automobils en este[a] sivdad.*
    'There are a lot of cars in this city.'

In examples (7)–(9), the nouns *kaza* 'house' and *sivdad* 'city' are iG[*fem*], but their corresponding adjectives, quantifiers, and demonstrative articles have failed to undergo a successful agree operation and have not been valued [*fem*] for gender phi-feature. The patterns in these valuations are the object of this study and will be discussed in section 5. However, the aforementioned cases of East Sutherland Gaelic, Warlpiri, Ocuilteco, Spanish, and the several varieties of Judeo-Spanish illustrate that variation in phi-feature agreement is present in a wide variety of endangered languages regardless of language family or contact language.

However, some variation patterns in phi-feature agreement are not inconsistent patchworks. As Dorian (1994) pointed out, "variation that is fundamentally linked to age and proficiency shows dramatic movement in variation use" (657). That is, the sociolinguistic conditions of some endangered languages are such that the older generation is more proficient and uses the endangered language more than the younger generation, and this may lead to sociolinguistic variation in which the younger generation displays a higher degree of change, that is, less phi-feature agreement. Variation governed by age and proficiency has been attested in a variety of endangered languages such as Dyirbal (Schmidt 1985) and Los Angeles Spanish (Silva-Corvalán 1994). Schmidt (1985) even labelled the endangered variety as "young people's Dyirbal," thereby emphasizing the group with the most variants. This type of age-proficiency linguistic variation may be rooted in the dynamics of linguistic domains. Besides a direct consequence of war and ethnic persecution, language endangerment and death may occur as a result of domain loss. A bilingual population may undergo language allocation, in which one language is assigned a certain social and functional range different from the other. For Dorian (1981), language endangerment begins when one language has fewer domains, such that the distribution is highly disproportionate, and, similarly for Schmidt (1985), the rapid reduction of a language's function, such that a new language replaces the former, over its entire functional range is the definition of language death (Schmidt 1985: 4). During most of the nineteenth century, Judeo-Spanish occupied most of the linguistic domains of the Sephardic communities in Turkey and elsewhere in the Ottoman Empire. Even the émigré communities that settled in New York City early in the twentieth century kept Judeo-Spanish as the language of most communal affairs, including a thriving press. Eventually, the sociolinguistic situation changed and Sephardim used Judeo-Spanish in fewer domains. The implication for this study is that the older generation acquired Judeo-Spanish when it was utilized in more domains than during the critical period of the younger generation. These different patterns of acquisition may have affected the way some grammatical features, such as phi-features, were processed or acquired with less competence by semispeakers, typically the younger members of the group. In the following section I will elaborate on the current linguistic domains in which Judeo-Spanish is still used among the three communities in question.

4. Methodology

Data were collected through a series of sociolinguistic interviews I conducted in Istanbul (2007), the Prince Islands (2009), and New York City (2013). Questions prompted informants on language use and linguistic attitudes. In addition, an oral translation task was also included, in which the researcher produced a sentence in Turkish (Istanbul and Prince Islands) or English (New York City) and asked the informant to translate it into Judeo-Spanish. The translation task sentences were not identical in all three communities, but it did contain similar sentences and vocabulary, which had been contrived to produce tokens relevant to gender agreement (among other morphological and syntactic features). For instance, the researcher uttered sentenced (10), and informants from Istanbul (11), the Prince Islands (12), and New York City (13) answered correspondingly:

(10) *Eski evim var.* / 'I have an old house.'

(11) *Yo tengo kaza vieja.*

(12) *Tengo una kaza vieja.*

(13) *Yo tengo una kaza viejo.*

The valuation of phi-features for uG[*val*] items with iG[*fem*] nouns was tabulated inside the DP. This included demonstrative and definite articles, prenominal adjectives, and post-nominal adjectives. Although other studies utilizing the minimalist approach to explore variation in gender agreement also included weak and strong quantifiers (Sessarego & Gutiérrez-Rexach 2011), there were not enough tokens in the Judeo-Spanish data to produce a statistically meaningful pattern.

Following the definitions postulated by Dorian (1973, 1978) and Grinevald (2003), informants in all three populations were divided into two groups: native fluent speakers and semispeakers. Native fluent speakers are bilingual, but Judeo-Spanish was learned first, usually as the home language. Semispeakers, on the other hand, are bilinguals whose dominant language is not Judeo-Spanish. Often times these are younger members of the speech community, and their variety is considered imperfect from the point of view of the older, more proficient members of the community. In many instances, they themselves do not think they know the language fluently, and many were surprised when I expressed interest in interviewing them (Grinevald 2003: 64–66; Dorian 1973: 417, 1978: 592). In terms of linguistic domains, native fluent speakers acquired Judeo-Spanish primarily in the home domain, with monolingual parents or other family members, and probably used Judeo-Spanish with friends and other social networks such as synagogue functions and entertainment. In contrast, semispeakers acquired Judeo-Spanish solely in the home domain, usually in a highly bilingual home or in a home already undergoing language shift. Judeo-Spanish was probably not spoken with the parents, but with an older monolingual or grandparent not fully fluent in Turkish or English. In fact, several semispeakers expressed that the only reason they are able to understand and know some Judeo-Spanish was because they grew up with a grandparent at home, which brought bilingualism into an otherwise Turkish/English monolingual home. The following examples are from Istanbul (14), the Prince Islands (15), and New York City (16). Speakers are identified throughout this chapter by gender (M/F) and age (number).

Table 9.1
Biographical characteristics of Judeo-Spanish informants.

Community	Gender		Age			Proficiency				Total
	Men	Women	<60	60+	age range	fluent	age range	semi-speaker	age range	
Istanbul	5	18	8	15	30–97	18	54–97	5	30–49	23
Prince Is.	1	10	6	5	27–73	7	53–73	4	27–47	11
NYC	1	7	3	5	51–80	3	74–80	4	51–64	8

(14) *Es lo ke me ambezí de la granmamá. A vezes se me está viniendo al tino, a vezes se me está olvidando.*
'It's what I learned from my grandmother. Sometimes it comes to mind, sometimes I forget it.' (F44)

(15) *Esto lingua es Ladino de mi granmamá. Kuando era chika yo, yo kon dingunos no avlava en Espanyol; solo mi granmamá avlava i kon mi madre, eos, las dos avlavan, mi madre kon mi padre i mi granmamá kon mi madre . . . solo los ninyos no avlavan, yo tanbién no avlava.*
'This language is Ladino from my grandmother. When I was small, I didn't speak Spanish with anyone, only my grandmother spoke Spanish with my mother, they, they both spoke [Spanish], my mother with my father, and my grandmother with my mother . . . only the children did not speak it, and I did not speak it either.' (F47)

(16) *De todos los inyetos, yo so yo avlo lo más muncho.*
'From all the grandchildren, I am the one who speaks more.' But I think that it's also because the others were not living with the grandparents. (F51)

Table 9.1 illustrates a summary of native fluent speakers and semispeakers for all three populations. The data reflects the endangered status of Judeo-Spanish, as most of the younger generations represent semispeakers, whereas the fluent speakers are mostly sixty and older. It also exemplifies the precarious situation for New York City Judeo-Spanish, as its semispeakers' age range is in the native fluent category in the Turkish communities. The distribution of the valuation of phi-features with G[*fem*] was recorded for both groups for all demonstratives, definite articles, and prenominal and post-nominal adjectives.

5. Results

The data from the three JS populations reveals an interesting pattern based on geographical location, as illustrated in Figure 9.1. Figure 9.1 shows a pattern of lower feminine gender agreement percentages in the semispeakers of all three populations. Moreover, the New York City population exhibits less agreement overall. However, Figure 9.1 also portrays very close results for all three populations. That is, the percentages in agreement for fluent (96.3–98.5%) and semispeakers (81.5–84.8%) do not seem to vary much across geography. In a previous, more detailed study between thirteen Istanbul participants and nine from the Prince Islands, within the same age range, these populations did not show a significant difference in gender agreement ($df = 18$, t-value 0.25, $p > 0.05$), and I had concluded they were actually part of the same linguistic community (Romero 2011b: 53, 55). The inclusion of six New York participants of similar age range in the Romero (2011b) data can provide a better understanding of the three communities, as in Figure 9.2. The inclusion of the New York City data provides a different statistical picture through a one-way ANOVA, as $df = 2$, $F = 4.18$, and $p = 0.03$. This implies that the differences among the three populations are statistically significant, but this seems to be driven mainly by informant F51 from New York, with only 63.3% of feminine gender agreement. Actually, if we take out her data, that analysis yields $p = 0.15$, thereby suggesting that the distribution of gender

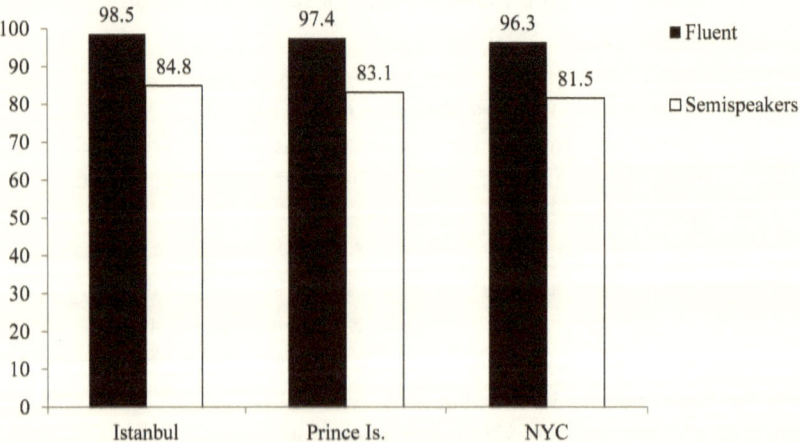

Figure 9.1
Percentage of feminine gender agreement in all three populations.

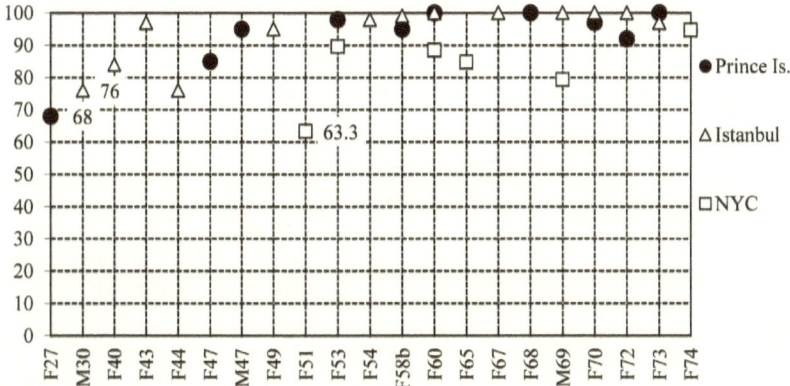

Figure 9.2
Percentage of feminine gender agreement per participant in the three communities.

agreement is nearly identical in the three geographical locations. Therefore, without looking at the distribution within the syntactic components of the DP, we could readily conclude that there are no major differences in the three Sephardic communities. However, this does not represent an accurate depiction of JS variation. We understand that JS semispeakers acquired the language in less-favorable sociolinguistic circumstances than their fluent counterparts, but geography (and thereby contact languages) cannot account for these differences. Even the generational gap, roughly 14% in all three communities, seems a bit optimistic. An analysis per syntactic category in the DP can provide additional insight into the variation between fluent and semispeakers. These distributions are illustrated through syntactic trees, since position inside the DP plays an important role in gender agreement.

Not surprisingly, the results for the Istanbulite native fluent speakers demonstrates that demonstratives, definite articles, prenominal adjectives, and post-nominal adjectives that are uG[*val*] undergo agree operations almost 100% successfully (the lowest was 97.3%). This is illustrated in Figure 9.3, where I have labeled as "stable gender feature domain" the aforementioned successfully valued items. On the other hand, the Istanbulite semispeakers (represented in Figure 9.4) exhibit lower percentages of phi-feature valuation in the prenominal and post-nominal adjective positions. I have labeled these as the vulnerable gender feature domain. The demonstrative and definite article position is still considered stable at 89%. The results for the Prince Islands were very similar to those of Istanbul both in

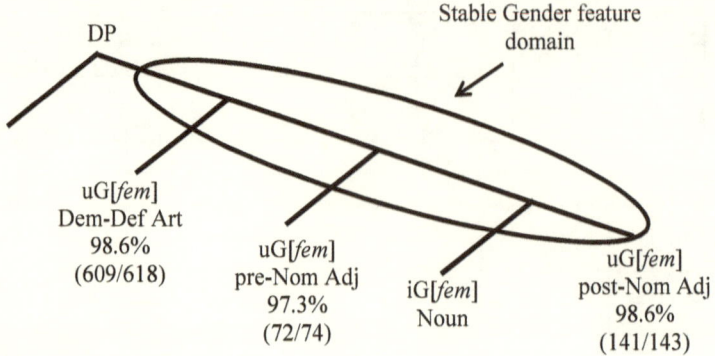

Figure 9.3
Istanbul fluent speakers (ages 54–97).

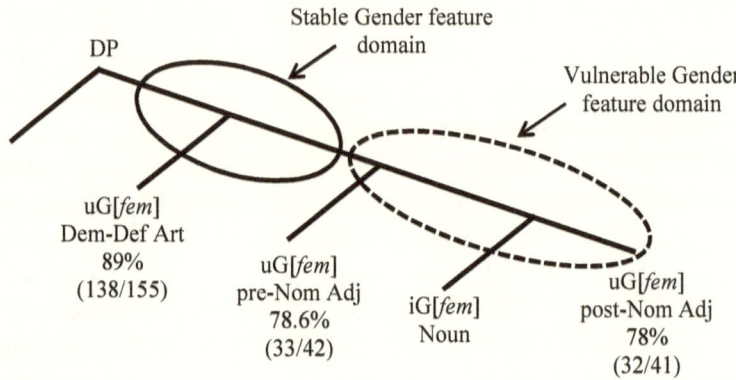

Figure 9.4
Istanbul semispeakers (ages 30–49).

percentages and fluent speakers vs. semispeakers patterns. This was probably expected given the proximity of both communities (a forty-five-minute catamaran ride) and how the social networks overlap during the summer months. Furthermore, the aforementioned study that compared the variation in gender and number agreement in the mainland and islands revealed that there were no clear differences between the communities, at least not at the morphological level (Romero 2011b, 55). Figure 9.5 depicts the percentages and token numbers per uG[*val*] category. A similar pattern emerges in the valuation of gender features in the Prince Island semispeakers (Figure 9.6).

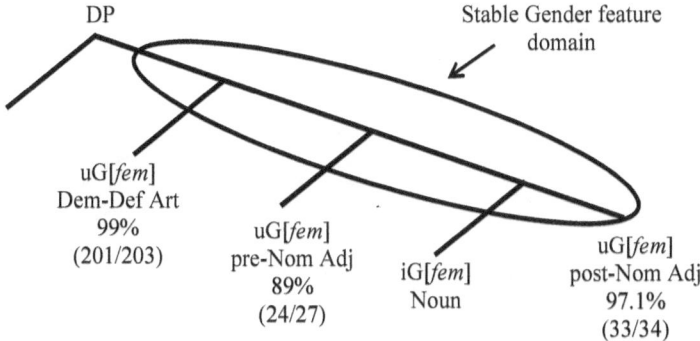

Figure 9.5
Prince Islands fluent speakers (ages 53–73).

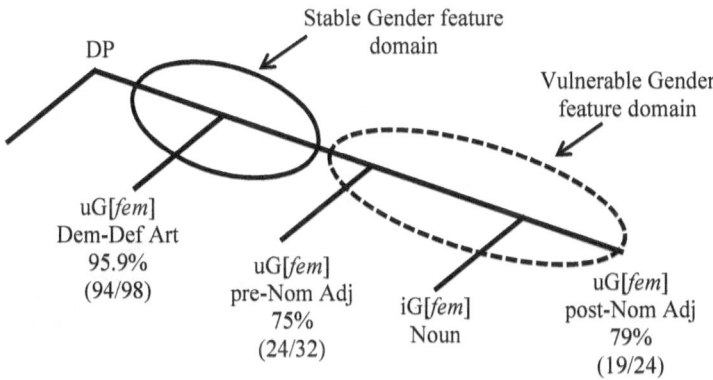

Figure 9.6
Prince Islands semispeakers (ages 27–47).

Prenominal and post-nominal positions are "vulnerable" and with a slightly lower percentage in the prenominal adjectival position. These similarities may be due to the common history and networks between Istanbul and the Prince Islands, but it is interesting that in both communities the adjectival positions present lower levels of agreement.

The data from New York City's fluent speakers (Figure 9.7) shows similar results in line with the fluent populations of Istanbul and the Prince Islands. And, similarly, the results for the semispeaker group in New York (Figure 9.8) showed the adjectival positions as being vulnerable. Since all three

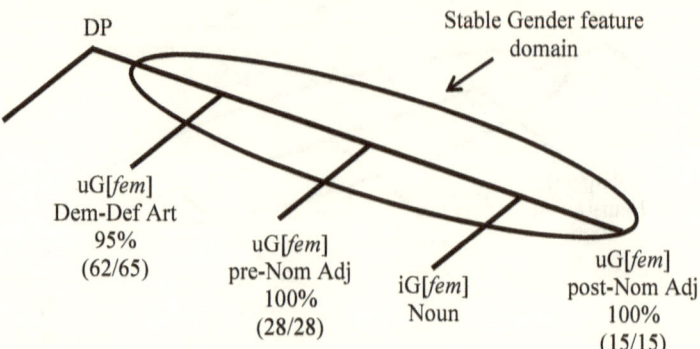

Figure 9.7
New York City fluent speakers (ages 74–80).

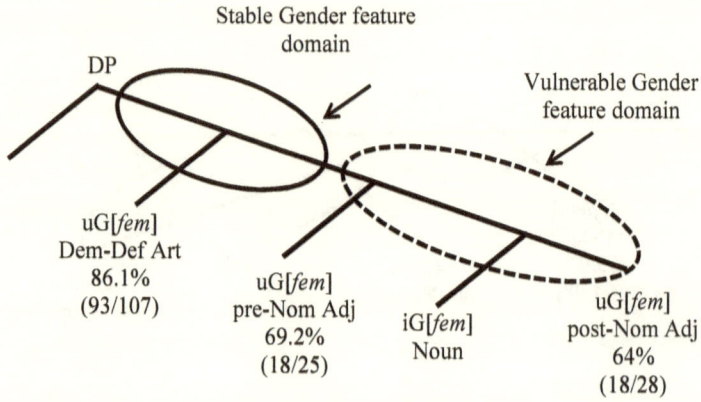

Figure 9.8
New York City semispeakers (ages 51–64).

populations display similar results in terms of speaker group characteristics and the syntactic positions most vulnerable in the semispeaker group, we can postulate that the differences in language acquisition dynamics are responsible for 1) maintaining gender phi-feature agreement inside the DP for the fluent JS group and 2) creating a vulnerable situation for agree operations in the prenominal and post-nominal adjective categories in the JS semispeaker group. Table 9.2 summarizes the data from Figures 9.3–9.8. I used the term "vulnerable" because agree operations have not ceased entirely in the uG[*val*] adjectives. Also, it is not the case that adjectives are coming from the lexicon as no-G[ ], or without a specification for gender, demonstrated in (17):

Table 9.2
Percentages of phi-feature valuation per uG[*val*] item per community.

Community	Fluent speakers			Semispeakers		
	Dem-Def Art.	pre-Nom Adj.	post-Nom Adj.	Dem-Def Art.	pre-Nom Adj.	post-Nom Adj.
Istanbul	98.6%	97.3%	98.6%	89%	78.6%	78%
Prince Is.	99%	89%	97.1%	95.9%	75%	79%
NYC	95%	100%	100%	86.1%	69.2%	64%

(17) [$_{DP}$ esta [$_{NP}$ kaza ermozo]
uG[*fem*] ... iG[*fem*] ... X ... no-G[ ]
'this beautiful house'

Statistically speaking, *most* adjectives are still undergoing valuation successfully, and significant changes in feature valuation have not taken place throughout the language.

However, Table 9.2 also mirrors the effect language shift and the lack of language domains have on the morphology of semispeakers. As previously stated, the semispeakers from New York City are within the age range considered as fluent speakers in the other two communities. This is the result of an unsuccessful intergenerational transmission that occurred much earlier than in Turkey, and it may be more difficult to reverse language shift and language death. The New York City semispeakers also have the lowest percentages of agreements in all three categories of demonstratives, definite articles, and adjectives, the lowest being 64% agreement for post-nominal adjectives. Although it is difficult to predict language change, post-nominal adjectives in New York City Judeo-Spanish are the most-likely elements to undergo feature valuation change from uG[*val*] to no-G[ ].

A central question to these results is why do adjectives tend to undergo successful valuation at a lesser rate than demonstratives and definite articles? Surprisingly, this pattern has also been observed in SLA research regarding the acquisition of gender agreement. Several studies with data from second language varieties and decreoleized varieties, namely those of Hawkins (1998), Bruhn de Garavito and White (2000), Franceschina (2005), and Sessarego and Gutiérrez-Rexach (2011), have demonstrated that learners produce gender agreement more consistently in determiners than in adjectives, and this preference may be rooted in universal language processability mechanisms.

6. Conclusion: "Dying with Morphological Boots on"

This study on gender agreement has attempted to illustrate the gravitational pull sociolinguistic variables such as age-proficiency have on morphological variation. By using syntactic derivations in line with the Minimalist Program, the notion that fluent and semispeakers may actually be operating different syntactic structures reveals another layer of variation between adjectives and determiners. Overall, the results of this study concur with research in other endangered languages in that variation in phi-feature agreement is a common characteristic in languages in shift and semispeakers, normally the younger generation, present less agreement. In addition, all three varieties of Judeo-Spanish exhibited similar patterns in stable and vulnerable gender feature domains, with prenominal and post-nominal adjectives being most likely to fail agree operations. As briefly stated, these patterns may be based on universal language acquisition processes.

Most interestingly, however, is that variation in gender agreement in Judeo-Spanish is not as radical or dramatic as in other endangered languages or even in Lipski's vestigial Spanish varieties from the Philippines, Guam, and Louisiana Isleños. We could have even expected lower rates of gender agreement through externally induced morphological change, given that Turkish and English, the contact languages, do not have a system of grammatical gender. Nevertheless, the Judeo-Spanish gender agreement system is quite robust, fluctuating from 64% to 79% in the most vulnerable adjectival positions in the morphology of the semispeakers. Dorian (1978) coined the phrase "dying with morphological boots on" to describe how an endangered language, albeit with a reduced number of language domains and a small population of speakers, has still managed to keep most of its structural morphology intact (Dorian 1978: 608). Perhaps this is the situation for modern Judeo-Spanish. The number of contexts in which the language is used is increasingly reduced, and the population of fluent speakers and semispeakers continues to dwindle, but, at least in gender feature valuation, the language has a stable, sometimes vulnerable, foothold.

10

Psych Predicates, Light Verbs, and Phase Theory
On the Implications of Case Assignment to the Experiencer in Non-*Leísta* Experience Predicates

Ricard Viñas de Puig

1. Introduction

In recent years, several excellent works on Hispanic linguistics have become an unavoidable part of the relevant literature in the field. However, some of these works present a heavy focus on sociolinguistic variation (Díaz-Campos 2011a, 2013), whereas others present a basic introduction to the different subdisciplines within the field (Azevedo 2009; Díaz-Campos 2013; Hualde et al. 2010).

The goal of this chapter is to fill a void in this recent literature. Along with other works in this volume, I analyze an understudied variety of current Spanish. Yet, in this case the variety under study is not determined by geographical factors, but rather by a morphosyntactic feature: I study the behavior of a non-*leísta* variety of Spanish, i.e., a variety in which the dative pronominal clitic *le* is not used in accusative constructions. From a methodological perspective, the work in this chapter also complements that by other authors in this volume by offering an analysis of an overlooked phenomenon from a minimalist theoretical framework.

In short, this chapter focuses on the study of experience predicates (i.e., those constructions that denote psychological or physical experiences) that surface as light verb constructions (i.e., with a verbal head that does not carry "meaning") in non-*leísta* varieties. The analysis presented not only provides evidence of some unnoticed features of these varieties, but also accounts for the occurrence of a phenomenon observed in the data.

1.1. THE ISSUE

Experience (or experiencer, or psych) verbs (or predicates) have been the object of extensive research in the generative literature (Pesetsky 1987, 1995; Belletti & Rizzi 1988; Rigau 1990; Masullo 1992; Arad 1999; McGinnis 2001; Pylkkänen 2002, 2008; Landau 2005; Adger & Ramchand 2006; Cuervo 2010; among many others). In Romance, and more specifically in Spanish, different authors have presented different views regarding the case assigned to the different arguments in the structure (see Franco 1990; Fernández-Ordóñez 1999; Parodi & Luján 2000; Rosselló 2002; Franco & Huidobro 2003; among many others). In this chapter I analyze experience predicates in non-*leísta* varieties of Spanish, as well as in Catalan, to shed further light on the case assigned to the Experiencer.

As noted in the literature, Experiencers in non-*leísta* varieties of Spanish (1) (as well as in other Romance languages that do not conflate dative and accusative case in animate third-person object pronouns, such as Catalan [2]) manifest a variation in the overt expression of case.

(1) a. *Le   molestan   los comentarios racistas.*
       DAT.3s   bother-PRES.3p   the comments racist.p
       'Racist comments bother her.'

   b. *Esos niños   la   molestan.*
       those children   ACC.3s.f   bother-PRES.3p
       'Those children bother her.'

(2) a. *Li   sorprenen   les notícies.*
       DAT.3s   surprise-PRES.3p   the news
       'This news surprises her.'

   b. *Els amics   la   van   sorprendre*
       the friends   ACC.3s.f   go-PRES.3p   surprise-INF

       amb una festa.
       with a party
       'Her friends surprised her with a party.'

In the examples above, the EXPERIENCER shows a variation in case. In the first sentence of each pair, the EXPERIENCER is assigned dative case; in the second sentence, however, the form of the pronominal clitic indicates that the EXPERIENCER receives accusative case. However, not all EXPERIENCERS allow for this case variation. In light verb experience constructions (henceforth, LVEC) (cf. Cuervo 2010; Viñas-de-Puig 2014), the EXPERIENCER argument can only surface as dative.

(3) a. *(A Luis)   La comida   le   hizo   daño.*
       (to Luis)   the meal   DAT.3s   do-PST.3s pain
       'The meal didn't sit well with Luis.' (lit. *The meal hurt Luis.*)
    b. **(A Luis)*   *Esos niños*   *lo*   *hicieron*   *daño.*
       (to Luis)   those children ACC.3s.m   do-PST.3p   pain
       'Those children hurt Luis.'

(4) a. *Li   fan   por   les amenaces.*
       DAT.3s do-PRES.3p fear   the threats
       'Threats scare her.'
    b. **(Aquells nens)*   *La*   *van*   *fer*   *por.*
       (those children)   ACC.3s.f   go-PRES.3p   do-INF   fear
       'Those children scared her.'

Note that the EXPERIENCER in the examples in (3) and (4) can only surface as dative: in both (3b) and (4b), the presence of an accusative EXPERIENCER yields an ungrammatical utterance. Given this contrasting behavior of the EXPERIENCER between full-fledged experience verbs and LVECs, the goal of this chapter is to provide a valid and up-to-date solution to the research question posed in (5).

(5) What motivates the lack of case variation on the EXPERIENCER in LVECs?

1.2. PHASE THEORY

One of the main claims that stem from the theoretical framework of the Minimalist Program is the fact that syntactic derivations do not happen seamlessly; instead, derivations are processed in recursive domains (or "chunks") of computation, what Chomsky (2001) labels as phases. According to this idea, given a set of items (or lexical array [LA]) that is pulled out of the lexicon to compute a syntactic derivation, this LA is divided into a series of lexical subarrays (LA_n), with only one being derived at a time. In other words, lexical subarray LA_2 cannot be derived until lexical subarray LA_1 is computed. Each derivation instantiation is a phase. Once a phase is computed, it becomes opaque to further computation, with only its edge (i.e., the specifier of the phase head) being available for a syntactic operation from the following phase.

This recursive operation of syntax is limited to heads that have propositional value. Chomsky (2001, 2008) argued that C and transitive v (or v^*), given their respective propositional properties, can be phase heads. On the other hand, and something that is crucial for the purposes of this chapter, other flavors of v, due to the fact that they are defective (i.e., do not introduce a full argument structure), cannot head a phase. More recently, Gallego (2010) has argued against this categorical division. However, many scholars, including Gallego, still consider experience v's (or v_{EXP}) to not be phase heads.

1.3. THE PROPOSAL

Based on the recent literature on experience predicates, I contend that the variation (or lack thereof) on the case assigned to the EXPERIENCER is dependent on two factors: 1) the argument structure of the predicate and 2) the event structure of the predicate. In the stative interpretations (i.e., when no further functional projection is merged on top of the experience structure) of incorporating predicates, the EXPERIENCER can only receive dative case; however, in eventive interpretations, the head of the eventive projection is responsible for assigning accusative case and, consequently, the EXPERIENCER receives the accusative. This possibility is not available in LVECs since, I argue, the EXPERIENCE is an independent argument generated in the lowermost structural position and, therefore, it can only be assigned accusative (or partitive) case by the functional projection v_{EXP}. Since accusative has already been assigned, the EXPERIENCER in these constructions (regardless of the eventive interpretation) can only surface as receiving inherent dative case. This serves as evidence that, contrary to recent views on the typology of phase heads, v_{EXP} is not unaccusative (cf. Rigau 1990), but rather a v^*, with full argument structure, and therefore a phase head.

1.4. METHODOLOGY

The data in this chapter, unless otherwise noted, have been provided by the author and checked with other native speakers when appropriate. I used traditional methodologies to explore the traditional empirical domain of generative linguistics; namely, intuitive grammaticality judgments, whose grammaticality values were confirmed through a small sampling of other native speakers. While more rigorous quantitative methods provide security against false generalizations (Gibson & Fedorenko 2013), it has been demonstrated that such traditional methods provide a reliable source of data (Sprouse & Almeida 2013).

2. A Basic Structure for Experience Predicates

In their already canonical work on psych(ological) verbs, Belletti and Rizzi (1988) present a classification of experience predicates, mainly based on the different cases assigned to the arguments present in the structure.

(6) a. Class I: Nominative EXPERIENCER; accusative THEME.
John loves Mary.
b. Class II: Nominative THEME; accusative EXPERIENCER.
The show amused Bill.
c. Class III: Nominative THEME; dative EXPERIENCER.
The idea appealed to Julie.

However, after a closer look to the possible expressions of experience predicates, we have to conclude that such a classification falls short, as it does not account for the existence of LVECs. Cuervo (2010) put forth an analysis according to which certain experience predicates (in Spanish) can be analyzed as a light verb construction.[1] I follow here Viñas-de-Puig's (2009, 2014) approach, based on Cuervo's, and argue for the existence of a structure that accounts for crosslinguistic evidence in support of the existence of experience predicates that surface as both full-fledged and light verbs. This BASIC EXPERIENCE STRUCTURE is shown in (7).

---

[1]. It should be noted, however, that all the light verb experience predicates that Cuervo (2010) presents, and that are also the object of this study, could be analyzed as being a subtype of Belletti and Rizzi's (1988) Class III of psych verbs: in both types of predicates, the EXPERIENCER (in its stative interpretation) surfaces as a dative argument.

(7) Basic experience structure

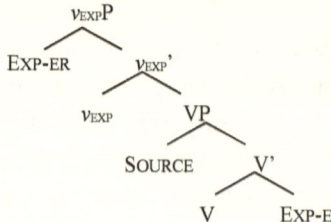

In the structure above, the EXPERIENCE (EXP-E) is an independent argument that merges with a V head (or root; cf. Hale & Keyser 1993, 2002). Another argument, the SOURCE, is externally merged at [Spec, VP], thus creating a predication-like structure (i.e., something, the EXPERIENCE, is being said about something else, the SOURCE). The last argument in the structure is the EXPERIENCER (EXP-ER), which, following various accounts on the introduction of external arguments (cf. Kratzer 1996; Arad 1999; McGinnis 2000; Pylkkänen 2002, 2008; Cuervo 2010), is introduced by a functional projection, namely v_{EXP}.

If we assume that this analysis is correct, we can then observe that it opens the door to two possibilities regarding the expression of the EXPERIENCE: either 1) the EXPERIENCE is incorporated on V or 2) the EXPERIENCE does not undergo incorporation and surfaces as an independent argument.

The first of the two possibilities for the expression of the EXPERIENCE is the one in which it undergoes a process of incorporation on V (akin to the incorporation onto a root proposed by Hale & Keyser [1993, 2002]), resulting in predicates with a full-fledged verb.

(8) Le   duelen   los brazos.
    DAT.3s   hurt-PRES.3p   the arms
    'Her arms hurt.'

(9) Em   molesten   aquests comentaris.
    DAT.1s   bother-PRES.3p   these comments
    'These comments bother me.'

In (8) and (9) above, the EXPERIENCE does not surface independently from the verb; rather, it creates a complex head with V, which results in an EXPERIENCE expressing the [Tense] and [Agr(eement)] features found on V.

The other two arguments, however, appear independently: the SOURCE is merged at [Spec, VP] (*los brazos* 'the arms' in [8]; *aquests comentaris* 'these comments' in [9]), while the EXPERIENCER is introduced by the functional projection v_{EXP} (*le* in [8], *em* in [9]).

The second possibility for the expression of the EXPERIENCE is the opposite from the one discussed above: the EXPERIENCE does not incorporate on V and, consequently, surfaces as an independent argument. Logically, this possibility entails the presence of a light verb.

(10) a. *Me   da   miedo   la oscuridad.*
        DAT.1s   give-PRES.3s   fear   the darkness
        'Darkness scares me.'
    b. *Me   dan   asco   las ratas.*
        DAT.1s   give-PRES.3p   disgust the rats
        'Rats disgust me.'

(11) a. *Em   fa   mal   la mà.*
        DAT.1s   do-PRES.3s   pain   the hand
        'My hand hurts.'
    b. *Em   fan   por   les serps.*
        DAT.1s   do-PRES.3p   fear   the snakes
        'Snakes scare me.'

In both examples above, the EXPERIENCE surfaces independently from V, which implies the surfacing of a light verb that is the element that provides a phonological output for [Tense] and [Agr] features.[2]

It is worth noting that in LVECs, the EXPERIENCE is a syntactically independent internal argument. As with other independent arguments, the EXPERIENCE can be quantified, as shown in (12) and (13). In both cases, the EXPERIENCE argument (but not the full predicate) is modified by a quantifier.

(12) *Me   da   mucho   miedo   la oscuridad.*
     DAT.1s   give-PRES.3s   much   fear   the darkness
     'Darkness scares me very much.'

---

2. The actual phonological output of the light verb (and its variation within and among languages) might actually be linked to other phenomena; namely, the features found in the EXPERIENCE argument and the event structure of the predicate. However, this issue is not fully developed here, as it does not have a significant impact on the analysis that is the object of this chapter.

(13) Em   fan   molt   mal   els ulls.
     DAT.1S   do-PRES.3P much   pain the eyes
     'My eyes hurt very much.'

The claim of the argumenthood of the EXPERIENCE is further supported with additional data. In Catalan, the EXPERIENCE argument can be replaced by a pronominal clitic, as in (14).

(14) No   me   'n   fan   gens   els ulls (, de mal).
     NEG   DAT.1S PART.3S   do-PRES.3P   at all   the eyes of pain
     'My eyes don't hurt at all.'

In (14) the EXPERIENCE is replaced by the partitive clitic *(e)n*. If we assume that only constituents can be replaced by proforms (e.g., pronominal clitics), we can affirm that the EXPERIENCE in these constructions is indeed an independent argument. It is worth noting that such a claim (i.e., the EXPERIENCE is an [internal] argument) is not only valid for Catalan; I contend that this is also true crosslinguistically. However, the pronominal test exemplified in (14) is not applicable in Spanish, since Spanish lacks the partitive pronominal observed in the Catalan data.

Once the argumenthood of the EXPERIENCE in LVECs has been established, we need to determine the type of argument it is. The examples (12), (13), and (14) provide some evidence on the nature of this argument: 1) the EXPERIENCE can be quantified (which indicates there is a projection higher than NP), and 2) the EXPERIENCE is replaced by a partitive clitic. Using these data as evidence, I argue against the idea that the EXPERIENCE is a DP. Consider the examples in (15) and (16).

(15) a. Me   dan   un   asco   espantoso   las ratas.
        DAT.1S   give-PRES.3P a   disgust   awful.m   the rats
        'Rats really disgust me.'
     b. *Me   dan   el   asco   espantoso   las ratas.
        DAT.1S   give-PRES.3P the   disgust   awful.m   the rats
        'Rats really disgust me.'

(16) a. Em   fan   un   mal   increïble   els ulls.
        DAT.1S   do-PRES.3P   a   pain   unbelievable the eyes
        'My eyes really hurt.'

b. *Em   fan   el   mal   increïble   els ulls.
   DAT.1s do-PRES.3p   the   pain   unbelievable   the eyes
   'My eyes really hurt.'

In the first sentence of each of the pairs above, the EXPERIENCE is preceded by an indefinite article. Yet, when the same EXPERIENCE is preceded by a definite article (which can be considered as a D head), the resulting utterance is ungrammatical. This evidence, along with the examples in (12) and (13), which show EXPERIENCE arguments can be quantified, demonstrates that the EXPERIENCE is not a DP, but a QP.

Since the EXPERIENCE is a nominal expression, it still needs to be assigned case. Because it is not a DP, the EXPERIENCE cannot be assigned full (accusative) case, leaving the only possibility, partitive case: in (14) the EXPERIENCE is replaced by the Catalan partitive clitic *(e)n*; however, if the EXPERIENCE is replaced by an accusative clitic, the sentence is then ungrammatical.

(17) —Et   fa   mal   la mà?
     DAT.2s do-PRES.3s   pain   the hand
     —*No   me'   l   fa   pro.
     NEG   DAT.1s ACC.3sm do-PRES.3s   pro
     '—Does your hand hurt?—No, it doesn't.'

In the answer in (17), the EXPERIENCE *mal* 'pain' in the question is replaced with an accusative pronominal clitic, which yields an ungrammatical utterance.

With all this evidence, we can therefore safely conclude that the EXPERIENCE in LVECs is an independent QP argument.

3. Eventive Experience Predicates

As widely noted in the literature (Belletti & Rizzi 1988; Franco 1990; Arad 1998, 1999; McGinnis 2001; Franco & Huidobro 2003; Pylkkänen 2008; among many others), certain (but not all) experience predicates allow different eventive interpretations: in some cases, the predicate is interpreted as a state; in other instances, the experience predicate presents an eventive (inchoative or causative) interpretation. This is a widespread crosslinguistic phenomenon, observed not only in Romance, but also in other linguistic families. Consider the Spanish examples in (18), the Catalan examples in (19), and the English examples in (20).

(18) a. *Le   molestaron   esos comentarios.*
       DAT.3s   bother-PST.3p   those comments
       'Those comments bothered her.'
    b. *Esos   niños   las   molestaron.*
       those   children   ACC.3pf   bother-PST.3p
       'Those children bothered them.'

(19) a. *Li   fan   por   les preguntes difícils.*
       DAT.3s   do-PRES.3p   fear   the difficult questions
       'Difficult questions scare him.'
    b. *Aquells nens   li   van   fer   por.*
       those children   DAT.3s   go-PRES.3p   do-INF   fear
       'Those children scared him.'

(20) a. My hand hurt yesterday.
    b. Those children hurt me yesterday.

Note that all the (a) utterances in the examples (18) to (20) above favor a stative interpretation; that is, these sentences convey a state (i.e., the EXPERIENCE) without any trigger or bound time. In contrast, the utterances in (b) are preferred under an eventive interpretation: in these sentences, an external (animate) CAUSER, *those children*, is responsible for triggering the EXPERIENCE (*molestar* 'to bother' in [18b], *fer por* 'to scare' in [19b], and *hurt* in [20b]).[3]

Following similar analyses in the recent literature (Arad 1998, 1999; McGinnis 2001; Franco & Huidobro 2003; Pylkkänen 2008; Viñas-de-Puig 2014), I contend that this variation in interpretation is structurally motivated. According to this proposal, then, the BASIC EXPERIENCE STRUCTURE presented in (7) above only yields stative readings (cf. Arad 1998, 1999). The eventive interpretations, which may be either inchoative or causative, are obtained when a functional projection is merged on top of v_{EXP}P: if an unaccusative v_{BECOME} is externally merged to v_{EXP}P, an inchoative interpretation (i.e., an event with no CAUSER or end-point) is obtained; additionally,

---

3. It is worth clarifying that the (b) utterances in examples (18) to (20) could also be interpreted as stative (i.e., the children are not AGENTS or CAUSERS, but "simply" the SOURCE of the experiences described). However, if that were the intended interpretation, it would have implications on the case assigned to the EXPERIENCER.

if a v_{CAUS} head, responsible for the introduction of an (external) CAUSER, is merged on top of v_{BECOME}P, the result is a causative interpretation (i.e., an event with a CAUSER and an end-point). The full-fledged eventive structure is shown in (21).

(21) Eventive experience structure

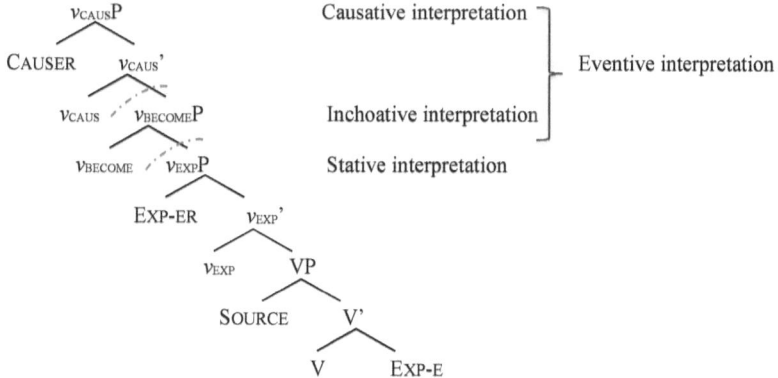

Let's go back to the examples in (18) to (20) above to test the actual validity of this proposal. If the (a) sentences in these examples are stative (as the result of not merging a causative projection on top of v_{EXP}P) and the (b) sentences are eventive (as the result of merging v_{CAUS}), we would expect different behaviors in each pair of utterances. Following canonical tests in the literature, we can confirm that this is indeed the case. According to Dowty (1979), states do not resist modification with an adjunct of the type *in X time*, which targets the end-point of an event. Consider the same examples modified with such an adjunct.

(22) a. */?*Le* molestaron esos comentarios en dos minutos.
DAT.3s bother-PST.3p those comments in two minutes
'Those comments bothered her in two minutes.'
b. *Esos niños* las molestaron en dos minutos.
those children ACC.3pf bother-PST.3p in two minutes
'Those children bothered them in two minutes.'

(23) a. */?Li* fan por les preguntes difícils
DAT.3s do-PRES.3p fear the difficult questions

en dos minuts.
in two minutes
'Difficult questions scare him in two minutes.'

b. *Aquells nens   li   van   fer   por*
   those children   DAT.3s   go-PRES.3p   do-INF   fear

   en dos minuts.
   in two minutes
   'Those children scared him in two minutes.'

(24) a. */?My hand hurt in two minutes yesterday
    b. Those children hurt me in two minutes yesterday.

In all the pairs of examples in (22) to (24) we observe a clear contrast of grammaticality. The (b) examples, when modified with the phrase *in two minutes*, result in grammatical utterances (since these utterances are the result of an eventive structure with an end-point)[4]; however, when the (a) examples are modified with the same phrase, the resulting utterance is not felicitous (since these utterances are states and, therefore, do not present the end-point triggered by the temporal phrase *in two minutes*). This therefore suggests that there is a difference in the eventive interpretation of the utterances in each pair.

Additional evidence further supports this claim. Always following Dowty (1979), causative (eventive) utterances may be modified by *deliberately/purposely* type adverbs (or phrases), since these adverbs (or phrases) target the AGENT (or CAUSER) of the event. States, on the other hand, due to the fact that they do not introduce a CAUSER in the structure, do not resist modification with such adverbs (or phrases). This contrast is manifested in the examples that follow.

(25) a. */?*Le*   *molestaron*   *esos comentarios*   *a propósito.*
       DAT.3s   bother-PST.3p   those comments   on purpose
       'Those comments bothered her on purpose.'
    b. *Esos niños*   *las*   *molestaron*   *a propósito.*
       those children   ACC.3pf   bother-PST.3p   on purpose
       'Those children bothered them on purpose.'

(26) a. */?Li*   fan   *por*   *les preguntes difícils*   *expressament*
       DAT.3s   do-PRES.3p   fear   the difficult questions   purposely
       'Difficult questions scare him on purpose.'

---

4. The (a) sentences in (22) and (23) may actually be grammatical only under an inchoative interpretation. In that case, the expression "in two minutes" does not trigger the end-point of the experience event, but the initial point of the experience state.

    b. *Aquells nens   li   van   fer   por*
       those children   DAT.3s go-PRES.3p do-INF fear

    expressament.
    purposely
    'Those children scared him on purpose.'

(27) a. */?My hand hurt on purpose yesterday.
    b. Those children hurt me on purpose yesterday.

Similar to what was observed in examples (22) to (24), the three pairs of examples above show a clear contrast in grammaticality. Note that in the (a) examples in (25), (26), and (27), the presence of the *deliberately/purposely* type phrase yields an ungrammatical utterance; yet, in the (b) sentences of the same examples, the presence of this modifier does not impact the grammaticality of the utterance. If we assume, following Dowty, that "only non-statives co-occur with the adverbs *deliberately, carefully*" (1979: 55), we demonstrate that each sentence in the pairs of experience predicates first presented in examples (18) to (20) yield different eventive interpretations, resulting from the EVENTIVE EXPERIENCE STRUCTURE put forth in (21).

4. Case Alternation in Incorporating Predicates

Let's return to the issue of case alternation on the EXPERIENCER. Consider again the examples introduced in Section 1 that manifest different case on the EXPERIENCER; these examples are repeated in (28) and (29).

    (28) a. *Le   molestan   los comentarios racistas.*
          DAT.3s bother-PRES.3p the comments racist.p
          'Racist comments bother her.'
       b. *Esos niños   la   molestan.*
          those children ACC.3s.f bother-PRES.3p
          'Those children bother her.'

    (29) a. *Li   sorprenen   les notícies.*
          DAT.3s surprise-PRES.3p the news
          'This news surprises her.'

b. *Els amics   la   van   sorprendre*
   the friends ACC.3s.f   go-PRES.3p   surprise-INF

   amb una festa.
   with a party
   'Her friends surprised her with a party.'

In these examples, as already noted, we observe a variation of the case on the EXPERIENCER: in the first utterance of each pair the EXPERIENCER is assigned dative case; conversely, in the second pair of each example, the EXPERIENCER is assigned accusative case. This difference, I argue (following different analyses of these structures), is based on the eventive interpretation of the predicate.

Recall from the previous section that states do not resist modification with *deliberately* type expressions. If we apply this test to the previous examples, we will observe a variation in the eventive reading of the predicates.

(30) a. **Le   molestan   los comentarios racistas*
        DAT.3s   bother-PRES.3p   the comments racist.p

        a propósito.
        on purpose
        'Racist comments bother her on purpose.'

     b. *Esos niños   la   molestan   a propósito.*
        those children   ACC.3s.f   bother-PRES.3p   on purpose
        'Those children bother her on purpose.'

(31) a. **Li   sorprenen   les notícies   expressament.*
        DAT.3s   surprise-PRES.3p   the news   deliberately
        'This news surprises her on purpose.'

     b. *Els amics   la   van   sorprendre*
        the friends   ACC.3s.f   go-PRES.3p   surprise-INF

        expressament amb una festa.
        deliberately with a party
        'Her friends surprised her on purpose with a party.'

In both (30) and (31), we observe a clear contrast in grammaticality between each pair with the inclusion of an expression of the *deliberately* type: the examples in the (a) sentences do not resist modification; the (b) sentences, on the other hand, are fully grammatical. Such a distinction indicates, following the differences in eventive interpretation presented in Section 2, that the first sentence in each pair above is a state (since states do not resist modification with a *deliberately* type expression), and the second sentence in each pair is an event.

Interestingly, the disparity in grammaticality observed in the pairs of sentences in (30) and (31) corresponds with the different value of case assigned to the EXPERIENCER. In the sentences that present a stative interpretation, the EXPERIENCER is assigned dative case, while in the examples in which the reading is that of an eventive predicate the EXPERIENCER surfaces as accusative. The relationship between case and eventive interpretation can be easily accounted for following the assumptions presented in the previous section (along with similar views observed in related literature).

Recall that the stative interpretation of experience predicates is the result of having the BASIC EXPERIENCE STRUCTURE, with no further functional (eventive) projection externally merged on top of v_{exp}P. For the purposes of this analysis, I assume that structural case is assigned via agree (cf. Chomsky 2001, 2008). In this view, we can suppose that the EXPERIENCER is assigned inherent dative case (as related to its θ-role), while the SOURCE is the first available goal of a nominative case assigning probe (i.e., T), as seen in (32).

(32) Eventive experience structure

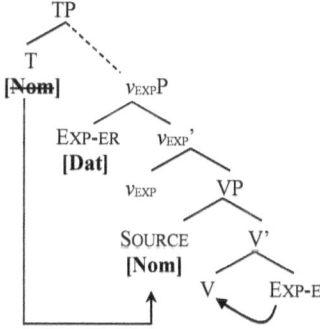

According to the structure in (32), in stative interpretations the EXPERIENCER is not the goal of any functional projection assigning (accusative) case and therefore is left with the inherent case related to its θ-role (as EXPERIENCER). The SOURCE, on the other hand, becomes a goal of the nominative assigning probe T and, as a consequence, is assigned nominative. This analysis, albeit it accounts for the facts repeated in (28a) and (29a), presents a problem: why isn't the EXPERIENCER the first goal of the probe T? The account that I propose to overcome this challenge is related with the information structure of the predicate. I argue that, following the lines proposed by Belletti (2004) accounting for new information focus interpretations, the SOURCE moves to a focus position above the verbal projection but below TP.[5] Assuming that case is the last operation before a phase is interpreted (cf. Brattico 2008), it is from this higher position above VP that the SOURCE becomes the first available goal for the nominative case assigning probe T and, therefore it is assigned nominative case. Assuming this account, then, the EXPERIENCER is no longer a possible goal for T.

For eventive readings, case assigning relations are significantly different. If we look back at the pairs of examples in (30) and (31), we can see how the eventive (causative) interpretation (as evidenced by the allowance of *deliberately* type phrases) corresponds to an EXPERIENCER being assigned accusative case. Recall from Section 3 that the eventive interpretation is the result of merging a v_{BECOME} functional projection and, in causative readings, a v_{CAUS} projection, which selects v_{BECOME}P and which is responsible for the introduction of the CAUSER. v_{BECOME} is an unaccusative head (it does not introduce an external argument and cannot assign case), while v_{CAUS} is a non-defective v (i.e., v^* in Chomsky's terms) and, therefore, a case assigning probe. Assuming this structure, the case relations accounting for the outputs observed in (30b) and (31b), with an accusative EXPERIENCER and a nominative CAUSER, are exemplified in the structure in (33).

(33) Eventive experience structure

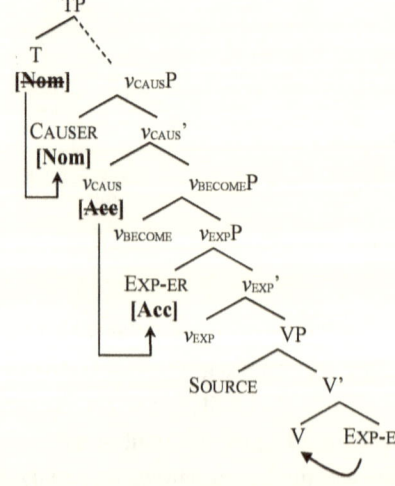

---

5. Note that if we only assume a movement of the SOURCE to a position between *v*P and TP, we would find that the word order is not what is observed in the examples presented (where

In this analysis, which stems from the approaches presented in earlier works in the literature dealing with experience predicates in Spanish (Franco 1990; Franco & Huidobro 2003; among others), the CAUSER is the first available goal of the nominative assigning probe T, while the EXPERIENCER becomes the first available goal of v_{CAUS}, which, as v^*, is a probe responsible for the assignation of accusative case. Since its case value has already been checked, the EXPERIENCER no longer surfaces as being assigned inherent (dative) case.

Similar to the analysis accounting for case relations in the stative reading of incorporating experience predicates, this analysis accounts for the data observed in (30b) and (31b). However, we should note that in these utterances there is no SOURCE (*esos niños* 'those children' in [30b] and *els amics* 'her friends' in [31b] are the CAUSERS of the experience event). I contend that this fact also has to do with the case relations with the different arguments. Consider the sentences in (34), adapted from the felicitous example in (30b).

(34) a. * *Esos niños   la   molestan   los brazos*
       those children   ACC.3s.f   bother-PRES.3p   the arms

   a propósito.
   on purpose
   'Those children bother her on her arms on purpose.'

   b. *Esos niños   la   molestan   en los brazos*
       those children   ACC.3s.f   bother-PRES.3p   on the arms

   a propósito.
   on purpose
   'Those children bother her on her arms on purpose.'

In the example in (34a), the inclusion of a possible SOURCE of the experience (*los brazos* 'the arms') results in an ungrammatical utterance. This is the case because this SOURCE, as a nominal expression, needs to be valued for case but there is no available case-assigning probe. If such a probe is introduced then the resulting sentence is grammatical. This is the case in (34b), where the P *en* 'on' serves as a probe and the SOURCE *los brazos* 'the arms' is its corresponding goal.

---

the SOURCE follows the [incorporated] predicate). To obtain the observed word order, we would have to assume that there is an additional step in the syntax: the V head, along with the EXPERIENCE argument, moves to the v_{EXP}, where it merges with the EXPERIENCER (if this surfaces as a clitic) and creates a complex head. In turn, this complex head moves to higher positions in the structure (i.e., T). Once these operations have taken place, the resulting word order is the one observed in the data.

5. Lack of Case Alternation in LVECs

Once we have analyzed the case relations in incorporating experience predicates, we need to take a look at what happens with LEVCs. In this regard, a similar analysis to the one presented in the previous section can be used to account for the lack of case variation on the EXPERIENCER in LVECs, with the difference being the overt presence of an "additional" argument; i.e., the EXPERIENCE.

(35) a. *(A Luis)* *La comida* *le* *hizo* *daño.*
 (to Luis) the meal DAT.3s do-PST.3s pain
 'The meal didn't sit well with Luis.' (lit. 'The meal hurt Luis.')
 b. **(A Luis)* *Esos niños* *lo* *hicieron* *daño.*
 (to Luis) those children ACC.3s.m do-PST.3p pain
 'Those children hurt Luis.'

(36) a. *Li* *fan* *por* *les amenaces.*
 DAT.3s do-PRES.3p fear the threats
 'Threats scare her.'
 b. **(Aquells nens)* *La* *van* *fer* *por.*
 (those children) ACC.3s.f go-PRES.3p do-INF fear
 'Those children scared her.'

As observed in the examples above, LVECs do not allow an accusative EXPERIENCER. In both Spanish and Catalan, the only possibility for the expression of the EXPERIENCER is if it surfaces as dative (as in [35a] and [36a]); if the EXPERIENCER is assigned accusative case, the resulting utterance is ungrammatical.

It is worth noting that this impossibility of having an accusative EXPERIENCER is not related to the event reading of the predicate: in both stative and eventive readings the only possibility for the EXPERIENCER is to surface as dative. If we introduce an expression to favor an eventive interpretation, again the only possibility is to have a dative EXPERIENCER.

(37) a. *(A Luis) Esos niños* *le* *hicieron* *daño*
 (to Luis) those children DAT.3s do-PST.3p pain

 a propósito.
 on purpose
 'Those children hurt Luis on purpose.'

b. *(A Luis) Esos niños   lo   hicieron   daño
   (to Luis) those children   ACC.3s.m   do-PST.3p   pain

   a propósito.
   on purpose
   'Those children hurt Luis on purpose.'

(38) a. (Aquells nens)   Li   van   fer   por
        (those children) DAT.3s   go-PRES.3p   do-INF   fear

   expressament.
   deliberately
   'Those children scared her on purpose.'
b. *(Aquells nens)   La   van   fer   por
   (those children)   ACC.3s.f go-PRES.3p   do-INF   fear

   expressament.
   deliberately
   'Those children scared her on purpose.'

Recall that *deliberately* type constructions target the CAUSER (or AGENT) of an event and, thus, are only possible if an eventive functional layer is merged on top of v_{EXP}P. Therefore, all the examples in (37) and (38) clearly favor an eventive interpretation, as marked with the presence of the expressions *a propósito* 'on purpose' and *expressament* 'deliberately.' However, in the utterances in (37b) and (38b), the presence of an accusative EXPERIENCER yields an ungrammaticality judgment, thus proving that the case on the EXPERIENCER cannot be linked to the event structure.

5.1. STATIVE LVECS

Following the general assumption presented in the previous sections, the stative reading is obtained when no further (eventive) projection is merged on top of v_{EXP}P. As already stated (and as it is obvious assuming the argument and eventive structure presented in Section 3), LVECs do indeed present non-eventive interpretations.

(39) a. #(A Luis) La comida   le   hizo   daño
        (to Luis) the meal   DAT.3s   do-PST.3s   pain

en cinco minutos.
in five minutes
'The meal didn't sit well with Luis in five minutes.'

b. *(A Luis) La comida   le   hizo   daño
   (to Luis) the meal   DAT.3S   do-PST.3S   pain

a propósito.
on purpose
'The meal didn't sit well with Luis on purpose.'

(40) a. #Li   fan   por   les amenaces   en cinc minuts.
        DAT.3S   do-PRES.3P   fear   the threats   in five minutes
        'Threats scare her in five minutes.'

    b. *Li   fan   por   les amenaces   expressament.
        DAT.3S   do-PRES.3P   fear   the threats   deliberately
        'Threats scare her on purpose.'

In all the sentences in (39) and (40) the presence of the expression "in five minutes" or of a purpose phrase forces an eventive interpretation, which results in ungrammaticality. Thus, both pairs of utterances above are concluded to be stative. In all these sentences the EXPERIENCER is assigned dative (not unlike the stative incorporating experience predicates analyzed in Section 4). Interestingly, though, the (QP) EXPERIENCE argument is assigned partitive case, as manifested with the possibility of it being replaced by a partitive clitic *(e)n* in Catalan (as shown in [41] below).

(41) Les amenaces,   te' n_i fan   molta ___$_i$
     the threats   DAT.2S   PART.3S   do-PRES.3P   much

(, de por).
of fear
'Threats scare you very much.'

I argue that all these data are evidence in favor of the structure shown in (42). According to this structure, v_{EXP} is not a defective v, unable to become a case assigning probe, but a v^* (contra Chomsky 2001, 2008; Gallego 2010; among others). This functional projection is the one responsible for assigning (partitive) case to the EXPERIENCE.

(42) Eventive experience structure

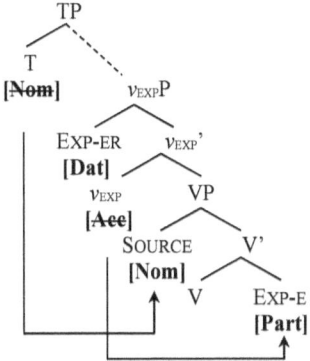

Following the tree in (42), the EXPERIENCE is assigned case by v_{EXP} and, since it is not a full DP, this case surfaces as partitive. The other two arguments in the structure, the SOURCE and the EXPERIENCER, are assigned case following a derivation similar to the one described in the previous section for stative incorporating experience predicates: the EXPERIENCER, since there is no available probe to assign case, surfaces with inherent (dative) case; the SOURCE, on the other hand, becomes the first available goal of the nominative assigning probe T. Again, this derivation is only possible if we assume movement of the SOURCE to a new information focus position between vP and TP (cf. Belletti 2004).

5.2. EVENTIVE LVECS

Akin to incorporating experience predicates, (some) LVECs allow for eventive interpretations. The (a) examples in (37) and (38) and the (b) examples in (39) and (40) are evidence of this: the Spanish LVEC *hacer daño* 'to hurt' and the Catalan LVEC *fer por* 'to scare' (among others) do indeed allow for a non-stative reading. In those examples, these LVECs are fully grammatical when modified with temporal expressions targeting the end point of the event, or when modified with expressions indicating purpose, which target the CAUSER (or AGENT) of the event.

However, LVECs display a different behavior from incorporating experience predicates: as noted, in LVECs the EXPERIENCER always surfaces displaying dative case, even when an obvious eventive interpretation is forced (again, note the contrast in grammaticality in the pairs of examples in [37] and [38]). The impossibility of having an accusative EXPERIENCER (as opposed to what was observed with incorporating predicates) is, I argue, directly related to the overt presence of the EXPERIENCE, as seen in (43).

(43) Eventive experience structure

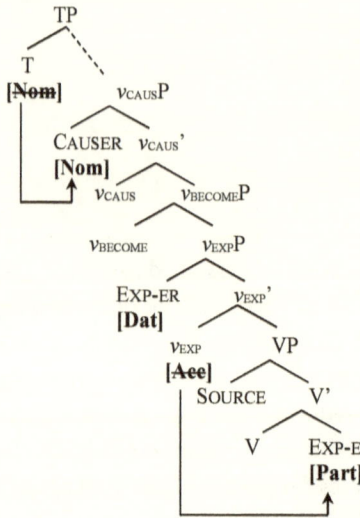

In (43), the EXPERIENCE is an independent argument and, therefore, it becomes the first available goal of an accusative assigning probe v_{EXP} (although the case surfaces as partitive since the EXPERIENCE is not a full DP). Since accusative case has already been assigned, the EXPERIENCER is left with no structural case and, consequently, it surfaces as displaying inherent (dative) case. Finally, the CAUSER, introduced by v_{CAUS}, becomes the first available goal of the nominative assigning probe T. In other words, the overt presence of the EXPERIENCE is what prevents the EXPERIENCER from being assigned accusative case.

Before moving on to the concluding remarks of the chapter, a word has to be said about the SOURCE in eventive LVECs. Note that in the structure in (48), the SOURCE is left with no case. I maintain that is actually the case: in eventive LVECs, the SOURCE cannot surface since there is no probe that can assign case to it; the only possibility for its surfacing is if a probe (e.g., a P) is introduced in the structure for which the SOURCE would be an available goal, as seen in (44).

(44) a. *Aquells nens   li   van   fer   mal
       those children   DAT.3s   go-PRES.3p   do-INF   pain

   la mà.
   the hand
   'Those children hurt her hand.'
  b. Aquells nens   li   van   fer   mal
     those children   DAT.3s   go-PRES.3p   do-INF   pain

   a la mà.
   on the hand
   'Those children hurt her hand.' (lit. 'Those children hurt her on the hand.')

In (44a) the SOURCE (*la mà* 'the hand') is introduced without its case being assigned, thus resulting in an ungrammatical utterance; in (44b), on the other hand, the introduction of the SOURCE is grammatical since its case is assigned by the P *en* 'on.'

6. Conclusions

This chapter contributes to the general vision of the current volume by offering a theoretically based account of a previously overlooked phenomenon from an understudied Spanish variety. Namely, in this chapter I have taken a look at the behavior of certain experience predicates in (a non-*leísta* variety of) Spanish and Catalan. According to the analysis that I propose here, experience predicates are the result of a BASIC EXPERIENCE STRUCTURE, which allows for two possibilities regarding the expression of the EXPERIENCE (incorporation vs. non-incorporation on V). Additionally, (some) experience predicates allow for both stative and eventive interpretations: the BASIC EXPERIENCE STRUCTURE can only yield stative readings; the eventive interpretations are the result of merging a functional eventive layer on top of v_{EXP}P.

Both the argument and the event structure of the predicate have a direct impact on the expression of the EXPERIENCER. In the eventive interpretations of incorporating experience predicates, v_{CAUS} is responsible for assigning accusative case to the EXPERIENCER, whereas in the stative interpretations of the same incorporating experience predicates, since there is no possible accusative case assigning probe (i.e., v_{CAUS}), the EXPERIENCER can only surface with its inherent (dative) case. Case relations in LVECs are somewhat different, due to the overt presence of an argument (i.e., the EXPERIENCE) that requires case: in both stative and eventive readings, the EXPERIENCE is the first goal of v_{EXP}, which is responsible for assigning accusative case (but which is displayed as partitive due to non-full DP status of the EXPERIENCE). In both readings of light verb experience predicates, then, the EXPERIENCER can only surface with its inherent (dative) case.

These case relations in LVECs serve as evidence that v_{EXP} is a non-defective type of v: v_{EXP} is responsible for case assignment, and all the theta roles within v_{EXP}P are assigned. Therefore, v_{EXP} is v^* and, consequently, a phase head.

This analysis opens an avenue for further research on the typology of (verbal) phase heads, as the data presented suggest that other types of v may also introduce a phase boundary. Also, considering the case relations outlined in this chapter, further research is necessary to have a better understanding of the stage in the derivation in which case assignment actually takes place.[6]

---

6. This chapter was supported in part by Grant FFI2012-31415 awarded by Spain's Ministry of Economy and Competitiveness. The views here expressed are my own, as are any errors.

Bibliography

Abreu de Carvalho, Ana Sofia. (2013). An overview of vocatives in European Portuguese. *Linguistica Atlantica* 32: 50–56.

Academia Nacional de Letras. (2011). *Diccionario del español del Uruguay*. Montevideo: Ediciones de la Banda Oriental.

Achugar, Mariana. (2003). Academic registers in Spanish in the U.S.: A study of oral texts produced by bilingual speakers in a university graduate program. In Ana Roca and Maria Cecilia Colombi (Eds.), *Mi lengua: Spanish as a heritage language in the United States, research and practice* (213–34). Washington, DC: Georgetown University Press.

Achugar, Mariana. (2008). *What we remember: The construction of memory in military discourse*. Amsterdam: John Benjamins.

Achugar, Mariana. (2009). Constructing a bilingual professional identity in a graduate classroom. *Journal of Language, Identity & Education* 8(2/3): 65–87.

Adger, David, and Gillian Ramchand. (2006). Psych nouns and predication. In Catherine Davis, Amy Rose Deal, and Youri Zabbal (Eds.), *Proceedings of the thirty-six annual meeting of the North East Linguistic Society, Volume 2* (89–102). Amherst, MA: University of Massachusetts, Amherst.

Adger, David, and Jennifer Smith. (2005). Variation and the minimalist program. In Leonie Cornips and Karen P. Corrigan (Eds.), *Syntax and variation: Reconciling the biological and the social* (149–97). Amsterdam: John Benjamins.

Agheyisy, Rebecca, and Joshua Fishman. (1970). Language attitude studies: A brief survey of methodological approaches. *Anthropological Linguistics* 12(1): 137–57.

Aguirre, Fausto. (2000). *El español del Ecuador*. Loja: Universidad Técnica Particular de Loja.

Alba-Juez, Laura. (2009). "Little words" in small talk: Some considerations on the use of the pragmatic markers *man* in English and *macho/tío* in Peninsular Spanish. In Donna Lardiere (Ed.), *Little Words* (171–81). Washington, DC: Georgetown University Press.

Almeida, Manuel. (2003). *Sociolingüística*. La Laguna: Universidad de la Laguna.

Alonso Cortés, Ángel. (1999). Las construcciones exclamativas. La interjección y las expresiones vocativas. In Ignacio Bosque and Violeta Demonte (Eds.), *Gramática descriptiva de la lengua española, Volume 3* (3993–4048). Madrid: Real Academia Española.

Alvar, Manuel. (1996). *Manual de dialectología hispánica*. Barcelona: Ariel.

Álvarez, Alexandra, and Enrique Obediente. (1998). El español caribeño: Antecedentes sociohistóricos y lingüísticos. In Matthias Perl and Armin Schwegler (Eds.), *América negra: Panorámica actual de los estudios lingüísticos sobre variedades hispanas, portuguesas y criollas* (40–61). Madrid: Iberoamericana-Vervuert.

Álvarez Nazario, Manuel. (1974). *El elemento afronegroide en el español de Puerto Rico*. San Juan: Instituto de Cultura Puertorriqueña.

Allen, W. Sidney. (1978). *Vox latina: A guide to the pronunciation of classical Latin* (2nd edition). Cambridge: Cambridge University Press.

Amado, Alonso, and Raimundo Lida. (1945). Geografía fonética: -l y -r implosivas en español. *Revista de Filología Hispánica* 7: 313–45.

Andersen, Henning. (2012). The new Russian vocative: Synchrony, diachrony, typology. *Scando-Slavica* 58 (1): 122–67.

Andersen, Roger W. (1982). Determining the linguistic attributes of language attrition. In Barbara F. Free and Richard Lambert (Eds.), *The loss of language skills* (83–118). Rowley: Newbury House.

Angel, Marc D. (1982). *La America: The Sephardic experience in the United States*. Philadelphia: The Jewish Publication Society of America.

Anscombre, Jean Claude, and Oswald Ducrot. (1976). L'argumentation dans la langue. *Langages* 42: 5.

Anthony, Laurence. (2013). *AntConc* (Version 3.2.4). Tokyo: Waseda University. Retrieved from http://www.antlab.sci.waseda.ac.jp.

Arad, Maya. (1998). Psych-notes. *UCL Working Papers in Linguistics* 10.

Arad, Maya. (1999). What counts as a class? The case of psych verbs. *MIT Working Papers in Linguistics* 35: 1–23.

Ariel, Mira. (1999). Cognitive universals and linguistic conventions: The case of resumptive pronouns. *Studies in Language* 23(2): 217–69.

Athanasiadou, Angeliki, Costas Canakis, and Bert Cornillie. (2006). Introduction. In Angeliki Athanasiadou, Costas Canakis and Bert Cornillie (Eds.), *Subjectification: Various paths to subjectivity* (1–13). Berlin: Mouton de Gruyter.

Azevedo, Milton. (2009). *Introducción a la lingüística española*. Upper Saddle River, NJ: Pearson.

Baker, Paul. (2010). *Corpus linguistics*. Edinburgh: Edinburgh University Press.

Banks, David. (2008). *The development of scientific writing linguistic features and historical context*. London: Equinox.

Bárkányi, Zsuzsanna. (2013). On the verge of phonetics and phonology: Pre-sonorant voicing in Spanish. Poster presented at *Phonetics and Phonology in Iberia 2013*, Universidade de Lisboa.

Barrenechea, Ana María, and Teresa Orecchia. (1977). La duplicación de objetos directos e indirectos en el español hablado en Buenos Aires. In Juan Miguel Lope Blanch (Ed.), *Estudios sobre el español hablado en las principales ciudades de América* (351–81). Mexico City: Universidad Nacional Autónoma de México.

Bartalesi-Graf, Daniela. (2011). *Voci dal sud: A journey to southern Italy with Carlo Levi and his Christ stopped at Eboli*. New Haven, NJ: Yale University Press.

Baumel Schreffler, Sandra L. (1989). *Una perspectiva del voseo: Una comparación de dos naciones voseantes, Guatemala y El Salvador*. Master's thesis, University of Florida.

Baumel Schreffler, Sandra L. (1995). The *voseo:* Second-person singular pronouns in Guatemalan speech. *Language Quarterly* 33(1–2): 33–44.

Bavin, Edith L. (1989). Some lexical and morphological changes in Warlpiri. In Nancy C. Dorian (Ed.), *Investigating obsolescence: Studies in language contraction and death* (267–86). Cambridge: Cambridge University Press.

Baxter, Alan. (1997). Creole-like features in the verb system of an Afro-Brazilian variety of Portuguese. In Arthur K. Spears and Donald Winford (Eds.), *The structure and status of pidgins and creoles* (265–88). Amsterdam: John Benjamins.

Behares, Luis E. (1981). Estudio sociodialectológico de las formas verbales de segunda persona en el español de Montevideo. In Adolfo Elizaincín (Ed.), *Estudios sobre el español del Uruguay* (29–49). Montevideo: Universidad de la República, Facultad de Humanidades y Ciencias.

Ben-Ur, Aviva. (2009). *Sephardic Jews in America: A diasporic history*. New York: New York University Press.

Benbassa, Ester, and Aron Rodrigue. (2000). *Sephardi Jewry: A history of the Judeo-Spanish community, 14th–20th centuries*. Berkeley: University of California Press.

Belletti, Adriana. (2004). Aspects of the low IP area. In Luigi Rizzi (Ed.), *The structure of IP and CP. The cartography of syntactic structures, Volume 2* (16–51). Oxford: Oxford University Press.

Belletti, Adriana, and Luigi Rizzi. (1988). Psych-verbs and theta-theory. *Natural Language & Linguistic Theory* 6: 291–352.

Bentivoglio, Paula. (2001). La variación sociosintáctica en español. *II Congreso Internacional de la Lengua Española*. Valladolid: Centro Virtual Cervantes.

Bentivoglio, Paula. (2003). Las construcciones "de retoma" en las cláusulas relativas: Un análisis variacionista. In Francisco Moreno-Fernández, José Antonio Samper Padilla, María Vaquero, María Luz Gutiérrez Araus, César Hernández Alonso, and Francisco Gimeno-Menéndez (Eds.), *Lengua, variación y contexto: estudios dedicados a Humberto López Morales* (507–20). Madrid: Arco Libros.

Bentivoglio, Paula. (2006). Los relativos con pronombre "de retoma" en un corpus del siglo XVI. In Concepción Company (Ed.), *Homenaje a José Moreno de Alba* (387–400). México City: UNAM.

Bentivoglio, Paula, and Manuel Sedano. (2011). Morphosyntactic variation in Spanish-speaking Latin America. In Manuel Díaz-Campos (Ed.), *The handbook of Hispanic sociolinguistics* (168–86). Malden, MA: Blackwell.

Bertolotti, Virginia. 2010. Notas sobre el *che*. *Lexis* 34 (1): 57–93.

Bertolotti, Virginia. 2011. La peculiaridad del sistema alocutivo singular en Uruguay. In Angela di Tullio and Rolf Kailuweit (Eds.), *El español rioplatense: Lengua, literatura, expresiones culturales* (23–47). Madrid: Iberoamericana-Vervuert.

Bertolotti, Virginia, and Magdalena Coll. (2003). A synchronical and historical view of the *tú/vos* option in the Spanish of Montevideo. In Silvina Montrul and Francisco Ordóñez (Eds.), *Linguistic theory and language development in Hispanic languages: Papers from the 5th Hispanic Linguistics Symposium and the 4th Conference on the Acquisition of Spanish and Portuguese* (1–12). Somerville, MA: Cascadilla Press.

Bhatia, Vijay. K. (2004). *Worlds of written discourse*. London: Continuum.

Biber, Douglas. (2006). *University language: A corpus-based study of spoken and written registers*. Amsterdam: John Benjamins.

Biber, Douglas, and Susan Conrad. (2009). *Register, genre, and style*. Cambridge: Cambridge University Press.

Blakemore, Diane. (2004). Discourse markers. In Laurence R. Horn and Gregory Ward (Eds.), *The handbook of pragmatics* (221–40). London: Blackwell.

Blanco de Margo, Mercedes. (1991). Actitudes hacia la lengua en la Argentina. Visión diacrónica. *Revista de Lingüística Teórica y Aplicada* 29: 197–214.

Blas Arroyo, José Luis. (1995). De nuevo el español y el catalán, juntos y en contraste. Estudio de actitudes lingüísticas. *Sintagma* 7: 29–41.

Blas Arroyo, José Luis. (1999). Las actitudes hacia la variación intradialectal en la sociolingüística hispánica. *Estudios filológicos* 34: 47–72.

Blas Arroyo, José Luis. (2011). Spanish in contact with Catalan. In Manuel Díaz-Campos (Ed.), *The handbook of Hispanic sociolinguistics* (374–94). Malden, MA: Blackwell.

Bolinger, Dwight. (1961). Contrastive accent and contrastive stress. *Language* 37: 83–96.

Bolívar, Adriana. (2005). Tradiciones discursivas y la construcción del conocimiento en las humanidades. *Signo y Seña* 14: 67–91.

Bonet, Eulàlia, and Maria-Rosa Lloret. (1998). *Fonologia catalana*. Barcelona: Ariel.

Boretti de Macchia, Susana H. (1989). Dequeísmo en el habla culta de Rosario. *Anuario de Lingüística Hispánica* 5: 27–48.

Borzi, Claudia, and Mabel Morano. (2009). Cláusulas relativas con duplicación del objeto. *Onomázein* 19(1): 71–88.

Borzone de Manrique, Ana María, and María Ignacia Massone. (1981). Acoustic analysis and perception of Spanish fricative consonants. *Journal of Acoustical Society of America* 69: 1145–53.

Bossong, Georg. (1985). *Empirische Universalienforschung. Differentielle Objektmarkierung in der neuiranischen Sprachen*. Tübingen: Narr.

Bourdieu, Pierre. (1991). *Language and symbolic power*. Cambridge: Polity.

Bradley, Travis. (2005). Sibilant voicing in Highland Ecuadorian Spanish. *Lingua(gem)* 2(2): 9–42.

Brattico, Pauli. (2008). Kayne's theory of case and Finnish DPs. *Nordic Journal of Linguistics* 31: 5–44.

Browman, Catherine, and Louis Goldstein. (1989). Articulatory gestures as phonological units. *Phonology* 6: 201–52.

Brown, Esther L., and Rena Torres Cacoullos. (2002). ¿Qué le vamoh aher?: Taking the syllable out of Spanish /s/ reduction. In Daniel R. Johnson (Eds.), *University of Pennsylvania working papers in linguistics: Papers from NWAV 30* (17–32). Philadelphia: University of Pennsylvania Press.

Brucart, José María. (1999). La estructura del sintagma nominal: Las oraciones de relativo. In Ignacio Bosque and Violeta Demonte (Eds.), *Gramática descriptiva de la lengua española* (395–522). Madrid: Espasa-Calpe.

Bruhn de Garavito, Joyce, and Lydia White. (2000). L2 acquisition of Spanish DP's: The status of grammatical features. In Catherine Howel, Sarah A. Fish, and Thea Keith-Lucas (Eds.), *Proceedings of the 24th Annual Boston University Conference on Language Development* (164–75). Somerville, MA: Cascadilla Press.

Bucholtz, Mary. (2009). From stance to style. In Alexandra Jaffe (Ed.), *Stance: Sociolinguistic perspectives*. (146–70). Oxford: Oxford University Press.

Bühler, Karl. (1934). *Sprachtheorie*. Jena: Fischer.

Burkhardt, Petra. (2005). *The syntax-discourse interface: Representing and interpreting dependency*. Amsterdam: John Benjamins.

Burns, Anne, Hellen Joyce, and Sandra Gollin. (1996). *'I see what you mean': Using spoken discourse in the classroom. A handbook for teachers*. Sydney: National Centre for English Language Teaching and Research (NCELTR).

Butt, John, and Carmen Benjamin. (2000). *A new reference grammar of modern Spanish*. Chicago: NTC Publishing Group.

Calle, Ana María. (2010). El fonema /s/, ¿sordo o sonoro? Un estudio de dos dialectos ecuatorianos. *Revista Pucara* 22: 187–206.

Campbell, Lyle, and Martha C. Muntzel. (1989). The structural consequences of language death. In Nancy C. Dorian (Ed.), *Investigating obsolescence: Studies in language contraction and death* (181–96). Cambridge: Cambridge University Press.

Campbell-Kibler, Kathryn. (2006). *Listener perceptions of sociolinguistic variables: The case of (ING)*. Doctoral dissertation, Stanford University.

Campos, Héctor, and Mary Zampini. (1990). Focalization strategies in Spanish. *Probus* 2(1): 47–64.

Campos-Astorkiza, Rebeka. (2014). Sibilant voicing assimilation in Peninsular Spanish as gestural blending. In Marie-Hélène Côté, Éric Mathieu, and Shana Poplack (Eds.), *Variation within and across Romance languages* (17–38). Amsterdam: John Benjamins.

Cantar de Mío Çid. (c. 1140). Retrieved from http://www.vicentellop.com/TEXTOS/miocid/miocid.htm.

Caravedo, Rocío. (2006). Sobre factores externos e internos en la lingüística de variación. In Mercedes Sedano, Adriana Bolívar, and Martha Shiro (Eds.), *Haciendo lingüística: homenaje a Paola Bentivoglio* (709–716). Caracas: Universidad Central de Venezuela.

Carbonell, Joan F. (1992). *Final devoicing and voicing assimilation in Catalan: An acoustic experiment*. Master's thesis, University College London.

Carrasco Gutiérrez, Ángeles. (2000). *La concordancia de tiempos*. Madrid: Arco Libros.

Carvalho, Ana M., Rafael Orozco, and Naomi Lapidus Shin (Eds.) (2015). *Subject pronoun expression in Spanish: A cross-dialectal perspective*. Washington, DC: Georgetown University Press.

Casesnoves Ferrer, Raquel, and David Sankoff. (2004). The Valencian revival: Why usage lags behind competence. *Language in Society* 33(1): 1–31.

Castellani, Arrigo. (1976). *I testi più antichi italiani*. Bologna: Patron.

Cerrón-Palomino López, Álvaro. (2006). Pronombres de retoma en cláusulas relativas del castellano peruano: un fenómeno de causación multiple. *Lexis* 30(2): 231–58.

Chafe, Wallace. (1987). The relation between written and spoken language. *Annual Review of Anthropology* 16: 383–407.

Chappell, Whitney. (2011a). The intervocalic voicing of /s/ in Ecuadorian Spanish. In Jim Michnowicz and Robin Dodsworth (Eds.), *Selected proceedings of the 5th Workshop on Spanish Sociolinguistics* (57–64). Somerville, MA: Cascadilla Press.

Chappell, Whitney. (2016a). On the social perception of intervocalic /s/ voicing in Costa Rican Spanish. *Language Variation and Change* 28(3): 357–78.

Chappell, Whitney. (2016b). Bilingualism and aspiration: Coda /s/ reduction on the Atlantic coast of Nicaragua. In Sandro Sessarego and Fernando Tejedo-Herrero (Eds.), *Spanish Language and Sociolinguistic Analysis* (261–82). Amsterdam: John Benjamins.

Chappell, Whitney, and Christina García. (In press). Variable production and indexical social meaning: On the potential physiological origin of intervocalic /s/ voicing in Costa Rican Spanish. To appear in *Studies in Hispanic and Lusophone Linguistics*.

Checa-García, Irene. (2012). Resumptive elements in Spanish relative clauses and processing difficulties. Poster presented at the 2012 *LSA Annual Meeting*, Portland.

Chomsky, Noam. (2000). Minimalist inquiries. In Roger Martin, David Michaels, and Juan Uriagereka (Eds.), *Step by step: Essays on minimalist syntax in honor of Howard Lasnik* (89–156). Cambridge, MA: MIT Press.

Chomsky, Noam. (2001). Derivation by phase. In Michael Kenstowics (Ed.), *Ken Hale: A life in language* (1–52). Cambridge, MA: MIT Press.

Chomsky, Noam. (2002). Beyond explanatory adequacy. *MIT Occasional Papers in Linguistics* 20: 1–28.

Chomsky, Noam. (2006). *Language and mind* (3rd edition). Cambridge, MA: MIT Press.

Chomsky, Noam. (2008). On phases. *Current Studies in Linguistics Series* 45: 133.

Ciapuscio, Guiomar. (2005). La noción de género en la lingüística sistémico funcional y en la lingüística textual. *Revista Signos* 38: 31–48.

Clivio, Gianrenzo, Marcel Danesi, and Sara Maida-Nicol. (2011). *An Introduction to Italian dialectology*. Munich: LINCOM.

Clopper, Cynthia, Brianna Conrey, and David B. Pisoni. (2005). Effects of talker gender on dialect categorization. *Journal of Language and Social Psychology* 24: 182–206.

Cogan, Ezequiel. (2013). Agarra charrúa. *Revista Olé*. Retreived from http://www.ole.com.ar/river-plate/futbol/titulo_0_1051094916.html.

Colina, Sonia. (2009). Sibilant voicing in Ecuadorian Spanish. *Studies in Hispanic and Lusophone Linguistics* 2(1): 3–29.

Colombi, Cecilia. (2006). Grammatical metaphor: Academic language development in Latino students in Spanish. In Heidi Byrnes (Ed.), *Advanced language learning: The contribution of Halliday and Vygotsky* (204–24). London: Continuum.

Comrie, Bernard, Martin Haspelmath, and Balthasar Bickel. (2008). *Leipzig glossing rules*. Retrieved from http://www.eva.mpg.de/lingua/resources/glossing-rules.php.

Cooper, Elizabeth. (2005). The geometry of interpretable features: Influence in English and Spanish. *Language* 81: 10–46.

Cooper, Robert, and Joshua Fishman. (1975). The study of language attitudes. *International Journal of the Sociology of Language* 136(3): 5–20.

Corominas, Joan, and José Antonio Pascual. (1980–91). *Diccionario crítico etimológico castellano e hispánico*. Madrid: Gredos.

Cowper, Elizabeth. (2005). The geometry of interpretable features: Infl in English and Spanish. *Language* 81(1): 10–46.

Cuartero Torres, Néstor. (1998). *Voicing assimilation in stop sequences in Catalan and English*. Master's thesis, Universitat Autónoma de Barcelona.

Cuartero Torres, Néstor. (2001). *Voicing assimilation in Catalan and English*. Doctoral dissertation, Universitat Autónoma de Barcelona.

Cubo de Severino, Liliana. (2002). Evaluación de estrategias retóricas en la comprensión de manuales universitarios. *Revista del Instituto de Investigaciones Lingüísticas y Literarias Hispanoamericanas*: 69–84.

Cuervo, María Cristina. (2010). Against ditransitivity. *Probus* 22(2): 151–80.

Daniel, Michael, and Andrew Spencer. (2009). The vocative: An outlier case. In Andrej Malchukov and Andrew Spencer (Eds.), *The Oxford handbook of case* (626–34). Oxford: Oxford University Press.

Davidson, Justin. (2014). A comparison of fricative voicing and lateral velarization phenomena in Barcelona: A variationist approach to Spanish in contact with Catalan. Unpublished manuscript.

Davies, Bethan L. (2005). Communities of practice: Legitimacy, membership and choice. *Leeds Working Papers in Linguistics and Phonetics* 10.

De Granda, Germán. (1968a). *Transculturación e interferencia lingüística en el Puerto Rico contemporáneo.* Bogotá: Instituto Caro y Cuervo.

De Granda, Germán. (1968b). La tipología criolla de dos hablas del área lingüística hispanica. *Thesaurus* 23(2): 193–205.

De Granda, Germán. (1970). Un temprano testimonio sobre las hablas "criollas" en África y América. *Thesaurus* 25(1): 1–11.

DellaPergola, Sergio. (2010). *Current Jewish Population Reports (No. 2, 2010).* Storrs, CT: North American Jewish Data Bank.

Díaz-Campos, Manuel (Ed.). (2011a). *The handbook of Hispanic sociolinguistics.* Malden, MA: Wiley-Blackwell.

Díaz-Campos, Manuel. (2011b). Introduction. In Manuel Díaz Campos (Ed.), *The handbook of Hispanic sociolinguistics* (1–6). Malden, MA: Wiley-Blackwell.

Díaz-Campos, Manuel. (2013). *Introducción a la sociolingüística hispánica.* Malden, MA: Wiley-Blackwell.

Díaz-Campos, Manuel, and Jason Killam. (2012). Assessing language attitudes through a matched-guise experiment: The case of consonant deletion in Venezuelan Spanish. *Hispania* 95(1): 83–102.

Dijk, Teun Adrianus van. (2008). *Discourse and context: A socio-cognitive approach.* Cambridge: Cambridge University Press.

Dikken, Marcel den. (2011). Phi-feature inflection and agreement: An introduction. *Natural Language and Linguistic Theory* 29(4): 857–74.

Dorian, Nancy C. (1973). Grammatical change in a dying dialect. *Language* 49: 413–38.

Dorian, Nancy C. (1978). The fate of morphological complexity in language death: Evidence from East Sutherland Gaelic. *Language* 54: 590–609.

Dorian, Nancy C. (1981). *Language death: The life cycle of a Scottish Gaelic dialect.* Philadelphia: University of Pennsylvania Press.

Dorian, Nancy C. (1994). Varieties of variation in a very small place: Social homogeneity, prestige norms, and linguistic variation. *Language* 70: 631–96.

Downing, Bruce. (1969). Vocatives and third-person imperatives in English. *Papers in Linguistics* 1(3): 570–92.

Dowty, David. (1979). *Word meaning and Montague grammar.* Dordrecht: Reidel.

Ducrot, Oswald. (1972). *Dire et ne pas dire.* Paris: Hermann.

Dworkin, Steven. (1985). From *-ir* to *-ecer* in Spanish: The loss of OSp. De-adjectival *-ir* verbs. *Hispanic Review* 53(3): 295–305.

Dworkin, Steven. (2012). *A history of the Spanish lexicon: A linguistic perspective.* Oxford: Oxford University Press.

El Cuarteto de Nos. (2004). Bo cartero. In *El Cuarteto de Nos.* Montevideo: Bizarro Records.

Eggins, Suzanne. (1994). *An introduction to systemic functional linguistics.* London: Pinter.

Eggins, Suzanne, and Diana Slade. (1997). *Analysing casual conversation.* London: Cassell.

Eggins, Suzanne, and F. Alcántara. (2002). *Introducción a la lingüística sistémica.* Logroño: Universidad de La Rioja.

Elizaincín, Adolfo, and Olga Díaz. (1981). Sobre tuteo-voseo en el español montevideano. In Adolfo Elizaincín (Ed.), *Estudios sobre el español del Uruguay* (83–86). Montevideo: Universidad de la República, Facultad de Humanidades y Ciencias.

Enfield, Nick. (2009). *The anatomy of meaning: Speech, gesture, and composite utterances.* Cambridge: Cambridge University Press.

Escobar, Anna María, and Kim Potowski (2015). *El español de los Estados Unidos.* Cambridge: Cambridge University Press.

Espinal, M. Teresa. (2013). On the structure of vocatives. In Barbara Sonnenhauser and Patrizia Noel Aziz Hanna (Eds.), *Vocatives! Addressing between system and performance* (109–32). Berlin: Walter de Gruyter.

Estigarribia, Bruno. (2006). Why clitic doubling? A functional analysis for Rioplatense Spanish. In Timothy Face and Carol Klee (Eds.), *Selected proceedings of the 8th Hispanic Linguistics Symposium* (123–36). Somerville, MA: Cascadilla Press.

Ethnologue. (2002). Retrieved from http://www.ethnologue.com/language/nap.

Fairclough, Norman. (1994). Conversationalization of public discourse and the authority of the consumer. In Russell Keat, Nigel Whitely, and Nicholar Abercombrie (Eds.), *The authority of the consumer* (235–49). London: Routledge.

Fernández-Ordóñez, Ignacio. (1999). Leísmo, laísmo y loísmo. In Ignacio Bosque and Violeta Demonte (Eds.), *Gramática descriptiva de la lengua española, Volume 1* (1317–98). Madrid: Espasa-Calpe.

Fernández Soriano, Olga. (1995). Pronombres reasuntivos y doblado de clíticos. In Patxi Goenaga (Ed.), *De grammatica generativa* (109–28). Gasteiz-Donostia: Universidad del País Vasco.

Fernández Soriano, Olga. (1999). El pronombre personal. Formas y distribuciones. Pronombres átonos y tónicos. In Ignacio Bosque and Violeta Demonte (Eds.), *Gramática descriptiva de la lengua española* (1209–74). Madrid: Espasa-Calpe.

Fierro, Aurelio. (1989). *Grammatica della lingua napoletana.* Milan: Rusconi.

File-Muriel, Richard. (2007). *The role of lexical frequency and phonetic context in the weakening of syllable-final lexical /s/ in the Spanish of Barranquilla, Colombia.* Doctoral dissertation, Indiana University-Bloomington.

Firth, John R., and Frank R. Palmer. (1968). *Selected Papers of J. R. Firth, 1952–59.* Bloomington: Indiana University Press.

Fontanella de Weinberg, María Beatriz. (1970). La evolución de los pronombres de tratamiento en el español bonaerense. *Thesaurus* 25: 12–22.

Fontanella de Weinberg, María Beatriz. (1971). El voseo en Buenos Aires en las dos primeras décadas del siglo XIX. *Thesaurus* 26: 495–514.

Fontanella de Weinberg, María Beatriz. (1976). Analogía y confluencia paradigmática en formas verbales de voseo. *Thesaurus* 31: 249–72.

Fontanella de Weinberg, María Beatriz. (1977). La constitución del paradigma pronominal del voseo. *Thesaurus* 32: 227–41.

Fontanella de Weinberg, María Beatriz. (1979). La oposición "cantes/cantés" en el español de Buenos Aires. *Thesaurus* 34: 72–83.

Fontanella de Weinberg, María Beatriz. (1987). *El español bonaerense. Cuatro siglos de evolución lingüística (1580–1980).* Buenos Aires: Hachette.

Fontanella de Weinberg, María Beatriz. (1992). Una variedad lingüística en busca de su propia identidad: El español bonaerense a lo largo del siglo XX. In María Beatriz Fontanella de Weinberg, Patricia Vallejos, and Yolanda Hipperdinger (Eds.), *Estudios sobre el español de la Argentina* (63–81). Bahía Blanca: Departamento de Humanidades, Universidad Nacional del Sur.

Fontanella de Weinberg, María Beatriz. (1993). Usos americanos y peninsulares de segunda persona singular. In Ana María Barrenechea, Luis Martínez Cuitiño, and Élida Lois (Eds.),

Actas del III Congreso Argentino de Hispanistas (144–53). Buenos Aires: Asociación Argentina de Hispanistas.

Fontanella de Weinberg, María Beatriz. (1996). Los sistemas pronominales de segunda persona en el mundo hispánico. *Boletín de Filología* 35: 151–62.

Franceschina, Florencia. (2005). *Fossilized second language grammars*. Amsterdam: John Benjamins.

Franco, Jon. (1990). Towards a typology of psych verbs: Evidence from Spanish. *MIT Working Papers in Linguistics* 12: 46–62.

Franco, Jon, and Susana Huidobro. (2003). Psych verbs in Spanish *leísta* dialects. In Silvina Montrul and Francisco Ordóñez (Eds.), *Linguistic theory and language development in Hispanic languages* (138–57). Somerville, MA: Cascadilla Press.

Fraser, Bruce. (2009). An account of discourse markers. *International Review of Pragmatics* 1(2): 293–320.

Frobert-Adamo, Monique. (2002). Humour in presentations. What's the joke? In Elija Ventola, Celia Shalom, and Susan Thompson (Eds.), *The Language of conferencing* (211–26). Frankfurt: Peter Lang.

Fuga en Helsinki. (n.d.). *Weblogs Clarín*. Accessed May 26, 2014. Retrieved from http://weblogs.clarin.com/data/podeti/archives/155990.php.

Galindo Solé, Mireia. (2003). Language contact phenomena in Catalonia: The influence of Catalan in spoken Castilian. In Lotfi Sayahi (Ed.), *First workshop on Spanish sociolinguistics* (18–29). Somerville, MA: Cascadilla Press.

Gallego, Ángel J. (2010). *Phase theory*. Amsterdam: John Benjamins.

Galmés de Fuentes, Álvaro. (1996). *Influencias sintácticas y estilísticas del árabe en la prosa medieval castellana*. Madrid: Gredos.

Gámez Elizondo, Maricela. (2013). *Jarchas*. Retrieved from http://www.jarchas.net/index.html.

García, Alison. (2013). *Allophonic variation in the Spanish sibilant fricative*. Doctoral dissertation, University of Wisconsin-Milwaukee.

García, Christina. (2011). *Intervocalic /s/ voicing in the Spanish of Loja, Ecuador*. Master's thesis, The Ohio State University.

García de Diego, Vicente. (1978). *Dialectología española*. Madrid: Ediciones Cultura Hispánica del Centro Iberoamericano de Cooperación.

García Marcos, Francisco Joaquín. (1999). *Fundamentos críticos de sociolingüística*. Almería: Servicio de Publicaciones de la Universidad de Almería.

García Mouton, Pilar, and Francisco Moreno Fernández. (1993). Sociolingüística en el atlas lingüístico (y etnográfico) de Castilla-La Mancha. In Ralph Penny (Ed.), *Actas del I Congreso Anglohispano* (139–49). Madrid: Castalia.

Geeslin, Kimberly. (2011). The acquisition of variation in second language Spanish: How to identify and catch a moving target. In Manuel Díaz-Campos (Ed.), *The handbook of Hispanic sociolinguistics* (303–19). Malden, MA: Wiley-Blackwell.

Gehman, Henry S. (1982). Arabic syntax of the relative pronoun in *Poema de mio Cid* y *Don Quijote*. *Hispanic Review* 50: 53–60.

Gibson, Edward, and Evalina Fedorenko. (2013). The need for quantitative methods in syntax and semantics research. *Language and Cognitive Processes* 28: 88–124.

Gimeno Menéndez, Francisco. (1990). *Dialectología y sociolingüística españolas*. Alicante: Servicio de Publicaciones de la Universidad de Alicante.

Gimeno Menéndez, Francisco, and José R. Gómez Molina. (2007). Spanish and Catalan in the community of Valencia. *International Journal of the Sociology of Language* 184: 95–107.

Goldberg, Adele. (2006). *Constructions at work: The nature of generalization in language.* Oxford: Oxford University Press.

González García, Luis. (2001). Construcciones de relativo anómalas y despronominalización. In Alexandre Veiga and María Rosa Pérez (Eds.), *Lengua española y estructuras gramaticales* (183–95). Santiago de Compostela: Universidade de Santiago.

González Martínez, Juan, and José Luis Blas Arroyo. (2011). Estabilidad y dinamismo en las actitudes lingüísticas de una comunidad bilingüe española (Els Ports, Castellón). *Hispania* 94(4): 663–79.

González Ollé, Fernando. (1962). *Los sufijos diminutivos en castellano medieval.* Madrid: Editorial Gómez.

Goodman, Leo A. (1961). Snowball sampling. *Annals of Mathematical Statistics* 32: 148–70.

Gradoville, Michael. (2011). Validity in measurements of fricative voicing: Evidence from Argentine Spanish. In Scott M. Alvord (Ed.), *Selected proceedings of the 5th conference on laboratory approaches to Romance phonology* (59–74). Somerville, MA: Cascadilla Press.

Gries, Stefan. (2013). Sources of variability relevant to the cognitive sociolinguist, and corpus—as well as psycholinguistic methods and notions to handle them. *Journal of Pragmatics* 52: 5–16.

Grinevald, Colette. (2003). Speakers and documentation of endangered languages. *Language documentation and description, Volume 1* (52–72). London: Hans Rausing Endangered Language Project.

Guirado, Krístel. (2006). Deixis proposicional en el habla de Caracas: Un análisis cuantitativo del (de)queísmo. *Boletín de Lingüística* 26: 130–56.

Guirao, Ramón. (1938). *Obrita de la poesía afrocubana 1928–1937.* Havana: Ucar García.

Güleryüz, Naim. (1992). *İstanbul Sinagogları.* Istanbul: Rekor.

Gutiérrez Ordóñez, Salvador. (1997). *Temas, remas, focos, tópicos y comentarios.* Madrid: Arco Libros.

Hale, Kenneth, and Samuel Jay Keyser. (1993). On argument structure and the lexical expression of syntactic relations. In Kenneth Hale and Samuel Jay Keyser (Eds.), *The view from Building 20: Essays in linguistics in honor of Sylvain Bromberger* (53–109). Cambridge, MA: MIT Press.

Hale, Kenneth, and Samuel Jay Keyser. (2002). *Prolegomenon to a theory of argument structure.* Cambridge, MA: MIT Press.

Halliday, Michael A. K. (1967). Notes in transitivity and theme in English. *Journal of Linguistics* 3: 199–244.

Halliday, Michael A. K. (1990). *Spoken and written language.* Oxford: Oxford University Press.

Halliday, Michael A. K. (2001). Literacy and linguistics: Relationships between spoken and written language. In Anne Burns and Caroline Coffin (Eds.), *Analysing English in a global context: A reader* (81–193). London: Routledge.

Halliday, Michael A. K., and Christian Matthiessen. (2014). *Halliday's introduction to functional grammar* (4th edition). New York: Routledge.

Harley, Heidi, and Elizabeth Ritter. (2002). Person and number in pronouns: a feature-geometric analysis. *Language* 78: 482–526.

Harrington, Karl P. (1972). *Mediaeval Latin.* Chicago: University of Chicago Press.

Hawkins, Roger. (1998). The inaccessibility of formal features of functional categories in second language acquisition. Paper presented at the *Pacific Second Language Research Forum*, Tokyo, March 1998.

Heestand Dustin, Ming Xiang, and Maria Polinsky. (2011). Resumption still does not rescue islands. *Linguistic Inquiry* 42: 138–52.

Hernández Campoy, Juan Manuel, and Manuel Almeida. (2005). *Metodología de la investigación sociolingüística*. Albolote: Comares.

Hernández, Gus. (n.d.) *El ojo de gran hermano*. Accessed August 30, 2013. Retreived from http://blogs.20minutos.es/gran-hermano/.

Herschensohn, Julia. (2000). *The second time around: Minimalism and L2 acquisition*. Amsterdam: John Benjamins.

Hill, Virginia. (2007). Vocatives and the pragmatics-syntax interface. *Lingua* 117: 2077–105.

Hoff, Mark (2014). Extended accusative a-marking in Argentine Spanish: Awareness, attitudes, and acceptability. Paper presented at *Diálogos XII*, Bloomington, IN.

Hoff, Mark (n.d.). *El empleo del presente de subjuntivo en lugar del imperfecto de subjuntivo en el español argentino*. Unpublished manuscript.

Holmquist, John. (2011). Gender and variation: Word-final /s/ in men's and women's speech in Puerto Rico's Western Highlands. In Manuel Díaz-Campos (Ed.), *The Blackwell handbook of Hispanic sociolinguistics* (230–43). Malden, MA: Wiley-Blackwell.

Hood, Susan. (2010). *Appraising research: Evaluation in academic writing*. Hampshire: Palgrave Macmillan.

Hood, Susan, and Gail Forey. (2005). Introducing a conference paper: Getting interpersonal with your audience. *Journal of English for Academic Purposes* 4(4): 291–306.

Hualde, José Ignacio, Antxón Olarrea, Anna M. Escobar, and Katherine E. Travis. (Eds.) (2010). *Introducción a la lingüística hispánica*. Cambridge: Cambridge University Press.

Hyland, Ken. (2000). *Disciplinary discourses: Social interactions in academic writing*. New York: Longman.

Konzett, Carmen. (2012). *Any questions? Identity construction in academic conference discussions*. Boston: De Gruyter Mouton.

Kratzer, Angela. (1996). Severing the external argument from the verb. In Johan Rooryck and Laurie Zaring (Eds.), *Phrase structure and the lexicon* (109–37). Dordrecht: Kluwer.

Jackendoff, Ray. (1997). *The architecture of the language faculty*. Cambridge, MA: MIT Press.

Jackendoff, Ray. (2002). *Foundations of language: Brain, meaning, grammar, evolution*. Oxford: Oxford University Press.

Jakobson, Roman. (1960). Closing statement: Linguistics and poetics. In Thomas A. Sebeok (Ed.), *Style in language* (350–77). Cambridge, MA: MIT Press.

Jiménez Fernández, Rafael. (1999). *El andaluz*. Madrid: Ibérica Grafic.

Johnson, Keith. (2004). Massive reduction in conversational American English. Spontaneous speech: Data and analysis. In K. Yoneyama and K. Maekawa (Eds.), *Proceedings of the 1st Session of the 10th International Symposium* (29–54). Tokyo: The National International Institute for Japanese Language.

Johnson, Mary, and John Grinstead. (2011). Variation in the *voseo* and *tuteo* negative imperatives in Argentine Spanish. *University of Pennsylvania Working Papers in Linguistics* 17(2): 99–104.

Jones, Sir William. (1786). *Third annual discourse before the Asiatic Society on the History and Culture of the Hindus*. n.p.

Kanwit, Matthew. (2012). Discourse topic and (de)queísmo: A variationist study of the Spanish of Caracas. *Indiana University Linguistics Club Working Papers* 12(1): 1–19.

Keenan, Edward L., and Bernard Comrie. (1977). Noun phrase accessibility and universal grammar. *Linguistic Inquiry* 8: 63–99.

Keller, Rudi. (1995). The epistemic weil. In Dieter Stein and Susan Wright (Eds.), *Subjectivity and subjectivisation: Linguistic perspectives* (16–30). Cambridge: Cambridge University Press.

Klee, Carol, and Andrew Lynch (2009). *El español en contacto con otras lenguas.* Washington, DC: Georgetown University Press.

Kovacci, O. (1992). Proposiciones completivas y estructuras alternantes. Sistema y norma en el español de Corrientes (Argentina). In Pilar García Mouton (Ed.), *El español de América* (433–44). Madrid: Consejo Superior de Investigaciones Científicas.

Kristiansen, Gitte, and Dirk Geeraerts. (2013). Context and usage in cognitive sociolinguistics. *Journal of Pragmatics* 52: 1–4.

Kühl de Mones, Ursula. (1981). Actitudes lingüísticas frente al español de Montevideo (Uruguay). *Revista de la Facultad de Humanidades y Ciencias. Serie Lingüística* 1(3): 37–60.

Labov, William. (1972). *Language in the inner city.* Philadelphia: University of Pennsylvania Press.

Labov, William. (1990). The intersection of sex and social class in the course of linguistic change. *Language Variation and Change* 2(2): 205–54.

Labov, William. (2001). *Principles of linguistic change, Volume II: Social factors.* Oxford: Blackwell.

Laca, Brenda. (2002). Spanish "aspectual" periphrases: Ordering constraints and the distinction between situation and viewpoint aspect. In Javier Gutiérrez-Rexach (Ed.), *From words to discourse: Trends in Spanish semantics and pragmatics* (61–93). New York: Elsevier.

Lafford, Barbara. (1986). Valor diagnóstico-social del uso de ciertas variantes de /s/ en el español de Cartagena, Colombia. In Rafael Núñez Cedeño, Iraset Páez, and Jorge Guitart (Eds.), *Estudios sobre la fonología del español del Caribe* (53–75). Caracas: La Casa de Bello.

Lakoff, Robin T. (1975). *Language and woman's place.* Oxford: Oxford University Press.

Lambert, Wallace E., R. C. Hodgson, Robert C. Gardner, and Samuel Fillenbaum. (1960). Evaluational reactions to spoken language. *Journal of Abnormal and Social Psychology* 60(1): 44–51.

Lambrecht, Kurt. (1994). *Information structure and sentence form. Topic, focus and the mental representations of discourse referents.* Cambridge: Cambridge University Press.

Landau, Idan. (2005). *The locative syntax of experiencers.* Unpublished manuscript, Ben Gurion University.

Langacker, Ronald W. (2006). Subjectification, grammaticization, and conceptual archetypes. In Angeliki Athanasiadou, Costas Canakis, and Bert Cornillie (Eds.), *Subjectification: Various paths to subjectivity* (17–40). Berlin: Mouton de Gruyter.

Lastra, Yolanda, and Pedro Martín-Butragueño. (2010). Futuro perifrástico y futuro morfológico en el corpus sociolingüístico de la ciudad de México. *Oralia* 13: 145–71.

Lavandera, Beatriz. (1978). Where does the sociolinguistic variable stop? *Language in Society* 7: 171–82. In Ledgeway, Adam. (2009). *Grammatica diacronica del napoletano.* Tübingen: Max Niemeyer Verlag.

Leumann, Manu. (1977). *Lateinische Laut- und Formenlehre.* Munich: Beck.

Lewis, M. Paul, Gary F. Simons, and Charles D. Fennig (Eds.) (2014). *Ethnologue: Languages of the world* (17th edition). Dallas: SIL International.

Liberman, Alvin M., Katherine S. Harris, Howard S. Hoffman, and Belver C. Griffith. (1957). The discrimination of speech sounds within and across phoneme boundaries. *Journal of Experimental Psychology* 54(5): 358–68.

Lindblom, Bjorn. (1963). Spectrographic study of vowel reduction. *JASA* (35): 1773–81.

Lipski, John M. (1985). Creole Spanish and vestigial Spanish: Evolutionary parallels. *Linguistics* 23: 963–64.

Lipski, John. (1987). The Chota Valley: Afro-Hispanic language in highland Ecuador. *Latin American Research Review* 22: 155–70.

Lipski, John M. (1989). /s/-voicing in Ecuadoran Spanish: Patterns and principles of consonantal modification. *Lingua* 79: 49–71.

Lipski, John M. (1993). Creoloid phenomena in the Spanish of transitional bilinguals. In John Lipski and Ana Roca (Eds.), *Spanish in the United States: Linguistic contact and diversity* (153–82). Berlin: Mouton de Gruyter.

Lipski, John. (1994a). *Latin American Spanish*. New York: Longman.

Lipski, John. (1994b). El español afroperuano: Eslabón entre África y América. *Anuario de Lingüística Hispánica* 10: 179–216.

Lipski, John. (2002). The role of the city in the formation of Spanish American dialect zones. *Arachne@Rutgers* 2(1): n.p.

Lipski, John. (2006a). Morphosyntactic implications in Afro-Hispanic language: New data on creole pathways. Paper presented at the *35th New Ways of Analyzing Variation Conference (NWAV35)*. Columbus: The Ohio State University.

Lipski, John. (2006b). Afro-Bolivian Spanish and Helvécia Portuguese: Semi-creole parallels. *Papia* 16: 96–116.

Lipski, John. (2008a). *Varieties of Spanish in the United States*. Washington, DC: Georgetown University Press.

Lipski, John. (2008b). *Afro-Bolivian Spanish*. Madrid: Iberoamericana-Vervuert.

Lloyd, Paul. (1987). *From Latin to Spanish, Volume 1: Historical phonology and morphology of the Spanish language*. Philadelphia: American Philosophical Society.

Lope Blanch, José Manuel. (1986). Duplicaciones pronominales en el habla culta de Madrid. *Estudios de lingüística española* (137–43). México City: UNAM.

Lope Blanch, José Manuel. (2001). Los relativos en problemas. *Lexis* 1/2: 159–72.

López Morales, Humberto. (1989). *Sociolingüística*. Madrid: Gredos.

Lorenzino, Gerardo. (1998). El español caribeño: antecedentes sociohistóricos y lingüísticos. In Matthias Perl and Armin Schwegler (Eds.), *América negra: Panorámica actual de los estudios lingüísticos sobre variedades hispanas, portuguesas y criollas* (26–39). Madrid: Iberoamericana-Vervuert.

Lyons, John. (1977). *Semantics*. Cambridge: Cambridge University Press.

MacEachern, Margaret. (1995). *Laryngeal similarity effects in Quechua and Aymara*. Unpublished manuscript, UCLA.

Madre reciente. (n.d.). Accessed August 30, 2013. Retreived from http://blogs.20minutos.es/madrereciente/.

Maiden, Martin. (1995). *A linguistic history of Italian*. London: Routledge.

Malmberg, Bertil. (1964). A propos du *che* argentin. Note sur la dite étymologie phonétique. *Studia Linguistica* 18(1): 47–54.

Marín, Diego. (1968). *Literatura española, Tomo I: Desde los orígenes hasta el Romanticismo*. New York: Holt, Rinehart, and Winston.

Martin, James R. (1994). Macro-genres: The ecology of the page. *Network* 21: 29–52.

Martin, James R. (1997). Analysing genre: Functional perspectives. In Francis Christie and J. R. Martin (Eds.), *Genre and institutions: Social processes in the workplace and school*. (3–39). London: Cassell.

Martin, James R. (2001). Technicality and abstraction: Language for the creation of specialized texts. In Anne Burns and Caroline Coffin (Eds.), *Analysing English in a global context: A reader* (211–28). London: Routledge.

Martin, James R., and David Rose. (2007). *Working with discourse: Meaning beyond the clause.* London: Continuum.

Martin, James. R., and David Rose. (2008). *Genre relations: Mapping culture.* London: Equinox.

Martín Zorraquino, María Antonia, and José Portolés Lázaro. (1999). Los marcadores del discurso. In Ignacio Bosque and Violeta Demonte (Eds.), *Gramatica descriptiva de la lengua española, Volume 3* (4051–213). Madrid: Espasa-Calpe.

Martinez Ibarra, Francisco. (2013). Why would I speak Valencian? Understanding language rejection in the Southern territories of the Autonomous Community of Valencia. *International Journal of the Linguistic Association of the Southwest* 34(2): 67–100.

Maslíah, Leo. (1999). Che, bo. In *Canciones desoídas.* Montevideo: Ayuí/Tacuabé.

Masullo, Pablo. (1992). *Incorporation and case theory in Spanish. A crosslinguistic perspective.* Doctoral dissertation, University of Washington.

Matsuda, Ken, Scott Sadowsky, and Omar Sabaj. (2012). Índice de palabras de contenido (IPC) y distribución porcentual de legomena (DPL) en artículos de investigación en español. *Revista Signos* 45: 70–82.

Matus-Mendoza, María de la Luz. (2004). Assibilation of /-r/ and migration among Mexicans. *Language Variation and Change* 16: 17–30.

Mayén, Norma. (2007). *Afro-Hispanic linguistic remnants in Mexico: The case of the Costa Chica Region of Oaxaca.* Doctoral dissertation, Purdue University.

Mazower, Mark. (2004). *Salonica, city of ghosts: Christians, Muslims, and Jews, 1430–1950.* New York: Vintage.

McCarthy, Corrine. (2008). Morphological variability in the comprehension of agreement: An argument for representation over computation. *Second Language Research* 24(4): 459–86.

McEnery, Tony, and Andrew Wilson (2001). *Corpus linguistics.* Edinburgh: Edinburgh University Press.

McGinnis, Martha. (2001). Semantic and morphological restrictions in experiencer predicates. In John T. Jensen and Gerard Van Herk (Eds.), *Proceedings of the 2000 CLA Annual Conference* (245–56). Ottawa: Cahiers linguistiques d'Ottawa.

McKinnon, Sean. (2012). *Intervocalic /s/ voicing in Catalonian Spanish.* Honors thesis, The Ohio State University.

Megenney, William. (1993). Elementos criollo-portugueses en el español dominicano. *Montalbán* 15: 3–56.

Megenney, William. (1999). *Aspectos del lenguaje afronegroide en Venezuela.* Madrid: Iberoamericana-Vervuert.

Mendoza, Reinhild. (2005). *Der Voseo im Spanischen Uruguays. Eine pluridimensionale Makro- und Mikroanalyse.* Kiel: Westensee-Verlag.

Meiser, Gerhard. (1998). *Historische Laut- und Formenlehre der lateinischen Sprache.* Darmstadt: Wissenschaftliche Buchgesellschaft.

Milroy, James, and Lesley Milroy. (1985). *Authority.* London: Routledge.

Milroy, Lesley. (1980). *Language and social networks.* Oxford: Blackwell.

Modismos de nuestra patria. (2010). *UnivisionForos.* Accessed on May 26, 2014. Retrieved from http://foro.univision.com/t5/Paint-Shop-Pro/Modismos-de-nuestra-patria/td-p/437790951/page/3.

Molinero, María del Mar, and Miranda Stewart (Eds.). (2006). *Globalization and language in the Spanish-speaking world.* New York: Palgrave MacMillan.

Montolío Durán, Estrella. (2008). *Conectores de la lengua escrita: Contragumentativos, consecutivos, aditivos y organizadores de la información*. Barcelona: Ariel.

Montoya Abat, Brauli, and Antoni Mas i Miralles. (2011). *La transmissió familiar del valencià a València*. Valencia: Acadèmia Valenciana de la Llengua.

Montrul, Silvina. (2004). *The acquisition of Spanish. Morphosyntactic development in monolingual and bilingual L1 acquisition and in adult L2 acquisition.* Amsterdam: John Benjamins.

Moreno Fernández, Francisco. (1998). *Principios de sociolingüística y sociología del lenguaje.* Barcelona: Ariel.

Morgan, Terrell A. (2010). *Sonidos en contexto: Una introducción a la fonética del español con especial referencia a la vida real.* New Haven, CT: Yale University Press.

Moris, Juan Pablo, and Federico Navarro. (2007). Género y registro en la lingüística sistémico funcional. Un relevo crítico. Paper presented at the *I Coloquio Argentino del Grupo ECLAR Texto y Género*, Universidad Nacional de la Plata, Argentina. Retrieved from http://discurso.files.wordpress.com/2009/03/moris-navarro2007genero-y-registro-en-la-lsfcoloquio-texto-y-genero.pdf.

Moro, Andrea. (2003). Notes on vocative case: A case study in clause structure. In Josep Quer, Jan Schroten, Mauro Scorretti, Petra Sleeman, and Els Verheugd (Eds.), *Romance languages and linguistic theory 2001: Selected papers from Going Romance* (251–65). Amsterdam: John Benjamins.

Moser, Karolin. (2003). En torno a las formas de tratamiento para la segunda persona en el español de Costa Rica. *Káñina: Revista de Artes y Letras de la Universidad de Costa Rica* 27(2): 153–61.

Moser, Karolin. (2008). Tres hipótesis sobre la (des)cortesía en el tratamiento diádico informal-familiar de San José, Costa Rica. *Revista Internacional de Lingüística Iberoamericana* 6.1(11): 129–45.

Moyna, María Irene, and Beatriz Vanni Ceballos. (2008). Representaciones dramáticas de una variable lingüística: Tuteo y voseo en obras de teatro del Río de la Plata (1886–1911). *Spanish in Context* 5(1): 64–88.

Murray, Denise E. (1988). The context of oral and written language: A framework for mode and medium switching. *Language in Society* 17: 351–73.

Narbona, Antonio, Rafael Cano, and Ramón Morillo. (1998). *El español hablado en Andalucía*. Barcelona: Editorial Ariel.

Narrog, Heiko. (2012). *Modality, subjectivity, and semantic change: A cross-linguistic perspective*. Oxford: Oxford University Press.

Navarro, Federico. (2011). *Análisis histórico del discurso. La evaluación en las reseñas del Instituto de Filología de Buenos Aires (1939–1989)*. Doctoral dissertation, Universidad de Valladolid.

Navarro Tomás, Tomás. (1962). *Atlas lingüístico de la Península Ibérica, I: Fonética*. Madrid: CSIC.

Navarro Tomás, Tomás. (1968). *Studies in Spanish phonology*. Coral Gables, FL: University of Miami Press.

Navarro Tomás, Tomás. (1977). *Manual de pronunciación española*. Madrid: CSIC.

Obaid, Antonio. (1967). A sequence of tenses?—What sequence of tenses? *Hispania* 50: 112–19.

Otheguy, Ricardo. (1973). The Spanish Caribbean: A creole perspective. In Charles-James Bailey and Roger W. Shuy (Eds.), *New ways of analyzing variation in English* (323–39). Washington, DC: Georgetown University Press.

Otheguy, Ricardo, and Ana Celia Zentella. (2012). *Spanish in New York: Language contact, dialectal leveling, and structural continuity.* Oxford: Oxford University Press.

O'Donnell, Michael. (2008). The UAM CorpusTool: Software for corpus annotation and exploration. In Carmen M. Bretones Callejas et al. (Eds.), *Applied linguistics now: Understanding language and mind / La lingüística aplicada hoy: Comprendiendo el lenguaje y la mente* (1433–47). Almería: Universidad de Almería.

Páez Urdaneta, Iraset. (1981). *Historia y geografía hispanoamericana del voseo.* Caracas: La Casa de Bello.

Painter, Robert Kenneth. (2011). *Acoustic and perceptual explanations for rhotacism in Latin and Germanic.* Doctoral dissertation, State University of New York-Buffalo.

Pander Maat, Henk, and Ted Sanders. (2000). Domains of use or subjectivity? The distribution of three Dutch causal connectives explained. *Topics in English Linguistics* 33: 57–82.

Pander Maat, Henk, and Liesbeth Degand. (2002). Scaling causal relations and connectives in terms of speaker involvement. *Cognitive Linguistics* 12(3): 211–45.

Parodi, Giovanni. (2007). Variation across registers in Spanish: Exploring the El Grial PUCV Corpus. In Giovanni Parodi (Ed.), *Working with Spanish Corpora* (11–53). London: Continuum.

Parodi, Claudia, and Marta Luján. (2000). Aspect in spanish psych verbs. In Héctor Campos, Elena Herburger, Alfonso Morales-Font, and Thomas J. Walsh (Eds.), *Hispanic linguistics at the turn of the millennium. Papers from the 3rd Hispanic Linguistics Symposium* (210–21). Somerville, MA: Cascadilla Press.

Pei, Mario. (1968). *The story of language.* New York: Touchstone.

Perez, Danae. (2015). Traces of Portuguese in Afro-Yungueño Spanish? *Journal of Pidgin and Creole Languages* 30(2): 307–43.

Perl, Matthias, and Armin Schwegler (Eds.) (1998). *América negra: Panorámica actual de los estudios lingüísticos sobre variedades hispanas, portuguesas y criollas.* Madrid: Iberoamericana-Vervuert.

Pesetsky, David. (1987). Binding problems with experiencer verbs. *Linguistic Inquiry* 18: 126–40.

Pesetsky, David. (1995). *Zero syntax: Experiencers and cascades.* Cambridge, MA: MIT Press.

Pesetsky, David, and Esther Torrego. (2007). The syntax of valuation and the interpretability of features. In Simin Karimi, Vida Samiian, and Wendy K. Wilkins (Eds.), *Phrasal and clausal architecture: Syntactic derivation and interpretation* (262–94). Amsterdam: John Benjamins.

Picallo, Carmen. (2008). Gender and number in Romance. *Lingue e Linguaggio* 1: 47–66.

Pieras, Felipe. (1999). *Social dynamics of language contact in Palma de Mallorca: Attitude and phonological transfer.* Doctoral Dissertation, Pennsylvania State University.

Piqueres Gilabert, Rosa María, and M. Fuss. (2016). Actitudes hacia la interferencia en el habla de los valencianohablantes. In Jeremy King and Sandro Sessarego (Eds.), *Varieties of Spanish: Language variation and contact-induced change.* Amsterdam: John Benjamins.

Pirello, Karen, Sheila E. Blumstein, and Kathleen Kurowski. (1997). The characteristics of voicing in syllable-initial fricatives in American English. *Journal of the Acoustical Society of America* 101: 3754–65.

Polinsky, María, Lauren E. Clemens, Adam M. Morgan, Ming Xiang, and Dustin Heestand. (2013). Resumption in English. In Jon Sprouse and Norbert Hornstein (Eds.), *Experimental syntax and island effects* (341–59). Cambridge: Cambridge University Press.

Potowski, Kim, and Richard Cameron (Eds.) (2007). *Spanish in contact: Policy, social and linguistic inquiries.* Amsterdam: John Benjamins.

Preminger, Omer. (2011). *Agreement as a fallible operation.* Doctoral dissertation, MIT.

Prieto, Pilar. (2004). *Fonètica i fonologia: els sons del català.* Barcelona: Editorial Universitat Oberta de Catalunya.

Prince, Ellen. (1990). Syntax and discourse: A look at resumptive pronouns. *Berkeley Linguistics Society: Proceedings of the 16th Annual Meeting* (482–97). Berkeley: University of California Press.

Privitera, Joseph. (2004). *Sicilian, the oldest Romance language.* New York: Legas.

Probus, Marcus Valerius. (3rd–4th century AD). *Appendix Probi.* Retrieved from http://www.ling.upenn.edu/~kurisuto/germanic/appendix_probi.html.

Pylkkänen, Liina. (2002). *Introducing arguments.* Doctoral dissertation, MIT.

Pylkkänen, Liina. (2008). *Introducing arguments.* Cambridge, MA: MIT Press.

Räisänen, Christine. (1999). *The conference forum as a system of genres: A sociocultural study of academic conference practices in automotive crash-safety engineering.* Göteborg: Acta Universitatis Gothoburgensis.

Ranson, Diana. (1999). Variación sintáctica del adjetivo demostrativo en español. In María José Serrano (Ed.), *Estudios de variación sintáctica* (121–42). Castellón: Servicio de Publicaciones de la Universidad Jaume I.

Real Academia Española. (2009). *Nueva gramática de la lengua española.* Madrid: Espasa-Calpe.

Real Academia Española. (n.d.). *Corpus diacrónico del español* (CORDE). Retrieved from http://corpus.rae.es/cordenet.html.

Recasens i Vives, Daniel. (1993). *Fonètica i fonologia* (2nd edition). Barcelona: Enciclopèdia Catalana.

Reinhart, Tanya. (2006). *Interface strategies: Reference-set computation.* Cambridge, MA: MIT Press.

Rigau, Gemma. (1990). Les propietats d'agradar: Estructura temàtica i comportament sintàctic. *Caplletra* 8: 7–20.

Rissel, Dorothy. (1989). Sex, attitudes, and the assibilation of /r/ among young people in San Luis Potosí, Mexico. *Language Variation and Change* 1: 269–83.

Rivera-Mills, Susana. (2011). Use of *voseo* and Latino identity: An intergenerational study of Hondurans and Salvadorans in the Western region of the U.S. In Luis A. Ortiz-López (Ed.), *Selected proceedings of the 13th Hispanic Linguistics Symposium* (94–106). Somerville, MA: Cascadilla.

Rivera-Mills, Susana, and Daniel Villa (Eds.). (2010). *Spanish of the US Southwest.* Madrid: Iberoamericana-Vervuert.

Roberts, Philip J. (2012). Latin rhotacism: A case study in the life cycle of phonological processes. *Transactions of the Philological Society* 110(1): 80–93.

Robinson, Kimball L. (1979). On the voicing of intervocalic s in the Ecuadorian Highlands. *Romance Philology* 33(1): 137–43.

Robinson, Kimball L. (2012). The dialectology of syllabification: A review of variation in the Ecuadorian Highlands. *Romance Philology* 66(1): 115–45.

Robles Garrote, Pilar. (2013). La conferencia como género monológico: análisis macroestructural en español e italiano. *Boletín de filología* 48: 127–46.

Rojas, Elena M. (1980). *Aspectos del habla en San Miguel de Tucumán.* Tucumán: Universidad Nacional de Tucumán.

Rojo, Guillermo. (1976). La correlación temporal. *Verba* 3: 65–89.

Romero, Joaquín. (1999). The effect of voicing assimilation on gestural coordination. In Maria-Josep Solé, Daniel Recasens, and Joaquín Romero (Eds.), *Proceedings of the Fifteenth International Congress of the Phonetic Sciences* (1793–96). Berkeley: University of California Press.

Romero, Joaquín, and Sidney Martín. (2003). Articulatory weakening as basis of historical rhotacism. In Maria-Josep Solé, Daniel Recasens, and Joaquín Romero (Eds.), *Proceedings of the Fifteenth International Congress of Phonetics Sciences* (2825–28). Barcelona: Causal Productions.

Romero, Rey. (2009). Lexical borrowing and gender assignment in Judeo-Spanish. *Ianua, Revista Philologica Romanica* 9: 23–35.

Romero, Rey. (2011a). Issues of Spanish language maintenance in the Prince Islands. In Alejandro Cortazar and Rafael Orozco (Eds.), *Lenguaje, arte y revoluciones ayer y hoy: New approaches to Hispanic linguistic, literary, and cultural studies* (162–87). Newcastle upon Tyne: Cambridge Scholars.

Romero, Rey. (2011b). Mainland vs. island: A comparative morphological study on Spanish-Turkish contact. In Jim Michnowicz and Robin Dodsworth (Eds.), *Selected proceedings of the 5th Workshop on Spanish Sociolinguistics* (50–56). Somerville, MA: Cascadilla Press.

Romero, Rey. (2012). *Spanish in the Bosphorus: A sociolinguistic study on the Judeo-Spanish dialect spoken in Istanbul*. Istanbul: Libra.

Rona, José Pedro. (1963). Sobre algunas etimologías rioplatenses. *Anuario de Letras* 3: 87–106.

Rona, José Pedro. (1967). *Geografía y morfología del "voseo."* Porto Alegre: Pontifícia Universidade Católica.

Rosenblat, Ángel. (1962). Origen e historia del *che* argentino. *Filología* 3: 327–401.

Rosselló, Joana. (2002). El SV, I: Verb i arguments verbals. In Joan Solà, Maria-Rosa Lloret, Joan Mascaró, and Manuel Pérez Saldanya (Eds.), *Gramàtica del català contemporani, Volum 2* (1853–1949). Barcelona: Empúries.

Rosy Runrún. (n.d.). Accessed August 30, 2013. Retreived from http://blogs.20minutos.es/rosyrunrun/.

Rowley-Jolivet, Elizabeth, and Shirley Carter-Thomas (2005). The rhetoric of conference presentation introductions: Context, argument and interaction. *International Journal of Applied Linguistics* 15(1): 45–70.

Rufo Sánchez, José Ramón. (2006). *Actitudes y creencias frente al rotacismo sevillano*. Master's thesis, University of Georgia, Athens.

Ruiz Asencio, José Manuel. (2010). *Los becerros gótico y galiciano de Valpuesta*. Real Academia Española y el Instituto Castellano y Leonés de la Lengua.

Ruiz García, Marta. (2001). *El español popular de Chocó: Evidencia de una reestructuración parcial*. Doctoral dissertation, University of New Mexico.

Ryan, E. B. & M. A. Carranza (1975). Evaluative reactions towards speakers of standard English and Mexican American accented English. *Journal of Personality & Social Psychology* 31(6): 855–63.

Sachar, Howard M. (1994). *Farewell España: The world of the Sephardim remembered*. New York: Vintage.

Samper Padilla, José Antonio, Clara Eugenia Hernández Cabrera, and Otilia Pérez Gil. (2005). Las construcciones "de retoma" en las cláusulas relativas en el español de Las Palmas de Gran Canaria. In César Alonso (Ed.), *Filología y lingüística: Estudios ofrecidos a Antonio Quilis, Vol. 1* (611–28). Madrid: CSIC.

Sanders, Ted. (2005). Coherence, causality and cognitive complexity in discourse. In Michel Aurnague and Miriam Bras (Eds.), *Proceedings of the First International Symposium on the Exploration and Modelling of Meaning* (31–46). Toulouse: Universite de Toulouse-le-Mirail.

Sanders, Ted, José Sanders and Eve Sweetser. (2009). Causality, cognition and communication: A mental space analysis of subjectivity in causal connectives. In Ted Sanders and Eve Sweetser (Eds.), *Causal categories in discourse and cognition* (19–59). Berlin: Mouton de Gruyter.

Sarnoff, Irving. (1966). Social attitudes and the resolution of motivational conflict. In Marie Jahoda and N. Warren (Eds.), *Attitudes* (279–84). Harmondsword: Penguin.

Schaden, Gerhard. (2010). Vocatives: A note on addressee-management. *University of Pennsylvania Working Papers in Linguistics* 16(1): 176–85.

Schleppegrell, Mary. (2004). *The language of schooling: A functional linguistics perspective*. Mahwah, NJ: Lawrence Erlbaum Associates.

Schmidt, Annette. (1985). *Young people's Dyirbal: An example of language death from Australia*. Cambridge: Cambridge University Press.

Schmidt, Lauren B., and Erik W. Willis. (2011). Systematic investigation of voicing assimilation of Spanish /s/ in Mexico City. In Scott M. Alvord (Ed.), *Selected proceedings of the 5th Conference on Laboratory Approaches to Romance Phonology* (1–20). Somerville, MA: Cascadilla Press.

Schwegler, Armin. (1999). Monogenesis revisited: The Spanish perspective. In John Rickford and Suzanne Romaine (Eds.), *Creole genesis, attitudes and discourse* (235–62). Amsterdam: John Benjamins.

Schwegler, Armin. (2014). Portuguese remnants in the Afro-Hispanic diaspora. In Patricia Amaral and Ana María Carvalho (Eds.), *Portuguese-Spanish interfaces: Diachrony, synchrony, and contact* (403–41). Amsterdam: John Benjamins.

Schwenter, Scott. (1999). Evidentiality in Spanish morphosyntax: A reanalysis of *dequeísmo*. In Manuel J. Serrano (Ed.), *Estudios de variación sintáctica* (65–87). Madrid: Iberoamericana-Vervuert.

Schwenter, Scott. (2011). Variationist approaches to Spanish morphosyntax: Internal and external factors. In Manuel Díaz Campos (Ed.), *The handbook of Hispanic sociolinguistics* (123–47). Malden, MA: Wiley-Blackwell.

Seco, Manuel (Ed.). (2003). *Léxico hispánico primitivo*. Madrid: Espasa Calpe.

Segura i Llopes, Josep Carles. (1996). *Estudi lingüístic del parlar d'Alacant*. Alicante: Institut de Cultura Juan Gil-Albert.

Segura i Llopes, Josep Carles. (1998). *El parlar d'Elx: Aproximacions a una descripció*. Elche: Ayuntamiento de Elche.

Serrano, María José (Ed.) (1999a). *Estudios de variación sintáctica*. Madrid: Iberoamericana-Vervuert.

Serrano, María José. (1999b). Nuevas perspectivas en variación sintáctica. In María José Serrano (Ed.), *Estudios de variación sintáctica* (11–49). Castellón: Servicio de Publicaciones de la Universidad Jaume I.

Serrano, María José. (2011). Morphosyntactic variation in Spain. In Manuel Díaz Campos (Ed.), *The handbook of Hispanic sociolinguistics* (187–204). Malden, MA: Wiley-Blackwell.

Sessarego, Sandro. (2008). Spanish concordantia temporum: An old issue, new solutions. In Maurice Westmoreland and Juan Antonio Thomas (Eds.), *Proceedings of the 4th workshop on Spanish sociolinguistics* (91–99). Somerville, MA: Cascadilla Press.

Sessarego, Sandro. (2009). On the evolution of Afro-Bolivian Spanish subject-verb agreement: Variation and change. *Sintagma* 21: 107–19.

Sessarego, Sandro. (2011a). On the status of Afro-Bolivian Spanish features: Decreolization or vernacular universals? In Jim Michnowicz and Robin Dodsworth (Eds.), *Proceedings of the 5th International Workshop on Spanish Sociolinguistics* (125–41). Somerville, MA: Cascadilla Press.

Sessarego, Sandro. (2011b). *Introducción al idioma afroboliviano: Una conversación con el awicho Manuel Barra*. Cochabamba/La Paz: Plural Editores.

Sessarego, Sandro. (2012). Vowel weakening in Yungueño Spanish: Linguistic and social considerations. *PAPIA: Revista Brasileira de Estudos Crioulos e Similares* 22(2): 279–94.

Sessarego, Sandro. (2013a). Afro-Hispanic contact varieties as conventionalized advanced second languages. *IBERIA* 5(1): 96–122.

Sessarego, Sandro. (2013b). On the non-creole bases for Afro-Bolivian Spanish. *Journal of Pidgin and Creole Languages* 28(2): 363–407.

Sessarego, Sandro. (2013c). *Chota Valley Spanish*. Madrid: Iberoamericana-Vervuert.

Sessarego, Sandro. (2013d). Chota Valley Spanish: A second look at creole monogenesis. *Revista Internacional de Lingüística Iberoamericana* 22(2): 129–48.

Sessarego, Sandro. (2014a). *The Afro-Bolivian Spanish determiner phrase: A microparametric account*. Columbus: The Ohio State University Press.

Sessarego, Sandro. (2014b). Afro-Peruvian Spanish in the context of Spanish creole genesis. *Spanish in Context* 11(3): 381–401.

Sessarego, Sandro. (2014c). On Chota Valley Spanish origin: Linguistic and sociohistorical evidence. *Journal of Pidgin and Creole Languages* 29(1): 86–133.

Sessarego, Sandro. (2016). A response to Pérez. *Journal of Pidgin and Creole Languages* 31(1): 201–12.

Sessarego, Sandro, and Fernando Tejedo-Herrero (Eds.) (2016). *Spanish language and sociolinguistic analysis*. Amsterdam: John Benjamins.

Sessarego, Sandro, and Javier Gutiérrez-Rexach. (2011). A minimalist approach to gender agreement in the Afro-Bolivian DP: Variation and the specification of uninterpretable features. *Folia Linguistica* 45(2): 465–88.

Sessarego, Sandro, and Javier Gutiérrez-Rexach (In press). Afro-Hispanic contact varieties at the interface: A closer look at Pro-Drop phenomena in Chinchano Spanish. In Jeremy King and Sandro Sessarego (Eds.), *The dynamics of language variation and change: Varieties of Spanish across space and time*. Amsterdam: John Benjamins.

Sessarego, Sandro, and Letania Ferreira (2016). Spanish and Portuguese parallels: Impoverished number agreement as a vernacular feature of two rural dialects. In Sandro Sessarego and Fernando Tejedo-Herrero (Eds.), *Spanish language and sociolinguistic analysis* (283–304). Amsterdam: John Benjamins.

Sessarego, Sandro, and Rey Romero. (In press). Hard come, easy go: Linguistic interfaces in Istanbul Judeo-Spanish and Afro-Ecuadorian Spanish. In Jeremy King and Sandro Sessarego (Eds.), *The dynamics of language variation and change: Varieties of Spanish across space and time*. Amsterdam: John Benjamins.

Sidwell, Keith. (1995). *Reading medieval Latin*. Cambridge: Cambridge University Press.

Silva-Corvalán, Carmen. (1984). Topicalización y pragmática en español. *Revista Española de Lingüística* 14(1): 1–19.

Silva-Corvalán, Carmen. (1989). *Sociolingüística. Teoría y análisis*. Madrid: Alhambra.

Silva-Corvalán, Carmen. (1994). *Language contact and change: Spanish in Los Angeles*. Oxford: Oxford University Press.

Silva-Corvalán, Carmen. (1996). Resumptive pronouns: A discourse explanation. In Claudia Parodi, Carlos Quicoli, Mario Saltarelli, and Maria Luisa Zubizarreta (Eds.), *Aspects of romance linguistics: Selected papers from the Linguistic Symposium on Romance Languages XXIV*. Somerville, MA: Cascadilla Press.

Silva-Corvalán, Carmen. (2001). *Sociolingüística y pragmática del español*. Washington, DC: Georgetown University Press.

Sinnott, Sarah. (In press). In Jeremy King and Sandro Sessarego (Eds.), *Varieties of Spanish: Language Variation and Contact-Induced Change*. Amsterdam: John Benjamins.

Siracusa, María Isabel. (1977). Morfología verbal del voseo en el habla culta de Buenos Aires. *Filología* 16: 201–13.

Slabakova, Roumyana. (2009). What is easy and what is hard to acquire in a second language? In Melissa Bowles, Tania Ionin, Silvina Montrul, and Annie Tremblay (Eds.), *Proceedings of the 10th Generative Approaches to Second Language Acquisition Conference* (280–94). Somerville, MA: Cascadilla Press.

Smith, Neilson V. (1973). *The acquisition of phonology*. Cambridge: Cambridge University Press.

Solé, Maria Josep. (1992). Experimental phonology: The case of rhotacism. In Wolfgang U. Dressier, Hans C. Luschutzky, Oskar E. Pfeiffer, and John R. Rennison (Eds.), *Phonologica 1988: Proceedings of the 6th International Phonology Meeting*. Cambridge: Cambridge University Press.

Sorace, Antonella, and Ludovica Serratrice (2009). Internal and external interfaces in bilingual language development: beyond structural overlap. *International Journal of Bilingualism* 19: 75–91.

Sprouse, Jon, and Diogo Almeida. (2013). The empirical status of data in syntax: A reply to Gibson and Fedorenko. *Language and Cognitive Processes* 28: 222–28.

SPSS for Windows. (2010). Rel. 17.0.2. Chicago: SPSS. Software.

Steffen, Joachim. (2010). El tratamiento en el Uruguay. In Martin Hummel, Bettina Kluge, and Virginia Laslop (Eds.), *Formas y fórmulas de tratamiento en el mundo hispánico* (451–64). Mexico City: El Colegio de México.

Steriade, Donca. (1997). *Phonetics in phonology: The case of laryngeal neutralization*. Unpublished manuscript, UCLA.

Stevens, Kenneth, Sheila Blumstein, Laura Glicksman, Marth Burton, and Kathleen Kurowski. (1992). Acoustic and perceptual characteristics of voicing in fricatives and fricative clusters. *Journal of the Acoustical Society of America* 91: 2979–3000.

Strycharczuk, Patrycja. (2012). *Phonetics-phonology interactions in pre-sonorant voicing*. Doctoral dissertation, University of Manchester.

Suárez Fernández, Mercedes. (2010). Cláusulas de relativo con pronombre personal anafórico en castellano medieval. *Nueva Revista de Filología Hispánica* 58(1): 1–37.

Suñer, Margarita. (2001). Las cláusulas relativas especificativas en el español de Caracas. *Boletín de Lingüística* 16: 7–43.

Suñer, Margarita, and José A. Padilla-Rivera. (1987). Sequence of tenses and the subjunctive, again. *Hispania* 70(3): 634–42.

Swales, John M. (1990). *Genre analysis: English in academic and research settings*. Cambridge: Cambridge University Press.

Swales, John M. (2004). *Research genres: Explorations and applications*. Cambridge: Cambridge University Press.

Swales, John M. (2009). Worlds of genre-metaphors of genre. In Charles Bazerman, Adair Bonini, and Débora Figueiredo (Eds.), *Genre in a changing world* (3–16). Fort Collins, CO: Clearinghouse.

Sweetser, Eve. (1990). *From etymology to pragmatics: Metaphorical and cultural aspects of semantic structure*. Cambridge: Cambridge University Press.

Taboada, Maria Teresa. (2004). The genre structure of bulletin board messages. *Text Technology* 13(2): 55–82.

Tagliamonte, Sali. (2006). *Analyzing sociolinguistic variation*. Oxford: Oxford University Press.

Tannen, Deborah (1985). Relative focus on involvement in oral and written discourse. In David Olson, Nancy Torrance, and Angela Hildyard (Eds.), *Literacy, language and learning: The nature and consequences of reading and writing* (124–47). Cambridge: Cambridge University Press.

Thompson, Geoff. (2014). *Introducing functional grammar* (3rd edition). London: Routledge.

Tippets, Ian. (2011). Differential object marking: Quantitative evidence for underlying hierarchical constraints across Spanish dialects. In Luis A. Ortiz-López (Ed.), *Selected proceedings of the 13th Hispanic Linguistics Symposium* (107–17). Somerville, MA: Cascadilla Press.

Torreblanca, Máximo. (1978). El fonema /s/ en la lengua española. *Hispania* 61: 498–503.

Torreblanca, Máximo. (1986). La "s" sonora prevocálica en el español moderno. *Thesaurus* 41: 59–69.

Torreira, Francisco, and Mirjam Ernestus. (2012). Weakening of intervocalic /s/ in the Nijmegen Corpus of casual Spanish. *Phonetica* 69: 124–48.

Torrejón, Alfredo. (1986). Acerca del voseo culto de Chile. *Hispania* 69(3): 677–83.

Torrejón, Alfredo. (2010). El voseo en Chile: Una aproximación diacrónica. In Martin Hummel, Bettina Kluge, and Virginia Laslop (Eds.), *Formas y fórmulas de tratamiento en el mundo hispánico* (413–27). México City: El Colegio de México.

Torres-Cacoullos, Rena, and Catherine Travis. (2015). Gauging convergence on the ground: Code-switching in the community. *International Journal of Bilingualism* 19(4): 365–86.

Traugott, Elizabeth. (2010). Revisiting subjectification and intersubjectification. In Kristen Davidse, Lieven Vandelanotte, and Hubert Cuyckens (Eds.), *Subjectification, intersubjectification and grammaticalization* (29–70). Berlin: Mouton de Gruyter.

Traugott, Elizabeth, and Richard Dasher. (2002). *Regularity in semantic change*. Cambridge: Cambridge University Press.

Travis, Catherine. (2005). *Discourse markers in Colombian Spanish: A study in polysemy*. Berlin: Mouton de Gruyter.

Trudgill, Peter. (1972). Sex, covert prestige and linguistic change in the urban British English of Norwich. *Language in Society* 1: 179–95.

Trujillo, Ramón. (1990). Sobre la supuesta despronominalización del relativo. *E. L. U. A.* 6: 23–45.

Valdés, Guadalupe, and M. Geoffrion-Vinci. (1998). Chicano Spanish: The problem of the "underdeveloped" code in bilingual repertoires. *The Modern Language Journal* 82(4): 473–501.

Valdés, Juan de. (1984). *Dialogo de la lengua*. Bilbao: Plaza y Janés.

Vassileva, Irina. (2002). Speaker-audience interaction: The case of Bulgarians presenting in English. In Elija Ventola, Celia Shalom, and Susan Thompson (Eds.), *The language of conferencing* (255–76). Frankfurt: Peter Lang.

Veiga, Danilo. (2010). *Estructura social y ciudades en el Uruguay: Tendencias recientes*. Montevideo: Universidad de la República, Facultad de Ciencias Sociales.

Ventola, Elija, Celia Shalom, and Susan Thompson (2002). *The language of conferencing*. Frankfurt: Peter Lang.

Viera Echevarria, Carolina (2014). *Academic Spanish in the United States: Discourse analysis of academic conference presentations*. Doctoral dissertation, University of California-Davis.

Viñas-de-Puig, Ricard. (2009). *The argument of experience: Experience predicates and argument structure in Catalan and Mayangna*. Doctoral dissertation, Purdue University.

Viñas-de-Puig, Ricard. (2014). Predicados psicológicos y estructuras con verbo ligero: Del estado al evento. *RLA. Revista de lingüística teórica y aplicada* 52(2): 165–88.

Viudas Camarasa, Antonio. (2003). El atlas lingüístico de la Península Ibérica y el dialectólogo Alonso Zamora Vicente. In Joan C. Rovira Soler (Ed.), *Actas del Congreso Internacional "La lengua, la Academia, lo Popular, los Clásicos, los Contemporáneos . . . ," Volumen 1* (285–300). Alicante: Servicio de Publicaciones de la Universidad de Alicante.

Vida Castro, Matilde, and Juan Andrés Villena Ponsoda. (2007). *El español hablado en Málaga*. Málaga: Editorial Sarriá.

Vo (lenguaje). (n.d.). *Wikipedia*. Accessed May 26, 2014. Retreived from http://es.wikipedia.org/w/index.php?title=Vo_%28lenguaje%29&oldid=74410637.

von Heusinger, Klaus, and Georg Kaiser. (2003). The interaction of animacy, definiteness, and specificity. In Klaus von Heusinger and Georg Kaiser (Eds.), *Proceedings of the Workshop "Semantic and Syntactic Aspects of Specificity in Romance Languages"* (41–65). Konstanz: Konstanz University.

Weyers, Joseph. (2009). The impending demise of *tú* in Montevideo, Uruguay. *Hispania* 92(4): 829–39.

Weyers, Joseph. (2012). *Voseo* in Montevideo's advertising: Reflecting linguistic norms. *Studies in Hispanic and Lusophone Linguistics* 5(2): 369–85.

Wheeler, Max. (1979). *Phonology of Catalan*. Oxford: Blackwell.

White, Lidia. (2011). Second language acquisition in the interfaces. *Lingua* 121(3): 577–90.

Widdison, Kirk A. (1995). The perception of voicing in Spanish sibilants. In *Eurospeech '95: Proceedings of the 4th European Conference on Speech Communication and Technology 3* (2289–92). Madrid: ISCA.

Widdison, Kirk A. (1996). Physical constraints on sibilant-voice patterning in Spanish phonology. In John Turley (Ed.), *Proceedings of the 1995 Desert Language and Linguistic Society Symposium* (37–42). Provo, UT: BYU Linguistics Dept.

Widdison, Kirk A. (1997). Phonetic explanations for sibilant patterns in Spanish. *Lingua* 102: 253–64.

Wineburg, Sam. (2004). Must it be this way? Ten rules for keeping your audience awake during conferences. *Educational Researcher* 33(4): 13–14.

Wölck, Wolfgang. (1973). Attitudes toward Spanish and Quechua in bilingual Peru. In Roger Shuy and Ralph W. Fasold (Eds.), *Language attitudes: Current trends and prospects* (129–47). Washington, DC: Georgetown University Press.

Woolard, Kathryn A. (1984). A formal measure of language attitudes in Barcelona. *International Journal of the Sociology of Language* 47(1): 63–71.

Woolard, Kathryn A., and T. Gahng. (1990). Changing language policies and attitudes in autonomous Catalonia. *Language in Society* 19(3): 311–30.

Zanoni, Leandro. (2006). Vo. *eBlog: Cibercultura, medios, periodismo*. Retreived from http://www.eblog.com.ar/1415/bo/comment-page-1/#comment-99481.

Zentella, Ana Celia (1997). *Growing up bilingual: Puerto Rican children in New York*. New York: Wiley-Blackwell.

Zwicky, Arnold. (1974). Hey! Whatsyourname! In Michael La Galy, Robert A. Fox, and Anthony Bruck (Eds.), *Papers from the Tenth Regional Meeting of the Chicago Linguistics Society* (787–801). Chicago: Chicago Linguistics Society.

Contributors

WHITNEY CHAPPELL earned her PhD from The Ohio State University in 2013 and is currently an Assistant Professor of Spanish linguistics in The University of Texas at San Antonio's Department of Modern Languages and Literatures. Specializing in sociophonetic variation across dialects of Spanish, Dr. Chappell addresses the following broad research questions: (i) Where does the phonetic variation occur and how can it be couched within linguistic theory to account for the phenomenon? (ii) How do phonetic realizations encode social or pragmatic meaning? (iii) What social or pragmatic meaning is encoded and how does it differ across dialects of Spanish? The pursuit of these questions sheds light on how different phonetic realizations are used to encode meaning and negotiate identity within a broader social setting, contributing to our understanding of sociolinguistics, phonetics, and dialectology. Her more relevant publications are "Linguistic Factors Conditioning Glottal Constriction in Nicaraguan Spanish," in the *Italian Journal of Linguistics* 27, no. 2 (2015): 1–42, and "The Intervocalic Voicing of /s/ in Ecuadorian Spanish," in the *Selected Proceedings of the 5th Workshop on Spanish Sociolinguistics*, edited Jim Michnowicz and Robin Dodsworth (Somerville, MA: Cascadilla Proceedings Project, document 250, 57–64).

IRENE CHECA-GARCÍA specializes in Hispanic linguistics, particularly in grammar and discourse, corpus linguistics, and conversation analysis of very young children. Her dissertation focused on measures of later syntactic development and social factors influencing it. Currently she is continuing this line of research with Prof. Guiberson in the Communication Disorders Department, researching how past tenses and mood are differential in bilingual children (Spanish-English) diagnosed with SLI (Specific Language Impairment). During her postdoc years she researched resumptive pronouns in the relative clauses of adult speech and adolescent writing. In her next project, she is working on grammaticality judgments and comprehension experimental studies of relative clauses with and without resumptive pronouns. She is also working on directives by very young children in a bilingual preschool. She is Assistant Professor of Spanish linguistics in the Department of Modern and Classical Languages of the University of Wyoming. Her publications include "Asking for Things without Words: Embodiment of Action Onset as a Toddlers' Communication Tool," in *Talk in Institutions: A LANSI Volume*, edited by Christine M. Jacknick, Catherine Box, and Hansun Z. Waring (Cambridge: Cambridge Scholars Publishing), and "Desarrollo sintáctico en la ciudad de Almería en adolescentes: Índices primarios e índices de error," in *Actas del VI Congreso de Lingüística General*, coordinated by Pablo Cano López (Madrid: Arco Libros, 181–90).

JUAN JOSÉ COLOMINA-ALMIÑANA is Assistant Professor in the Department of Mexican American and Latina/o Studies, and has developed the Language & Cognition track at The University of Texas at Austin. His research focuses on the semantic and pragmatic basis of language, the connection between language and thought, and the representation and perception of speech. Currently, he is working on several projects about the grammaticalization of Indigenous languages from Meso-America because of their contact with Spanish and English, the linguistic ideologies and attitudes of migrants and heritage speakers in the United States, and paleo-archeological research of the syntax and semantics of Guanche, among other investigations. His more recent publications are "Scope and Partitivity of Plural Indefinite Noun Phrases in Spanish," in *Pragmatics and Society* 8, no. 1 (2017): 109–30, "Disagreement and the Speaker's Point of View," in *Language and Dialogue* 5, no. 2 (2015): 224–46, and "A Solution-Based on Ordinary Language to the Psychological Objection," in *Linguistic and Philosophical Investigations* 12 (2015): 25–48 (coauthored with David P. Chico).

MARK HOFF is a PhD student in Hispanic linguistics at The Ohio State University. His specializations include pragmatics and morphosyntactic variation, especially as they pertain to the Southern Cone. Hoff's most recent work examines differential object marking and variable mood use in Argentine Spanish.

FRANCISCO MARTÍNEZ IBARRA is a sociolinguist and Assistant Professor of Spanish at Towson University. His research interests include language variation, multilingualism, language use and attitudes, and language contact between Spanish and other languages, particularly English and Catalan. He earned his PhD in Spanish linguistics from the State University of New York at Buffalo in 2011. He is the author of "Why Would I Speak Valencian? Understanding Language Rejection in the Southern Territories of the Community of Valencia," in *International Journal of the Linguistic Association of the Southwest* 32, no. 1 (2013): 67–100.

MARÍA IRENE MOYNA is Associate Professor of Hispanic linguistics, and Head of the Department of Hispanic Studies at Texas A&M University. Moyna's research explores variation and change in Spanish, particularly in word formation, personal address systems, and the history of Spanish in the United States. Her main research interest lies in the relationship between society, cognition, and acquisition as factors behind language change. Professor Moyna teaches courses on topics such as phonology, morphology, dialectology, Spanish in the United States, bilingualism, and linguistic methods, as well as advanced grammar and Spanish for the professions. She is coeditor (with A. Balestra and G. Martínez) of *Recovering the U.S. Hispanic Linguistic Heritage* (Houston: Arte Público Press), and her articles include "Back at the *Rancho*: Language Maintenance and Shift among Spanish Speakers in Post-Annexation California (1848–1900)," in *Revista Internacional de Lingüística Iberoamericana* 7, no. 1: 165–84 and "Can We Make Heads or Tails of Spanish Endocentric Compounds?," in *Linguistics* 42, no. 4: 617–37.

ROSA M. PIQUERES GILABERT is a PhD student at Indiana University. Her specializations include sociolinguistic variation with a focus on language contact between Catalan and Spanish. She also works on second language acquisition, phonetics, and pragmatics. Her most recent work focuses on a usage-based approach when analyzing pluralization of "haber" in Venezuelan Spanish. Her most recent article, "Actitudes hacia la interferencia en el habla de los valencianohablantes" (coauthor with R. Fuss), is forthcoming in *Varieties of Spanish: Language Variation and Contact-Induced Change*, edited by Jeremy King and Sandro Sessarego (Amsterdam: John Benjamins).

REY ROMERO earned a PhD in Spanish linguistics from Georgetown University in Washington, DC, focusing on Spanish language contact varieties. His monograph, *Spanish in the Bosphorus: A Social Linguistic Study on the Judeo-Spanish Dialect Spoken in Istanbul* (Libra, 2012), analyzes the sociolinguistic characteristics of the Sephardic community in Istanbul, focusing on patterns of transmission and structural change. He has published articles on Judeo-Spanish in several conference proceedings, chapters in Hispanic linguistics volumes, and linguistic journals such as *Ianua. Revista Philologica Romanica* and *Studies in Hispanic and Lusophone Linguistics*. He is Assistant Professor of Spanish linguistics at the University of Houston-Downtown, where he teaches courses on linguistics, translation, and Spanish for heritage speakers.

JOHN M. RYAN earned his PhD in rhetoric, composition, and linguistics at Arizona State University in Tempe, Arizona, in 2008. He earned his Master's degree in Spanish linguistics, also from Arizona State in 1991. He earned his Bachelor of Science degree in Spanish from Georgetown University's School of Languages and Linguistics in Washington, DC in 1985. He is currently Assistant Professor of Spanish linguistics at the University of Northern Colorado. His research on the acquisition of verbs by children and adults has been published in such journals as the *Journal of Child Language and Development* and *Hispania*, and his first book, *The Genesis of Argument Structure: Observations from a Child's Early Speech Production in Spanish* (Saarbrücken: Lambert, 2012), traces the emergence of the verb phase in the developing language of a monolingual child learning Peninsular Spanish. Other interests include historical news discourse of the Italian American community and the reconstruction of proto-Ibero Romance. Dr. Ryan is a member of the Linguistic Society of America, the Rocky Mountain Modern Language Association, the Linguistic Association of the Southwest, and the Italian American Historical Society.

SANDRO SESSAREGO is Assistant Professor in the Department of Spanish and Portuguese at the University of Texas at Austin and Freiburg Institute for Advanced Studies. He teaches undergraduate and graduate courses on Hispanic linguistics. He primarily works in the fields of contact linguistics, sociolinguistics, and syntax. His current research focuses on Afro-Hispanic contact varieties and on the syntax and semantics of the determiner phrase (DP). He is the author of *Introducción al idioma afroboliviano: Una conversación con el awicho Manuel Barra* (Plural Editores, 2011), *Chota Valley Spanish* (Iberoamericana/Vervuert, 2013), *The Afro-Bolivian Spanish Determiner Phrase: A Microparametric Account* (The Ohio State University Press, 2014), and *Afro-Peruvian Spanish: Spanish Slavery and the Legacy of Spanish Creole* (John Benjamins, 2015). He is also the coeditor of *Current Formal Aspects of Spanish Syntax and Semantics* (Cambridge Scholars Publishing, 2012), *New Perspectives on Hispanic Contact Linguistics in the Americas* (Iberoamericana/Vervuert, forthcoming), *Varieties of Spanish around the World: Language Variation and Contact-Induced Change* (John Benjamins, in progress), and *Spanish Language and Sociolinguistic Analysis* (John Benjamins, in progress). He has published more than twenty articles in international journals on Hispanic linguistics.

SARAH SINNOTT is Assistant Professor of Spanish and Hispanic linguistics at the University of Sioux Falls. She received a BA and a MA in Spanish language and literature from the University of Northern Iowa, and earned a PhD in Hispanic linguistics from The Ohio State University. Her most recent article is forthcoming in *Varieties of Spanish: Language Variation and Contact-Induced Change*, edited by Jeremy King and Sandro Sessarego (Amsterdam: John Benjamins).

CAROLINA VIERA received her PhD in Spanish linguistics at the University of California, Davis, with a Designated Emphasis in second language acquisition (SLA) in 2014. She also holds a Master's degree in Hispanic linguistics from the University of New Mexico and a Bachelor's degree in education from the Instituto de Profesores Artigas in Montevideo, Uruguay. She is an Assistant Professor of Spanish linguistics in Boise State University. Her main areas of research include sociolinguistics, discourse analysis, applied linguistics, corpus linguistics, and Spanish in the United States. Her current research projects examine advanced oral academic proficiency of speakers of Spanish in the United States. Future/current projects include research in a collected corpus of heritage students of Spanish in regard to the development of academic registers mediated by technology-assisted tools.

RICARD VIÑAS-DE-PUIG is Assistant Professor in the Department of Hispanic Studies at the College of Charleston. He earned a BA in translation and interpreting at the Universitat de Vic in 1998, and an MA in Spanish linguistics in 2001 and a PhD in linguistics in 2009 at Purdue University. As part of his linguistic outreach efforts, in 2012 and 2014 he organized IMLD@ECU, a series of events aimed at promoting linguistic awareness and language diversity at the local, state, and global level.

His research endeavors are divided in two different but related areas. From a theoretical linguistics perspective, Dr. Viñas de Puig looks at the argument structure of experience predicates and their possible manifestations cross-linguistically. In his dissertation, using Romance (Catalan, Spanish) and Misumalpan (Mayangna) data, he proposed a universally available structure for experience predicates, allowing for predicates with an incorporated experience argument and predicates with a non-incorporated experience, which result in light verb constructions. In his second line of research, as codirector of the

SoCIOLing (Study of Community Involvement and Outreach & Linguistics) Lab, based at East Carolina University, Dr. Viñas de Puig follows a sociolinguistic methodology. He is currently working on different projects aiming at the study of Spanish varieties in immigrant settings in the United States. He is also interested in establishing collaborative efforts with the community in the promotion of immigrant indigenous languages in Hispanic settings in the Carolinas. His most representative publications are "Predicados psicológicos y estructuras con verbo ligero: Del estado al evento," *Revista de Lingüística Teórica y Aplicada* 52, no. 2: 165–88, "Internal and External Calls to Immigrant Language Promotion: Evaluating the Research Approach in Two Cases of Community-Engaged Linguistic Research in Eastern North Carolina," in *Responses to Language Endangerment. In honor of Mickey Noonan*, edited by Elena Mihas, Bernard Perley, Gabriel Rei-Doval, and Kathleen Wheatley (Amsterdam: John Benjamins, 157–74), and "Agentivity and Experiencer Verbs in Catalan and Mayangna and the Roles of 'Little V,'" *Journal of Portuguese Linguistics* 7, no. 2: 151–72.

Index

academic conference presentations. *See* conference presentations in Spanish in the U.S.
accusative *a* marking of inanimates. *See* differential object marking (DOM) use with inanimates
Adger, David, 176, 178, 179
Afro-Bolivian and Afro-Hispanic languages. *See* Yungueño Spanish, subject-verb agreement in
age and generation: subject-verb agreement in Yungueño Spanish and, 173, 174, 175 table 8.3, 174–75; *voseo* vocatives and, 137, 138 fig. 6.3, 138
agree operation (Minimalist Program), 175–76, 178, 188
Alcántara, F., 156
Almeida, Manuel, 4
a-marked inanimates. *See* differential object marking (DOM) use with inanimates
Andalusian Spanish, rhotacism in, 48–49
Andersen, Henning, 126
Andersen, Roger W., 189
AntConc software, 155, 159

Appendix Probi (Probus), 22
Arabic, medieval, 65
Aramaic, 185
Argentine Spanish, linguistic attitudes in: conclusions and further research, 122–23; discussion, 119–22; introduction, 101; matched-guise technique, 107–9; methodology, 110–13; previous literature, 102–9; research questions and hypotheses, 109–10; results, 113–19, 114 fig. 5.1, 119 fig. 5.11, 114–19
Argentine Spanish, vocatives in, 132
Athanasiadou, Angeliki, 85
Atlas Lingüístico de la Península Ibérica (ALPI), 2
attitudes, linguistic. *See* Argentine Spanish, linguistic attitudes in; Montevideo Spanish, *voseo* vocatives in
authentic speech technique, 144

Balearic Catalan, 48–49
Barrenechea, Ana María, 103
Baxter, Alan, 170–71, 173
Belletti, Adriana, 205, 205n1, 216

Benjamin, Carmen, 82–83
Bentivoglio, Paula, 102
Berceo, Gonzalo de, 23n4
Bertolotti, Virginia, 127
bilingual speakers and language-contact studies, 6
Blas Arroyo, José Luis, 107, 109, 110, 112
Bolinger, Dwight, 73
Bolivian Spanish, 105, 166. *See also* Yungueño Spanish, subject-verb agreement in
Bonaerense Spanish. *See* Argentine Spanish, linguistic attitudes in
Boretti de Macchia, Susana H., 102
Borzi, Claudia, 69, 72
Bossong, Georg, 103
bo/vo. *See* Montevideo Spanish, *voseo* vocatives in
Brucart, José María, 66
Bruhn de Garavito, Joyce, 199
Buenos Aires Spanish, vocatives in, 131–32
Buenos Aires Spanish and linguistic attitudes. *See* Argentine Spanish, linguistic attitudes in
Burns, Anne, 152
Butt, John, 82–83
Büyükada, Prince Islands, 186

Campbell-Kibler, Kathryn, 122
El Cantar del Mío Çid, 18, 19 fig. 1.1, 19
Capusotto, Peter, 141n1
Carrasco Gutiérrez, Ángeles, 105
Cartularios de Valpuesta, 18, 19 fig. 1.1, 19
Casesnoves Ferrer, Raquel, 108
case variation in non-*leísta* experience predicates. *See* experience predicates, light verbs, and case assignment in non-*leísta* varieties
Castilian Spanish, rhotacism in, 48–49
Catalan: Elche Spanish study and, 51, 54; experience predicates in, 202, 208, 209, 210; light verb experience constructions (LVECs) in, 218, 221; linguistic attitudes and, 107; rhotacism in Balearic Catalan, 48–49; /s/ voicing in, 45–48

causal relations, 86–87, 92–95
Cerrón-Palomino López, Álvaro, 67–68, 75, 78
che. *See* Montevideo Spanish, *voseo* vocatives in
Checa-García, Irene, 65
Chomsky, Noam, 4, 204, 216
Clopper, Cynthia, 108
Comrie, Bernard, 67, 70
conative vocatives, 126
conference presentations in Spanish in the United States: active bilingualism, dialectical diversity, and genre, 148–49; conclusions, 160–61; genre analysis, 151–52, 155–57; methodology, 153–55; register analysis, 152–53, 154 table 7.1, 153–55; results, 155–60; theoretical framework and discourse analysis, 149–53, 154 table 7.1, 154
Conrey, Brianna, 108
consecutio temporum, 105
contrastiveness, 73–75, 78–79
CORLEC (Corpus de Referencia de la Lengua Española Contemporánea), 71–72
Cowper, Elizabeth, 177
creoles and creole-like features, 167–70
Cuartero Torres, Néstor, 47
Cuba, 169
Cuervo, María Cristina, 205, 205n1

Dasher, Richard, 96
Davidson, Justin, 47
Degand, Liesbeth, 81–82, 86–88, 90
De Granda, Germán, 167–69
(de)queísmo, 102–3, 113–23, 114 fig. 5.1–5.2, 116 fig. 5.6, 118 fig. 5.9, 119. *See also* Argentine Spanish, linguistic attitudes in
Díaz-Campos, Manuel, 4, 109, 120, 122
differential object marking (DOM) use with inanimates, 103–4, 113–23, 114 fig. 5.1–5.2, 117 fig. 5.7, 118 fig. 5.10, 119. *See also* Argentine Spanish, linguistic attitudes in
diminutive suffix in Neapolitan, 27–28
discourse analysis, 150–53, 160. *See also* conference presentations in Spanish in the United States

discourse marker variation, role of subjectivity in: conclusions, 96–97; introduction, 81–82; methodology, 88–91; previous research, 82–85; results and discussion, 92–96, 93 table 4.1–4.2, 94 table 4.3–4.4, 95 table 4.5–4.6, 95; subjectivity, 85–88

domain theory, 84–85, 88

Dorian, Nancy C., 188–92, 200

Dowty, David, 211–13

Dutch, 84, 88

Dyirbal, 190

East Sutherland Gaelic, 188–89, 190

Eggins, Suzanne, 154–55, 156

Elche Spanish, rhotacism of /s/ in: conclusions, 60–61; demographics and language use in Elche, 44–45; introduction, 43–44; methodology and data analysis, 50–54, 52 fig. 2.1, 53 table 2.1; participant demographics, 61–62; results and discussion, 54–60, 55 table 2.2, 56 fig. 2.2, 57 fig. 2.3, 57 table 2.3, 58 fig. 2.4, 59 fig. 2.5; rhotacism in Romance, Germanic, and Sanskrit languages, 48–50; /s/ voicing in standard Spanish and Catalan, 45–48

English: matched-guise technique and, 108; rhotacism in American English, 49–50; stative experience predicates, 210; usage of, in Spanish-language conference presentations, 158, 159–60

epistemic causality, 87

Ernestus, Mirjam, 47

Etheria (or Egeria), 18, 19 fig. 1.1, 19

eventive light verb experience constructions (LVECs), 221–23

eventive vs. stative experience predicates, 209–17

experience predicates, light verbs, and case assignment in non-*leísta* varieties: a basic structure for experience predicates, 205–9; case alternation in incorporating predicates, 213–17; conclusions, 223–24; eventive experience predicates, 209–13; introduction, 201–5; lack of case alternation in light verb experience constructions (LVECs), 218–23; methodology, 205; phase theory, 203–4

feature-geometry approach, 176–79

Fernández Soriano, Olga, 75

first-person present tense indicative form, multi-syllabic, in Neapolitan, 29–31

Fontanella de Weinberg, María Beatriz, 102

formal texts, 158, 159

Franceschina, Florencia, 199

French, 108, 186

friend-of-a-friend method, 50

Fuss, M., 107–13

Gaelic, 188–89, 190

Gahng, T., 108, 110

Gallego, Ángel J., 204

Galmés de Fuentes, Álvaro, 65

Gehman, Henry S., 65

gender agreement in Judeo-Spanish. *See* Judeo-Spanish, phi-feature valuation and gender agreement in

gender assignment in Judeo-Spanish, 188n1

gender as variable (male and female): rhotacism of /s/ in Elche Spanish and, 57 fig. 2.3, 57 table 2.3, 58 fig. 2.4; subject-verb agreement in Yungueño Spanish and, 172, 174, 175 table 8.3, 174–75; *voseo* vocatives and, 136–37, 136 fig. 6.1, 137 fig. 6.2, 138 fig. 6.3, 138

genre, 148–49, 152, 155–57

Genre and Register, theory of, 151–53, 154 table 7.1

German, 84, 177

Germanic languages, rhotacism in, 49–50

Gimeno Menéndez, Francisco, 45

Glosas Emilianenses y Silenses, 18, 19 fig. 1.1, 19, 35n9

Gollin, Sandra, 152

Gómez Molina, José R., 45

González García, Luis, 66, 69, 71

González Martínez, Juan, 107, 109

Grinevald, Colette, 192

Guamanian Spanish, 189, 200

Guaraní, 127, 132

Guirado, Krístel, 103

Gutiérrez Ordóñez, Salvador, 72–73, 73n7
Gutiérrez-Rexach, Javier, 199

Hale, Kenneth, 206
Halliday, Michael A. K., 73
Harley, Heidi, 179
Hawkins, Roger, 199
Hebrew, 185, 186
Helvécia Portuguese, 170
Highland Bolivian Spanish, 166
Hoff, Mark, 103, 105

imperfect subjunctive, present subjective in place of, 104–5, 113–23, 115 fig. 5.4, 117 fig. 5.8, 119 fig. 5.11. See also Argentine Spanish, linguistic attitudes in
inanimates, DOM use with, 103–4, 113–23, 114 fig. 5.1–5.2, 117 fig. 5.7, 118 fig. 5.10. See also Argentine Spanish, linguistic attitudes in
inchoativization of pre-inchoative infinitives in Neapolitan Ibero Romance, 28–29
indirect objects: as resumptive elements, 79; sematic roles of, in simple clauses, 75–76
information newness, 72–73
interfaces, 180–81
interviews as method, 2–3, 50–51
Isleño Spanish, 189–90, 200
Istanbul, Judeo-Spanish in. See Judeo-Spanish, phi-feature valuation and gender agreement in
Italian mainland vernaculars. See Proto-Ibero-Romance and southern Italian mainland vernaculars

Jakobson, Roman, 126
Jarchas, Las, 18, 19 fig. 1.1, 19
Joyce, Hellen, 152
Judeo-Spanish, phi-feature valuation and gender agreement in: conclusions, 200; introduction, 183–85; Istanbul, Prince Islands, and New York City communities, 185–87, 193; methodology, 191–93, 193 table 9.1; phi-features in endangered languages, 187–91; results, 194–99, 194 fig. 9.1–198 fig. 9.8, 199 table 9.2

Kaiser, Georg, 103
Kanwit, Matthew, 102, 103
Keenan, Edward L., 67, 70
Keller, Rudi, 83–84
Keyser, Samuel Jay, 206
Killam, Jason, 109, 120, 122
Kovacci, O., 102

Labov, William, 2, 4, 179
Laca, Brenda, 103
Ladino. See Judeo-Spanish, phi-feature valuation and gender agreement in
Lambert, Wallace E., 107–8, 144
Lambrecht, Kurt, 72, 73, 73n7, 80
Langacker, Ronald W., 85
language acquisition: Afro-Hispanic languages of the Americas and, 166, 169–70, 179–82; Judeo-Spanish and, 191, 192, 195, 198, 200; nature of language interfaces and, 180–81
language contact, study of variation in, 5–6. See also *specific studies*
Latin, Neapolitan, and Proto-Ibero-Romance. See Proto-Ibero-Romance and southern Italian mainland vernaculars
Latin: post-tonic vowels, weakening vs. full syncope of, 19, 22–27, 25 table 1.1; rhotacism in, 48
lexicons: academic, 151, 153; Judeo-Spanish, 188, 198; Neapolitan, 36–38; phase theory and, 204; subject-verb agreement in Afro-Bolivian Spanish and, 176, 178
light verb experience constructions (LVECs). See experience predicates, light verbs, and case assignment in non-*leísta* varieties
linguistic variation, history of study of, 2–6. See also *specific studies*
Lipski, John M., 170, 171, 173, 179, 189–90, 200
Lope Blanch, José Manuel, 2–3, 65
Los Angeles Spanish, 190

Madrileño Spanish, 47
Martial, 18, 19 fig. 1.1, 19
Martin, James R., 152
Martín, Sidney, 49–50
Martín Zorraquino, María Antonia, 82
matched-guise technique, 107–9, 122–23, 144
Matus-Mendoza, María de la Luz, 106
McCarthy, Corrine, 176
McKinnon, Sean, 47
merge operation (Minimalist Program), 175–76, 178
methodology: authentic speech, 144; discourse analysis, 150–53, 160; friend-of-a-friend method, 50; genre analysis, 151–52, 155–57; interviews, 2–3, 50–51; matched-guise technique, 107–9, 122–23, 144; quantitative-qualitative mix, 63; questionnaires, 2–3, 133, 137–42, 143; register analysis, 152–53, 154 table 7.1, 153–55; snowball technique, 50; surveys, 45, 125, 133–37, 143–44. *See also specific studies*
Milroy, James, 106
Milroy, Leslie, 106
Minimalist Program approach, 175–76, 184, 187–88, 192, 200, 203–4
monogentetic hypothesis, 169
Montevideo Spanish, *voseo* vocatives in: conclusions and future directions, 144; discussions, 142–43; introduction, 124–26; methodology, 133–35; odds ratio by gender, 147 table 6.2; participant demographics, 146 table 6.1, 146; questionnaire items, 145–46; results, 136–42, 136 fig. 6.1, 137 fig. 6.2, 138 fig. 6.3; vocatives and Río de la Plata Spanish, 126–33
Morano, Mabel, 69, 72
morphosyntactic variation, in history of linguistic variation studies, 4–5
move operation (Minimalist Program), 175–76
Muestro Espanyol. *See* Judeo-Spanish, phi-feature valuation and gender agreement in

Narrog, Heiko, 85
Neapolitan: lexicon, 36–38; morphology, 27–38; phonological characteristics, 21–27; syntax, 32–36, 37 fig. 1.2; as term, 20; Tuscan vs., 20–21
New York City, Judeo-Spanish in. *See* Judeo-Spanish, phi-feature valuation and gender agreement in
non-*leísta* experience predicates. *See* experience predicates, light verbs, and case assignment in non-*leísta* varieties

occluded genres, 149
Ocuilteco, 189, 190
Orecchia, Teresa, 103
Ottoman Empire, 184

Palo Monte ritual language (Cuba), 169
Pander Maat, Henk, 81–82, 84–91
Perez, Danae, 169, 171–72, 173, 179
Peruvian Spanish, 105
phase theory, 203–4
phatic vocatives, 126
phi-feature valuation. *See* Judeo-Spanish, phi-feature valuation and gender agreement in
Philippine Spanish, 200
pidgin, 167–69
Piqueres Gilabert, Rosa María, 107–13
Pisoni, David B., 108
por tanto and *por lo tanto*. *See* discourse marker variation, role of subjectivity in
Portolés Lázaro, José, 82
Portuguese: Helvécia, 170; proto-Afro-Portuguese pidgin, 167–69
possessive adjectives, post-nominal placement of, 33
post-tonic Latin vowels, weakening vs. full syncope of, 19, 22–27, 25 table 1.1
pragmatics: *bo* vocative and, 125; discourse marker variation and, 81, 97; subjectivity and, 85; vocatives and, 126–27. *See also* Montevideo Spanish, *voseo* vocatives in; resumption strategy in Spanish relative clauses
predicates, experience. *See* experience predicates, light verbs, and case assignment in non-*leísta* varieties

PRESEEA (*Proyecto para el estudio sociolingüístico del español de España y América*), 5
present subjective in place of imperfect subjunctive, 104–5, 113–23, 115 fig. 5.4, 117 fig. 5.8, 119 fig. 5.11. *See also* Argentine Spanish, linguistic attitudes in
Prince, Ellen, 70, 72
Prince Islands, Judeo-Spanish in. *See* Judeo-Spanish, phi-feature valuation and gender agreement in
Probus, Marcus Valerius, 22
proto-Afro-Portuguese pidgin, 167–69
Proto-Ibero-Romance and southern Italian mainland vernaculars: conclusions, 38–40; historical texts from the Iberian Peninsula, 17–18, 19 fig. 1.1, 19; methodology, terminology, and research methods, 20–21; morphology, 27–38; phonology, 21–27; present-day languages as evidence for earlier language forms, 18; purpose and objectives, 20; syntax, 32–36, 37 fig. 1.2, 37
Proyecto de estudio coordinador de la norma lingüística culta de las principales ciudades de Iberoamérica ("Norma culta"), 2–3
Proyecto para el estudio sociolingüístico del español de España y América (PRESEEA), 5
psych predicates. *See* experience predicates, light verbs, and case assignment in non-*leísta* varieties

Quechua, 106
questionnaires as method, 2–3, 133, 137–42, 143
Quijote, El, 19 fig. 1.1, 19
Quintilian, 18, 19 fig. 1.1, 19

Recasens i Vives, Daniel, 55
register analysis, 152–53, 154 table 7.1, 153–55
Reinhart, Tanya, 180, 181 fig. 8.1, 181
relative clauses, resumption strategy in. *See* resumption strategy in Spanish relative clauses
resumption strategy in Spanish relative clauses: contrastiveness and resumptive elements, 78–79; hypotheses, 76; indirect objects as resumptive elements, 79; methodology, 71–76; old information and resumptive elements, 76–78, 78 table 3.1; pragmatic factors affecting presence of resumptive pronouns, 66–71; pragmatics and simple clause parallelism, weight of, 79–80; resumption and resumptive pronouns, 64–65
rhotacism of /s/ in Elche Spanish. *See* Elche Spanish, rhotacism of /s/ in
Río de la Plata Spanish. *See* Montevideo Spanish, *voseo* vocatives in
Risell, Dorothy, 106
Ritter, Elizabeth, 179
Rizzi, Luigi, 205, 205n1
Rojas, Elena M., 102
Rojo, Guillermo, 105
Role Phrase, 127
Romanian, 48
Romero, Joaquín, 49–50, 188n1, 194
Rose, David, 152
Royal Spanish Academy (Real Academia Española), 104

/s/, rhotacism of. *See* Elche Spanish, rhotacism of /s/ in
Sanders, José, 86
Sanders, Ted, 81–82, 84–91, 97
Sankoff, David, 108
Sanskrit languages, rhotacism in, 49
Sardinian, 18
Saussure, Ferdinand, 4
Schmidt, Annette, 190–91
Schwegler, Armin, 169
Schwenter, Scott, 102–3
Sedano, Manuel, 102
Sefarad I, II, and III, 184
Segura i Llopes, Josep Carles, 55
semi-formal texts, 158
Seneca, 18, 19 fig. 1.1, 19
Sephardic communities. *See* Judeo-Spanish, phi-feature valuation and gender agreement in

Sessarego, Sandro, 105, 172, 173–74, 199
Sevillian Spanish, 48
Sicilian, 18
Silva-Corvalán, Carmen, 4, 69n4, 74
Simposio sobre corrientes actuales en dialectología del Caribe hispánico (1976), 3
Sinnott, Sarah, 84–85, 89, 95
Slabakova, Roumyana, 177
Slade, Diana, 154–55
Smith, Jennifer, 176, 178, 179
snowball technique, 50
sociolinguistics: language-contact studies and, 5–6; linguistic variation, expanded interest in, 3–4; theoretical linguistics and, 125; vocatives, sociolinguistic value of, 127. *See also specific studies*
southern Italian mainland vernaculars. *See* Proto-Ibero-Romance and southern Italian mainland vernaculars
Speech Act Shells, 127
speech community attitudes. *See* Argentine Spanish, linguistic attitudes in; Montevideo Spanish, *voseo* vocatives in
spontaneous-dialogic texts, 158
stative light verb experience constructions (LVECs), 219–21
stative vs. eventive experience predicates, 209–17
Suárez Fernández, Mercedes, 65
subjectivity theory, 85–88. *See also* discourse marker variation, role of subjectivity in
Subject of Consciousness (SOC), 86–87, 90–95
subject-verb agreement in Afro-Bolivian Spanish. *See* Yungueño Spanish, subject-verb agreement in
surveys as method, 45, 125, 133–37, 143–44
Swales, John M., 149
Sweetser, Eve, 83–84, 86, 88
systemic functional linguistics (SFL), 152

Taboada, Maria Teresa, 154–55
thematization, 66
Tippets, Ian, 103
Torreira, Francisco, 47
Traugott, Elizabeth, 85, 95
Trinidadian Spanish, 189
Trujillo, Ramón, 67
Turkish, 185
Tuscan, 20, 24. *See also* Proto-Ibero-Romance and southern Italian mainland vernaculars

UAM Corpus Tool, 155, 159
Universidad Autónoma de Madrid Corpus of Peninsular Spanish, 71–72
Uruguayan Spanish. *See* Montevideo Spanish, *voseo* vocatives in
U.S. conference presentations. *See* conference presentations in Spanish in the United States

Valencian, 107, 108
variation, history of study of, 2–6. *See also specific studies*
Venezuelan Spanish, 109
Viñas-de-Puig, Ricard, 205
vocative particles. *See* Montevideo Spanish, *voseo* vocatives in
volitionality in causal relations, 86–87, 92–95, 93 table 4.1–4.2, 94 table 4.3–4.4, 94
von Heusinger, Klaus, 103
voseo vocatives. *See* Montevideo Spanish, *vosea* vocatives in

Warlpiri, 189, 190
White, Lydia, 199
Wölck, Wolfgang, 106
Woolard, Kathryn A., 108, 110

Yungueño Spanish, subject-verb agreement in: conclusions, 182; data collection and qualitative methodology, 172–73; discussion, 178–82; introduction, 165–67; nature and origins of Yungueño Spanish and Afro-Hispanic languages of the Americas, 167–70, 168 table 8.1; qualitative findings, 170–72; statistical results, 173–74, 174 table 8.2, 175 table 8.3, 175; theoretical assumptions and feature-geometry approach, 175–78

THEORETICAL DEVELOPMENTS IN HISPANIC LINGUISTICS
Javier Gutiérrez-Rexach, Series Editor

This book series aims to be an outlet for monographs or edited volumes addressing current problems and debates within Hispanic linguistics. The series will be open to a wide variety of areas and approaches, as long as they are grounded in theoretical goals and methodologies. Contributions from the disciplines of syntax, semantics, pragmatics, morphology, phonology, phonetics, etc. are welcome, as well as those analyzing interface issues or the historical development, acquisition, processing, and computation of grammatical properties. Research topics of interest are those dealing with Spanish or other Hispanic languages, in any of their dialects and varieties.

Contemporary Advances in Theoretical and Applied Spanish Linguistic Variation
    EDITED BY JUAN J. COLOMINA-ALMIÑANA

Advances in the Analysis of Spanish Exclamatives
    EDITED BY IGNACIO BOSQUE

The Afro-Bolivian Spanish Determiner Phrase: A Microparametric Account
    SANDRO SESSAREGO

Interfaces and Domains of Quantification
    JAVIER GUTIÉRREZ-REXACH

www.ingramcontent.com/pod-product-compliance
Lightning Source LLC
Chambersburg PA
CBHW030109010526
44116CB00005B/165